# eCommerce Inbound Marketing

## HOW TO
## SELL
### BETTER THAN
## AMAZON

**Sam Mallikarjunan | Mike Ewing**

INFINITY
PUBLISHING

Copyright © 2012 by Sam Mallikarjunan and Mike Ewing

ISBN 978-0-7414-8148-1  Paperback
ISBN 978-0-7414-8149-8  Hardcover
ISBN 978-0-7414-8150-4  eBook

Printed in the United States of America

Published December 2012

INFINITY PUBLISHING
1094 New DeHaven Street, Suite 100
West Conshohocken, PA 19428-2713
Toll-free (877) BUY BOOK
Local Phone (610) 941-9999
Fax (610) 941-9959
Info@buybooksontheweb.com
www.buybooksontheweb.com

# Contents

# Foreword

New technologies often change society and business drastically, but it usually takes longer than people expect for the full effect of the changes to set in, and the changes often come in waves. Telephone technology was first developed in the 1840's, and perfected in the 1870's. The first wave of this technology was telephone lines being leased as a point to point connection between just 2 parties, not as part of a shared network connecting everyone. Only in the early 1900's did the telephone really start to resemble the devices and network we know today. And it took decades after that before the telephone became an effective selling and marketing tool.

The Internet has changed the way we live our lives, consume information and purchase products. But again, it took time for the full effects of this new technology to be felt. The first wave of using the internet to sell products involved basically taking existing catalog-style business practices and putting them on the web. Customer acquisition went from direct mail to email, from offline ads to online ads, the static paper catalog became a static website, the paper order form became a digital order form. My job as an ecommerce marketer in 1999 was still to spend money to buy ad space next to something people wanted to read, try my best to distract them from that media with my advertisement and put something in the virtual shopping cart. This wave probably ran from 1994 when Amazon was founded until 2001 when the dot-com bubble burst with a stock market crash combined with the September 11 terrorist attacks which sent the economy into recession for a few years.

The next wave is far more interesting, and this is the opportunity that exists for every business today. WordPress blogging software first appeared in 2003, Facebook was founded in 2004, and YouTube was founded in 2005. Normal everyday people were starting to use the Internet to not only consume information, but to produce, publish, share and discuss information. Along with this new use of the Internet came other technologies – caller ID, spam and ad blocking software, TiVo and the DVR - giving consumers more and more control over what information they consume and how. Today Facebook now has over 1 billion active users, YouTube delivers over 4 billion hours of video a month, and there are over 170 million blogs, 86% of people skip TV ads and 200 million people are on the US do not call list.

In this wave companies are starting to leverage the real power of the internet to sell products in an entirely new way, using inbound marketing. People have become accustomed to controlling their consumption of information. Why watch ads on TV when I can fast forward through them using my DVR? Why watch something I don't enjoy on one of my 200 cable TV stations if there are over 100,000 videos uploaded to YouTube each day? Why read the mainstream news that the New York Times publishes for everyone, when I can find 20 blogs about some narrow topic that is exactly what I want to read? Why get interrupted by telemarketers when I can use caller ID and let it go to voicemail? Why get distracted by email blasts when I can interact with the people I trust on Facebook and Twitter? Why subject myself to marketing I don't love?

Today's leading marketers have changed the way they think and they are using inbound marketing to attract customers to their business using marketing people love. They create their own content and they become what their potential customers are interested in, not ads that they try to ignore. They personalize the shopping experience to segments of buyers, adapting the website and email to each type of buyer. These inbound marketers are getting higher ROI and grow faster at a lower cost. This new paradigm of inbound marketing is what this book is all about.

I had the good fortune to work alongside Mike and Sam for a long time as we built HubSpot, and I know that they are each experts in inbound ecommerce marketing. Mike and Sam are part of a new breed of ecommerce marketing professionals who are blazing the path toward inbound ecommerce marketing. They understand how to use content to attract more customers at a lower cost and how to use context to drive personalization which raises your conversion rates. They have both run marketing at ecommerce companies, rolling up their sleeves and getting into the details of how to do it right. And, they have both coached and worked alongside hundreds of HubSpot customers who implemented inbound marketing. You want to learn to fly an airplane from a pilot with a lot of flight time, and you want to learn inbound marketing from someone who has a lot of experience doing it. Well, Mike and Sam have a lot of inbound marketing flight time.

It really is possible today for a small business to use an inbound approach to ecommerce and perform better than the big guys, even Amazon. Turn the page and you too can learn how.

-   Mike Volpe, HubSpot CMO

# Preface:
## How to Read This Book

This book is intended to be a fairly comprehensive exploration of the changes in and factors of effective, modern e-commerce marketing campaigns. We've done our best to balance the advanced concepts with fairly basic and actionable tips on how you can improve your marketing efforts, but there are some sections that will be inapplicable to the primary opportunities that your particular firm needs to address right now.

Although we don't want to discourage reading the book in its entirety, the text covers some highly advanced topics designed for larger enterprise-level marketing concerns, and you should feel free to skip to chapters that address topics where you've identified the potential to improve and implement new strategies specific to you. If you have any questions about the more advanced sections, we encourage you to take advantage of the multiple ways to contact the authors and ask us questions:

Text us at: (518) 966-2678

Tweet us at: @Mallikarjunan or @InboundCommerce

E-mail us at: info@eCommerceMarketingBook.com

Fill out our form at: bit.ly/eCommBook

Conversely, some marketers may find certain sections to be more basic than your current needs. However, if you have advanced questions about any of the topics that we cover, we also encourage you to contact us with questions or in search of further, more advanced material.

# Chapter 1:

## How to Sell Better Than Amazon

$97,680.10.

That's a decent amount of money by almost anyone's standards. For many eCommerce companies, that may represent an entire month's sales revenue, or even quarterly revenue. But according to their filings, for Amazon.com, the towering, titanic juggernaut of the eCommerce world, that's roughly the amount of revenue that they made during every minute of every day during Q2 of 2012.

For a long time, the way to make money on the Internet was to run lean. The average profit margin for eCommerce companies in 2012 was a mere 6.8 percent according to IBISWorld. The idea was that eCommerce companies could create an economy of scale that would enable massive profit volume even if profit per transaction was low. With more than seven out of ten US consumers shopping online, eCommerce companies had a massive market with which to scale this process, and the race to the bottom began. eCommerce companies based their entire business models on having the cheapest prices and even wrote scripts to scan competitors' websites and adjust their prices to constantly be lower.

Price-sensitive consumers were always an attractive market to eCommerce companies because of their velocity. In the overall consumer buying cycle, consideration of pricing by vendors falls at the very bottom, and therefore the number of those consumers who would hit a site, find a product, and buy right away was extremely high. Because eCommerce companies chose to engage in this arms race of low margins, their main streams of revenue were built around high-velocity, low-profit consumers making individual, one-time transactions.

The advent of product and price aggregators such as Google Shopping vastly accelerated this process. Consumers no longer even had to shop around for the lowest price; by simply entering the product they were looking for into a search engine and clicking "sort by price," they could instantly find the website with that product for the cheapest cost. This led to the inevitable breakdown of this business model as a viable revenue stream. When your main focus is price-sensitive consumers, and the race to the bottom gets out of control, you're confronted with a singular, unavoidable, and ultimately devastating fact: there's always someone willing to make less money than you.

This corporate obsession with the acquisition and conversion of price-sensitive eCommerce consumers also led to another phenomenon—sometimes colloquially called "getting Amazoned." Most product, vertically oriented websites (websites oriented around specific industries or product groups) by their nature and definition were infinitely better than Amazon at providing information to consumers in higher phases of the buying cycle, where they were researching exactly which product would address their need or pain point (the problem or reason that the consumer wanted to address by purchasing the product). Knowing that they were losing the short-tail and price-point race, eCommerce firms halfheartedly invested in blogs or—for the very advanced—even a single buyer's guide on their websites that would attract and help consumers identify which product they needed. However, once consumers had educated themselves and decided what product to buy, a significant portion would then leave the site and go to Amazon (or another highly price-oriented website) and buy the product there. This meant that a significant amount of the traffic that was coming to the vertically oriented eCommerce sites wasn't converting there, and firms concluded that content marketing wasn't, in fact, the war to end all price wars.

However, eCommerce firms that don't invest in content and insist on continuing to fight the pricing war are making a grave and—in the long term—fatal error. Amazon has a massive strength in its *long-tail* inventory offering, but that strength is also its weakness. The long-tail theory is one that's most frequently heard in relation to keyword strategy for search engine optimization; that is, it is orders of magnitude easier to rank for "best television to connect to a PlayStation for first person shooter gaming" than it is to rank for "best television." For firms without massive resources or existing domain authority, focusing on long-tail keywords with multiple words makes it plausible that they can be competitive with larger, more-established firms.

The long-tail theory also refers to the amount of inventory that an eCommerce store can carry and offer as opposed to a conventional brick-and-mortar store. Large conventional bookstores, for example, can carry around 130,000 titles. However, Amazon (who sold only books in its early days online) attributes more than half of its revenue to titles outside of its top 130,000 best sellers. In the same way that long-tail keyword phrases allow firms to capitalize on the innumerable permutations of keyword queries that consumers are looking for answers to, long-tail inventory strategy enables firms to capitalize on the innumerable specific product offerings that appeal to the vast number of online shoppers.

However, this great strength of Amazon's is also its greatest vulnerability. Although it's difficult for anyone with Amazon's dominant market share and positioning (not to mention its massive gross revenues, as we discussed earlier) to feel a great sense of urgency in altering their business model, Amazon has key weaknesses that provide significant opportunity to eCommerce firms. Quite simply, Amazon's long tail is so massive that it's been unable to effectively address the higher phases of the buying cycle, where education to aid consumer research and topical credibility are key. Also, Amazon has been unable to address the long-term value of consumers due to their weak, price-specific value proposition and inability to adequately define and target buyer personas.

This book will focus on how to be competitive in the eCommerce marketing battle space without focusing primarily on product price to drive traffic and conversions. In the opinion of the authors, Amazon and the other major long-tail eCommerce firms have effectively won the race to the bottom and will continue to dominate online transactions for highly price-sensitive consumers. If you're committed to being competitive in an eCommerce price war, then this book will have little value to you; we focus on how modern eCommerce firms can compete by shining a light on the inherent weaknesses in long-tail eCommerce business models.

# eCommerce Consumer Long-Term Value

We once had an eCommerce marketing team come to us with a confusing and devastating problem: their competitor was massively outspending them per click in Google search engine advertising, which both this team and their competitor relied on to drive the majority of their business.

The team's members were very confused because they knew that they had the same product supplier and roughly the same cost of goods sold (COGS). They also knew that their competitor's website had roughly the same visit-to-customer conversion rate. There was no way that they could think of that their competitor was able to afford to spend so much to acquire each customer.

To explain this to them, we told them about a quote from one of our favorite eCommerce marketers, Matt Lauzon, at Gemvara. Lauzon's prediction is that effective eCommerce marketers will very soon have to think of eCommerce revenue models from the perspective of SaaS (Software as a service) economics, where the cost to acquire a customer is only one-half of the economic equation—and arguably not the most important half.

SaaS companies express their unit economics using the ratio formula COCA:LTV (cost of customer acquisition to long-term value). It's the balance of the numbers in this ratio that defines the economic value of the enterprise. Since most SaaS firms are on monthly recurring revenue (MRR) models, the average LTV is a simple function of their average sale price and their revenue churn coupled with their ability to upgrade customers along whatever their secondary axis of pricing is.

However, most eCommerce firms express their unit economics using COCA:ASP (cost of customer acquisition to average sale price). This ratio formula is fundamentally flawed and overly simplistic. Although most eCommerce marketers understand and acknowledge intellectually that cross-selling, upselling, and reselling to existing customers is important, very few of them model or bake this fact into the way that they consider the unit economics of their business.

For our customer's competitor, however, we were able to identify how they were using social media and e-mail marketing automation to very effectively stimulate repeat and recurring purchases from their existing customers, thereby vastly increasing the LTV of their individual customer contacts. Whether or not they were doing this on purpose, they'd effectively out-leveraged our customer, who was very focused on customer acquisition and price competitiveness, in the grand equation of COCA:LTV unit economics. Quite simply, they could afford incredibly slim—or even negative—profit margins on the individual transaction because they were being very effective at increasing the LTV of their individual customer contacts.

Long-tail eCommerce firms like Amazon have a fundamental weakness here because the best way to improve customer LTV is through content and engagement. Amazon, like many eCommerce marketers, relies on the somewhat lazy fallback of discounts and price incentives to drive buyer behavior. The traditional eCommerce method for extracting value from a list of existing customer contacts is to blast the list twice a week with special discounts and sales. This method is dangerous because it has the potential to turn customers that aren't already highly price sensitive into ones that are by framing the entire conversation from the perspective of competitive price. Also, it fails to address the fact that consumer buying cycles aren't a linear continuum. In fact, consumer buying cycles are a dynamic function of the many products and accessories that are related to their buyer personas, which we'll discuss in-depth in a later chapter.

Amazon, because of its diverse inventory and product offerings, has a massive challenge in identifying and nurturing micro personas in a highly targeted and effective way. They're fairly good at identifying related products or offering product suggestions based on historic purchase patterns, although they've been known to fail at this rather spectacularly as well. For example, Amazon sent an e-mail to a user recommending they buy a book called "Crafting With Cat Hair" – even though that user neither owned a cat nor was particularly crafty. While the specific factor of their algorithm triggered that suggestion isn't clear, a real human would never have recommended that particular item to this user if they'd had a micro-persona defined for him.

However, they've historically avoided entirely using any kind of related-content nurturing in e-mail automation (much less social media nurturing) that helps address the dynamic buying cycles involved in selling interrelated or upgraded products. The sheer scale of what they're selling makes it implausible that they'll be able to compete with a vertically oriented eCommerce marketer who truly understands all the dimensions of his or her buyer personas and has an inherent expertise and experience in the factors and topics related to their product categories and accessories.

# Research-Phase eCommerce Marketing

eCommerce websites traditionally have very low visit-to-customer conversion rates, averaging between 2 percent and 5 percent for many websites. However, most Internet traffic is no longer arriving at websites accidentally or from unqualified sources. With somewhere north of one trillion web pages on the Internet, and the primary methods of page discovery being search engines, referral links, and social media, the traffic to websites is self-selecting to be fairly well targeted and qualified. For example, if you're searching for information on flat-screen TVs using a search engine, you're very unlikely to end up at a website about baking homemade apple pies.

Then why are conversion rates on eCommerce websites so low? If the traffic that's arriving at eCommerce sites is coming from a qualified source, why is so little of that traffic converting into customers?

The simple fact is that the vast majority of the Internet's eCommerce website traffic is in a higher, non–price sensitive phase of the buying cycle. Most of the people visiting eCommerce websites are only somewhat aware of the fact that they have a need and have identified a product category that will address that need—much less a specific product. We'll discuss later specific strategies for how to address this top-of-the-funnel (a.k.a. TOFU) traffic and how eCommerce marketers can be competitive by widening the tops of their funnels.

This is another example of how long-tail eCommerce firms like Amazon are handicapped by their sheer scale. As this book will discuss, effectively attracting and converting research-phase traffic involves defining effective buyer macro personas and creating a volume of content that targets each persona. In addition to the massive challenge of creating that volume of content across a wide variety of product categories, long-tail firms are handicapped by the simple fact that they don't possess the knowledge or expertise required to effectively address the research-phase needs of consumers within any given product vertical.

Although Amazon may move logistically into new consumer product verticals by adding more products to their long-tail inventory, competing in a content battle with every eCommerce marketer dedicated to a specific product vertical would involve such a massive and unscalable operation on their part that it's highly improbable that they'll ever make such a fundamental shift in their marketing—and even less likely that they'll succeed should they try.

In this book we'll teach you how to attract research-phase consumer traffic, lower your COCA while improving your customer contact LTV using persona-driven content and marketing automation and avoid the mutually destructive race-to-the-bottom of a price war. Amazon and other long-tail firms will continue to dominate the price-sensitive consumer segment for the foreseeable future, but this book will teach you how your firm can go toe-to-toe with long-tailed monsters like Amazon and win by creating a unit economics model that they simply can't compete with across the vastness of their inventory offerings.

# Chapter 2:
## Persona-Driven Marketing

Personas should be the guiding light of any good marketing program and, in fact, any good business plan in general. Fundamentally, different types of visitors and customers react to different messaging and provide different levels of enterprise value for your business. Most marketers may know this intellectually but still fail to define and differentiate these customer types, and in doing so, they miss the opportunity to make marketing and operational decisions that leverage their differences.

Although it may sound strange, developing entire fictional characters with distinct behavior patterns, values, pain points, budgets, and even skill levels can prove a significant help in segmenting your market and targeting the types of visitors, leads, and customers that will best increase your website's economic output. Personas developed by B2B marketing teams almost universally include a job title, demographics, and education level for the purpose of improving customer-focused marketing efforts and support. Personas are incredibly underutilized in eCommerce marketing, despite their prevalence in the B2B marketing realm. It may seem odd to carefully craft fictitious clients with names and backstories, but defining these characters and their attributes will help identify valuable types of visitors and customers and enable you to coordinate the efforts of the various parts of your company in extracting maximum value.

Marketers have been claiming to "know" the customers and prospects for a long time—the concept of buyer personas isn't new. However, we've typically restricted ourselves to the demographic analysis of buyer personas because that's the information that was most readily available when we were trying to develop targeting parameters for campaigns. Television stations, radio stations, print media outlets, and the other traditional methods of interruption-oriented outbound marketing all gathered and provided this information to marketers to help them determine if, when, and how to sponsor their media. However, the advent and increasing importance of inbound marketing has renewed an interest in defining buyer personas because inbound marketing is attraction based. That is, inbound marketing relies on creating content and messaging that attracts visits, converts leads, and creates successful customers.

The key difference in outbound marketing buyer personas and inbound marketing buyer personas is that attraction isn't primarily a demographic characteristic—it's a *psychographic* characteristic. That is, it's dependent on the values, pain points, responsiveness to stimuli, and other behavioral and psychological characteristics of consumers, as opposed to being dependent on who they are from the demographic perspective of age, income, gender, etc. The major development of inbound marketing in recent years has been the increasing ability to identify, define, test, refine, and leverage these psychographic characteristics to attract the types of visitors, convert the types of leads, and close the types of customers who are going to drive true enterprise value for the business.

However, the science behind *what* psychographic characteristics to define and leverage is still being developed and is very much in its infancy. Also, in much the same way that knowing the position of every particle in the universe wouldn't necessarily help you predict the future, even if you were able to specifically define and track every conceivable psychographic variation within a group of consumers, you still wouldn't be able to perfectly predict their behavior. Social and behavioral science simply doesn't allow for that level of precision. To accommodate for this, marketers create detailed character backstories for buyer personas to help the members of the marketing team, as well as the other members within an organization who find defined buyer personas empowering, use the *context* of the buyer persona to draw on personal social experiences and memories to help them "know" the persona in a way that helps them make intelligent decisions that attract and influence the persona in the proper way.

This is particularly useful for the segments outside of the marketing team of a business organization that can benefit strongly from "knowing" the persona but don't need a detailed breakdown. For example, customer service organizations can use buyer personas to understand how to handle customer inquiries. Sales teams can benefit strongly from training that emphasizes the product value and key pain points for a persona. Product and inventory management teams can use the buyer personas to know what types of products are going to appeal to the company's most valuable customers. IT and web-development teams can leverage "knowing" the customer personas into creating richer, smoother, more effective user interfaces that will reduce the transactional resistance in the buying experience and convert more visitors into sales. With character backstories for buyer personas, marketers and other key personnel can fill in the psychographic dimensions of a buyer persona and answer, "Does what I'm doing add value for this persona?" even if the exact factor of the question isn't defined and measurable by drawing on their personal experiences with similar persons.

Personas are often oversimplified as a means of improving the "quality" of leads and customers. While any buyer persona has some value, and therefore many businesses skip distinguishing one from another and simply group them all into "customers," defining specific personas can help you target the types of customers who will bring greater economic value to your company. Based on their responses to messaging, conversion rates, buying cycle, purchase values, and buying patterns, different buyer personas will have different levels of value based on the cost to acquire them as well as differences in their long-term value. Personas have been heavily used by leads-oriented B2B companies with a strong sales culture for decades. Identifying a customer's persona can help sales teams find which value propositions can be leveraged in closing a deal as well as in upselling or cross-selling.

There are two primary types of buyer personas that marketing organizations can leverage: "macro" personas, which have fairly general characteristics that are used to guide net-new traffic and customer generation, and "micro" personas, which focus on the unique and specific differences that drive changes in the long-term value of a customer (such as relevant accessories for cross-selling).

As with PR firms and advertising agencies, the main characteristics that people have used to define and identify personas are demographic—who the consumer is based on sex, age, ethnicity, income, etc. This is certainly valuable information to include in a buyer persona profile because it is an easy way to separate large groups of people. Since demographic information is the easiest information to define, collect, and analyze, it's the most easily researched and accessible. Its ease of access also makes it the most commonly provided characteristic for advertising and paid-traffic or contact generation. Direct-mail companies, for example, typically exclusively provide demographic characteristics on which you can segment your mailings. To use a less archaic example, Facebook Ads essentially allow you to plug exact demographic parameters into their advertising platform; age, sex, and location, as well as education and other traditional demographic parameters, are built right into their platform.

Aggregating demographic information about your buyer personas is therefore very easy. Most census and market research reports focus primarily on these characteristics and track them by industry. Also, since it's fairly well understood by consumers that this data is collected and leveraged, the self-reporting and survey data for this information is typically easily collected within your own systems (such as your shopping cart's checkout process).

However, just because it's the most commonly used persona parameter doesn't make it the most effective! After all, what does that really tell you? Simple demographic characteristics alone will only empower you to target outbound—or "interruption-based"—advertising based on the information that the advertisement provider is providing. For effective eCommerce inbound marketing, you need much more.

Fundamentally, inbound marketing is based on attraction. Attraction is, by definition, not a demographic trait. Instead, attraction is primarily a psychographic trait. Psychographic characteristics—how consumers think and feel, what they want, how they react to specific stimuli, what makes them happy or frustrated—may sound like the indefinable, airheaded, fluffy priorities from the Mad Men of yesteryear. These kinds of psychic insights were what old-school advertisers used to defend their positions and ideas in the absence of data.

Although the field of psychographic persona development does need further growth and research, the dawn of so-called *big data* (an IT term for very large and complex data sets) as well as advancements in progressive profiling for contacts have, however, brought what has historically been thought of as pseudoscience further into the light. We are increasingly gaining the ability to define, test, and track psychographic hypotheses with a high level of accuracy.

The place to start collecting psychographic information is from your frontline staff. Your sales and services teams typically have much greater and more personal interaction with individual customers and prospects, and therefore greater exposure to their psychographic characteristics. Your marketing team should start the process of creating a buyer persona profile based on their assumptions, experience, and exposure, and then bring that profile to your frontline employees and ask, "Does this person sound familiar?"

Since your frontline employees have more personal exposure, they'll be able to more accurately address the assumptions needed for an initial buyer persona profile. Sales reps will be able to say what value propositions and use cases prospects respond to, what true pain points your product solves for, what truly delights your customers, and other emotional information that's the inevitable result of developing rapport with prospects. Customer service representatives will have an even more in-depth exposure to your customers postsale—after the purchase "honeymoon" is over—and be able to identify the actual use cases and reactions that they encounter. They'll also be the best qualified to identify the characteristics of exclusionary personas.

Exclusionary personas are types of consumers that detract value from your organization. They may add an unsustainable load on your services organization (your customer service reps know who the high-maintenance customers are), have an unscalable buyer behavior such as low price point or infrequent reorder pattern, or simply be contacts who are highly unlikely to become actual customers. Defining exclusionary buyer personas, and identifying what marketing activities are attracting them, is an equally important part of the persona profiling exercise. Marketers tend to think of all traffic and contacts generated as "good," but from a business planning perspective, that's simply not true. There are types of contacts and customers that you can attract to your company that just don't make for good business.

The number of variations in psychographic characteristics is too large a topic to cover in this book and varies so widely among individual business that attempting to define specific characteristics that you should track wouldn't be a useful exercise here. However, some examples may include customers' responsiveness to humor versus serious messaging, their reactions to assertive marketing and sales, their level of technical sophistication, their primary-use cases for technology and social media, their responsiveness to groupthink and social proof, or even their reactions to various types of incentives (such as the endowment effect versus action incentives) can all be valuable characteristics to define, track, and test. These function in addition to the more standard characteristics of pain points and the motivations that spur customers to love your company and product (or love your company but not your product, or your product but not your company, and so forth).

Once your marketing organization has created initial profiles and modified them based on the feedback from your sales and services departments, you can begin to develop methods of identifying, tracking, and testing these assumptions. There is no set number of macro personas that you should define, but since each buyer persona is considered as a unique marketing segment and economic ecosystem, you should define as many as you are able to support independent operations for as a marketing team. A marketing team of one or two people may only be able to create content and offers to attract and convert three or so buyer personas, whereas a larger team may be able to work with more. Defining more characteristics than you can support isn't a bad thing, as it allows you to track and analyze different personas to identify potential opportunities, but you should identify which personas are most beneficial to your organization and focus your resources there.

Let's dive into some practical examples of the development and application of buyer personas. These short synopses of buyer-persona profiles aren't as detailed as a proper exercise would produce, but they provide enough of a high-level overview for our purposes here.

Charlie is a twenty-seven-year-old sales professional living in Boston who wants to buy a flat-screen TV. He has just been hired by a major BioTech firm as a senior sales associate, and is eager to use some of his new-found income to upgrade the small TV he's been carrying around since he graduated from college. Our eCommerce website sells a huge variety of televisions—an imposing proposition for someone not familiar with the different types of modern TVs. There are all the features that one has to consider when buying a television—hardware features such as contrast ratio, and software features such as preinstalled applications for accessing Internet content. Because of the variations in sophistication for televisions, the price points also vary wildly.

Whereas a buyer who's already highly educated about televisions and precise in his desire for functionality might go straight to Amazon for the TV he knows he wants, Charlie needs to increase his product knowledge so that he can be sure to select the right one. Like many consumers, Charlie is going to research his purchase online before even beginning to make a decision about where to buy from. This is where we have a significant advantage over sites like Amazon. Because we're specialized for TV sales, we have product knowledge, and have dedicated time to creating content that's going to build domain authority for his research phrases and attract him to our website. Because we know what questions and concerns buyers like Charlie have when trying to choose a TV (because we've interviewed our frontline employees), we can provide opportunities for Charlie to download an e-book, checklist, or other educational material in exchange for his contact and persona-qualifying information. We can then nurture Charlie through his buying cycle using messaging specific to his persona—such as defining hardware features and educating him on use cases for preinstalled applications—until he feels confident in making a purchase.

We'll go into how to leverage that buyer research cycle in greater depth later, but at this point we have the unique opportunity to separate Charlie from micro personas similar to the macro persona of Charlie. Developing micro personas that further segment your market into more specialized areas can provide enormous benefit, particularly for eCommerce organizations that offer a wide range of products or services. The more targeted and specific you can make the messaging and nurturing of existing customers, the more likely you will be to increase their propensity for making a purchase. Micro personas aren't scalable at the top of the funnel because their psychographic characteristics aren't distinct enough that you'd need to create entirely different types of content and offers to attract and convert them. Instead, micro personas allow us to identify and nurture contacts and customers that we already have with messaging that is highly targeted to their subtle differences and improve their conversion and reconversion opportunities using highly targeted mediums, such as e-mail or social nurturing. Micro persona profiling allows us to identify and separate Charlie from "Charles" and "Chuck."

Charlie, Charles, and Chuck may all have the same buyer research priorities and challenges, as well as similar demographic characteristics, but identifying these three micro personas can help us leverage additional lifetime value from these customers beyond the initial sale. Whereas Charlie primarily wants to use his television to play video games in high definition, Chuck is mostly interested in watching sports, and Charles is mostly interested in high-quality cinematic experience. The same content may, at the top of the funnel, attract all three, but when we're trying to tailor messaging specific to their use cases or even trying to sell them accessories after the sale, knowing their specific-use cases can help us segment and target them with messaging and offers that they'll actually find valuable.

Since it's not practical to ask a wide array of qualifying questions on a landing page where the value offer is a simple e-book or checklist, this profiling occurs after they've initially converted. Even though the initial conversion opportunity might only capture their name and e-mail address, using educational content for nurturing and landing page reconversion can allow us to identify in greater detail what messaging will be required to convert and reconvert them into transactional customers.

The same general approach applies for B2B eCommerce. Since the most valuable buyer personas to define are usually the decision makers and influencers in a purchase process, two types of personas that are often created by classic B2B organizations include the CEO and the department head. For the purpose of illustration, we'll identify a CEO and a training manager who are both customers of our eCommerce organization that specializes in developing custom training materials. CEO Christopher and Trainer Therese have widely varying goals and roles in their respective companies. Defining the differences in customer value for Christopher and Therese can help the marketing manager make intelligent decisions about how to attract the kinds of customers that will offer the highest financial potential over time. In the following narratives, we'll give brief examples of possible personas for our fictional companies.

CEO Christopher runs a sales-focused organization that has 120 employees, including a relatively large sales team. Employee development is one of many hats that Christopher will wear in a given day. Organizational growth and increasing the bottom line are among Christopher's primary goals for his company in the next years. Christopher purchases basic training materials, such as "Top 10 Tips for Closing a Sale." Christopher is primarily attracted to our organization's products and services because they save him time and money, allowing him to focus on his overall goal of growth.

Trainer Therese works at a midsized company with around 1500 employees. Her sole role is ensuring that all employees receive the initial and ongoing training required for success. While Therese majored in human resources in college, she has been out of school for a few years and relies on our organization to provide a constant flow of relevant, modern information. She will likely request materials on needs assessment, negotiation skills, and understanding buying styles. While Therese is also a busy member of her organization, current and comprehensive training is her priority and specialty.

It's easy to quickly recognize that Therese offers more monetary value as a customer than Christopher. Based on the sheer volume of materials purchased, landing and maintaining Therese as a client will lead to far more sales than will courting Christopher.

A smart marketer would never encourage their customer service or sales representatives to neglect customers who match the persona of Christopher, but they would focus their marketing efforts to attract more leads like Therese. Since we know in part what attracts Therese to our website in the first place—educational resources that keep her up to date on what types of training resources to provide—we know that producing a steady stream of this content will help us attract more visitors, contacts, and customers like Therese. At the top of the funnel, this macro persona helps us identify what we need to do to attract the Thereses that bring significant economic value to our organization.

Let's examine another micro persona scenario. While Trainer Therese's company may be a SaaS organization primarily focused on educating its sales team about its software and the use cases and tactics that appeal to its customers by training the sales team using short, illustrated process materials, Trainer Tiffany's company is a multinational organization with more than 350,000 employees worldwide, and she's primarily responsible for supplying her company's 350 regional management employees with long, detailed training manuals that break down the economic conditions affecting their business around the globe. A profiling question on a landing page such as "How many employees are you responsible for educating?" might inaccurately lump these different personas together, even though they might be attracted by similar types of content.

Since one of the services offered by Trainer Tiffany's company is custom market research and data analysis, it would make sense to nurture Trainer Tiffany with messaging about how accurate data can improve her training materials and how our research teams provide an easy and integrated process for this. Trainer Therese wouldn't respond at all to those messages, and if we nurture her with those, she'll become disengaged from our nurturing, or worse, stop thinking of us as a vendor that's in touch with what she needs.

We can create a scalable method of distinguishing between Tiffany and Therese using progressive profiling throughout their lives as customers of our company. A key differentiating factor here is business size—different-size businesses have fundamentally different needs for training materials. We could also ask them, at some point, what their "biggest training material development challenge" is and create custom nurturing based on answers like "process retention" versus "data collection and analysis." Although these two characteristics may not differentiate Tiffany and Therese enough to warrant separate macro personas to drive traffic and nontransactional leads, they're certainly enough to warrant separate nurturing programs to improve their long-term value to our company.

Personas aren't just useful for determining which types of customers can increase your bottom line the fastest; they can also help you develop a more customer-centric business model that increases efficiency and satisfaction at all levels of operations. Depending on the scope and breadth of your products or services, you could have from two to twenty unique personas among your current contacts. Consider which aspects of each persona are required to ensure that each level of your organization's team is providing the most customer-centric services possible. For an eCommerce organization marketing an array of organic food products, such as coconut oil, raw nuts, and grass-fed beef, there could be a wide number of very distinct personas among the customer contacts. From middle-class, middle-aged vegans who prioritize earth-friendly packaging to young consumers with allergies and who are on a tight budget, each customer brings very distinctive needs, pain points, and value assessments to the table.

Initially drawing up personas requires an analytical look at three crucial elements of your current customers: their demographics, needs, and behaviors. Each of these categories has a variety of subsets that will also shape the initial personas. Start your process of developing personas by examining the various ages, genders, and geographic locations of your contacts. Smaller pieces of demographic data, such as marital status, annual household income, and family size, can also dramatically affect a customer's behavior and purchase patterns and create a persona grouping. Once you have begun to recognize patterns among your customers' demographics, envision a typical day in their lives and the reasons why they may have converted from website visitors to leads in the first place.

The organic food eCommerce organization can reasonably conclude that forty-five-year-old executives in San Francisco aren't likely to be motivated to purchase organic food products online due to budgetary constraints or a lack of product availability in their hometown. Identifying that these consumers are likely to choose products online due to time constraints and convenience can help you focus marketing efforts to this group that will highlight your organization's convenience and its availability of overnight shipping. An automatic delivery program could offer exceptional appeal to individuals who don't have to worry about whether their bank account balance will have sufficient funds for high-end, organic products in three months. Stay-at-home mothers of large families living in remote areas, on the other hand, are likely to make occasional bulk purchases with the intent of feeding their families organically on a tight budget. These customers are likely to be motivated by special offers, such as free shipping or samples of other related foods.

The organic food organization could identify four main personas among their current customers based on their demographics, needs, and behavior patterns. Developing these initial personas can aid in more advanced analyses of each buyer's motivations and habits. Even if your eCommerce organization isn't focused on providing products and services to businesses, envisioning each persona's position description and work-life balance can help significantly in bringing each sketch to life. When the persona profile and narrative is complete, every member of your company should be able to say, "Is what I'm doing valuable to the persona I'm working with?"

Executive Edgar works sixty-hour weeks managing a software company in San Francisco. Success in the workplace is his top priority, followed by living a healthy lifestyle. He lives alone, goes to bed early, and usually heads to the gym for swimming and weights before each workday. Edgar likes top-notch organic products delivered to his door that are easily converted into foods that power his lifestyle, such as protein shakes or kale sauteed in coconut oil. Budgeting is no concern to Edgar, though he'd rather attend networking events after work than spend thirty minutes sorting through the products at a supermarket.

Allergic Allie is a graduate student and lifelong healthy eater who was recently diagnosed as having a gluten intolerance. She needs products that are convenient and certified gluten free, but is on a budget and doesn't have time to read labels to find such items at her local organic supermarket. Allie's coursework in economics has taught her the importance of buying in bulk. She purchases entire cases of roasted cashews or grass-fed beef jerky that will fuel her between office hours, lectures, and all-night study sessions.

Vegan Vic works as an assistant at an environmentally focused nonprofit organization in a remote area. He carefully avoids all animal products, including body care items tested on animals and shoes made from leather. His budget is small, but his motivation to save the planet is huge. Vic buys organic online because he needs the guarantee that all his groceries are cruelty free. Vic's hometown only offers two major supermarkets, and, while there is an organic cooperative in the nearest major metropolitan area, he can't access it via bike or bus.

Budget Bridget is a stay-at-home mother to four young children. She strives to feed her kids all-natural, organic foods on her husband's income. She is attracted to natural living due to the economical benefits and the fact that she wants to set a good example for her children. Bridget spends time researching the best deals and waits for sales to ensure she gets the most value for her dollar. Bridget feels that she has no choice but to head to her local grocery stores several times weekly, but she buys online when the prices are better.

These buyer personas developed by the organic food eCommerce marketing companies offer unique and important value. All of these customers will contribute to the bottom line in an important fashion. Whether they are motivated by convenience, dietary restrictions, savings, or personal beliefs, these four distinct groups are valued customers with real needs. Considering ways to customize marketing materials and landing pages to increase sales to each persona follows the initial construction. Use the images you have drawn of these customers to really envision their experiences shopping online to meet their needs. Focus on ways that you can bring these personas to your web page before they are drawn to the sites of competitors online or in real life. Avoid fixating on initial conceptions of buyer personas as slightly silly, and work toward developing actionable intelligence by putting yourself in the shoes of each of your organization's valued customers. This exercise should result in trackable, measurable, and testable psychographic characteristics that are anything but silly or fluffy.

After envisioning the typical day-to-day experiences of each of your personas and their motivations, consider their pain points and add values. If each of the four personas had an unlimited amount of your product or service in their home, they wouldn't need to go online and purchase another. What is the need they are choosing to pay their money to resolve?

For Executive Edgar, his busy schedule of presentations, conferences, and training his new assistant means that he needs to choose between buying groceries and finishing all fifty of his bicep curls at the health club. Edgar buys soy protein powder and vitamin D online from you because it is quick, easy, and can be accomplished between e-mails to clients. Vegan Vic has limited choices that he can access in his hometown, so he buys online from your organic food company because of its reputation for selling quality products and the content on your blog, which details your commitment to green practices in packaging and operations. Allergic Allie keeps coming back because you offer a combination of factors that she needs: gluten-free snacks that can keep her sufficiently energized for a busy day on campus, and convenience. Bridget Budget doesn't really need your product since she has plenty of time to research the best local sales while her kids are in school, but she's happy to take advantage of your spring specials and limited-time offers.

Buyer motivations can be divided into three categories: improvement, compliance, and savings. Combinations of some or all of these factors are possible. Edgar is motivated by an improvement in his weekly schedule, while Allie is motivated by compliance to her new, gluten-free diet, improvement in her schedule, and the savings of buying in bulk. Vic hopes to comply with his vegan diet and save money on transportation out of town. Bridget is solely driven by saving money to pay for summer camps. It is easy to understand how an individual's pain points are directly related to the reason for his initial conversion from site visitor to lead and how initial motivation affects his value points. Think of values as smaller aspects of each buyer persona's main motivation. Values are often surprisingly unrelated to each pain point, though the individual factors offer value when considered in tandem.

Value points are defined as multiple aspects of your organization's unique business plan that influence the lead-to-customer conversion process. Your organic food company may have three competitors that offer a gallon of coconut oil within pennies of your price, but why precisely do your customers choose you above your competition? Values can be as major as having a website with a user-friendly interface or as minor as the fact that your chief financial officer is a vegetarian.

Executive Edgar purchases through your website because he can have soy protein powder shipped to his house every two weeks without having to log-in and ask for the order to be reshipped. Bridget found the website initially by searching various terms about the cheapest bulk organic groceries available for purchase. While many value propositions are admittedly related to a company's marketing reach, considering ways you can identify each persona's value propositions offers real power to beating out your competitors.

Ask yourself next how each of these buyer personas performs research to make purchase decisions. Is each of these personas active on social media? Do they have time to commit to reading blog content? Most important, how active are each of these personas online? Some consumers perform thorough research through more traditional methods of marketing, such as word of mouth or print media. Identifying which sources of information these consumers use can help you tailor your approach to bring in more similar leads.

Of all the buyer personas identified by the organic food eCommerce company, Budget Bridget dedicates the most time to performing research online. She uses social media and blog content to research the best deals. She also scours her Facebook news feed on a daily basis looking for information on sales and content offered by the many brands and eCommerce organizations she has subscribed to. By identifying that many of their active social media users are motivated by sales and savings instead of information on their commitment to quality, the organization can significantly increase social media engagement by running a series of contests or content on savings.

Similarly, Vegan Vic is an avid follower of animal rights blogs and loves directing his income toward products that offer a guarantee of ethical processing and testing methods. Allergic Allie and Executive Edgar's schedules significantly limit their availability to perform extensive research. Due to their busy lifestyles and inflexible needs, searching for "gluten-free goods" or "soy protein powder" may be all the research they can afford to perform. Keyword analysis and search engine optimization (SEO) methods on salient landing pages offer the best chances of winning the business of these personas.

Ask yourself what objections these customers could have during their initial visit to your website. eCommerce organizations marketing services or operating on a leads-based model can tailor follow-up contact by addressing these common objections. Organizations focused on selling products face a stronger challenge in dealing with the top objections of their identified personas. These types of companies need to ensure that landing page content and product descriptions address these objections without being overly wordy. Vegan Vic may be horrified to learn that the organic food organization sells beef jerky, as he dedicates a lot of his free time to educating others about the cruelties he perceives in the meat industry. By playing up the fact that their beef is sourced from cruelty-free, independent farmers, the organization decreases the likelihood that Vic will contribute to the landing page's bounce rate. The organization should do everything possible to portray their support of meat-free and ethical meat practices to avoid losing the business of vegans and vegetarians.

User experience also plays a strong role in determining the conversion rates of each buyer persona. Ask yourself what sort of experience these personas need for their initial conversion to leads or customers. Certain aspects of experience, such as a user-friendly interface, an attractive landing page, and a visible commitment to excellence aren't likely to drive away anyone, regardless of needs, pain points, and objections. Delve a little deeper into the minor aspects of user experience to really tailor your marketing methods to each persona. Ask yourself exactly why these consumers are choosing to buy online, or buy from you instead of competitors. Both Budget Bridget and Allergic Allie need the savings and convenience that purchasing in bulk offers. Vegan Vic is forced to buy online because the grocery stores in his small town don't offer the guarantee that products are humanely tested. Once you have a user-friendly experience and visible commitment to customer service, focus on tweaking your content and landing pages to address each of these specific desires for experience.

Identifying each persona among your website visitors, social media followers, and current leads is critical to making sure that your tailored approach to user experience, refuting objections, and meeting value points isn't in vain. Identifying personas can offer a particular challenge for eCommerce organizations that often don't have the benefit of personal conversations with their leads. Many B2B organizations are able to quickly and conveniently identify a buyer persona at the time of introduction based on an individual's tone of voice, attire, or job description. eCommerce organizations often take advantage of keyword analysis, social media engagement, and page views to pin personas on their leads. However, the greatest benefit in defining eCommerce buyer personas will be feedback from frontline employees, such as customer service representatives. Combining real-world interaction with data-driven analysis will enable low- or no-touch sales processes such as eCommerce businesses to create and define specific and accurate buyer personas.

Keyword analysis offers significant value to identifying personas based on raw search engine traffic. Keep abreast of the search terms and industry trends that are driving traffic to your page and the pages of competitors. The organic food company could make a strong effort to include blog content that addresses their offerings of bulk, gluten-free snacks to bring allies on board. Check out social media engagement, including comments, retweets, and shares to fit your followers into personas. Finally, an individual website visitor's pattern of page views can help you identify his priorities. If a website visitor views cruelty-free coconut oil, vegan snack bars, and toothpaste that hasn't been tested on animals, chances are that he is a Vegan Vic.

Macro-level buyer personas are often vague due to the nature of eCommerce business. While more specialized buyer personas have a great deal of value for converting customers into dedicated regulars, it is essential to visualize personas as a pyramid. The initial handful of buyer macro-personas should be at the top of the pyramid because, in the initial stages of customer interaction, subtle persona variations make little difference. More specific micro personas have value for precise forms of targeting, such as e-mail campaigns and social media, while subtle variations have little value in the initial stages. These top-of-the-funnel marketing activities include imprecise marketing mediums, such as blog content and landing pages. Creating an abundance of TOFU content to meet the interests of twenty different micro personas simply isn't a practical solution for eCommerce organizations, nor are the variances in content going to be significant enough to attract significantly different proportions of individual micro personas.

While search terms and the source of the traffic to a given landing page can often reveal some information about buyers' motivations and demographics, minute aspects of personas cannot easily be defined. Before the initial sale, many eCommerce businesses focus on courting customers based on the motivations and pain points of no more than four or five buyer personas. Once leads are converted into customers through initial sales, you should take advantage of every possible method of tailoring how you nurture customers' interests and persona characteristics. By funneling customers through a process of progressive profiling, you can gradually derive information for the best chances of developing dedicated buyers.

Progressive profiling is a highly valuable concept for marketers who don't want to drive away potential or new customers with overly enthusiastic (which site visitors may perceive as overly invasive) efforts to gain valuable data. Many leads are converted through a simple sign-up for e-mail communications that requests no more information than visitors' first name and e-mail address. Requiring leads to fill out a complex form that asks for their geographic location, interests, profession, and annual household income would drive away conversions without adding any value to the initial sales nurturing process. Progressive profiling is a gradual approach to data mining that slowly adds important information to contact records by asking for more information over time. Progressive profiling is inspired by real-life interactions, which allow individuals to gain knowledge over the course of an acquaintance instead of in the first moments of an interaction, where in-depth personal details are neither useful nor readily forthcoming. Advancements in the logging and storage of customer contact and persona data have decreased the need to capture information all at once, instead enabling the ability to ask only questions we don't already know the answer to in exchange for content and offers that the contact finds valuable based on the profiling previously completed.

A key fact to note is that progressive profiling is primarily powered through useful and engaging content—just like the top of the funnel. People's information has value to them, and you need to offer them something of value in return. Progressive profiling on repurchases is fine, and using coupons can be effective, even if lazy and oversimplistic. Creating content that's probably valuable to the contact based on the information you've already gathered, and using that as an incentive to provide more information, is the most effective method of garnering further data and insight to identify which micro persona applies to a specific contact.

After an initial sale is the perfect time to launch progressive profiling efforts. If your organization has adopted buyer personas, follow-up e-mail efforts are likely to be already targeted. You already have some information on geography (which is necessary for order fulfillment) and the sale price range (which is part of the sales process) that can help to segment customer contacts. The open rate and click-through rate of e-mail marketing efforts can also provide valuable data on the objections, interests, and pain points of each client. Offer clients opportunities to provide feedback or receive deals by filling out brief questionnaires that can yield insight into their micro personas. Polls and qualifying questions on landing pages further define your leads into more specialized personas. For example, something as simple as asking them to enter their birthday to receive a special birthday coupon can help you determine age if age is an important differentiating demographic characteristic of your buyer persona. Asking your customers what they prioritize in a shopping experience can help you define their persona. Progressive profiling is driven by a more direct approach than allowed by initial search engine traffic or paid clicks. The key is to never overwhelm leads with too many questions during the initial site visit but rather to glean information through follow-up communications after the initial conversion or sale.

The organic food company follows initial sales with an e-mail to clients asking for input on the company's stock and selection. Customers are invited to provide input on which grocery items they need and which aspects of a buying experience are most valuable. They could discover that a customer initially pegged as an Allergic Allie actually chooses to purchase online in bulk due to strong environmental convictions against excessive packaging. E-mail communications to this micro persona should also include information about the organization's commitment to green practices and earth-friendly packaging, in addition to gluten-free products and specials. Further interactions with this client through social media interaction could reveal that she avoids pork by-products. E-mail campaigns and offers directed at this micro persona can be tailored to avoid any mention of certain meats.

For eCommerce organizations, repeat buyers and dedicated customers offer the most value. It's simply easier to gain additional value from existing relationships than it is to acquire new customers. In the grand economics model of an eCommerce business where the enterprise value is defined as COCA:LTV (cost of customer acquisition to lifetime value), increasing the LTV is typically an easier point of leverage. Also, existing buyers are most likely to promote your organization through social media shares, testimonials, and word-of-mouth marketing (which are aspects of LTV that are difficult to track and define, although still incredibly valuable). Converting a first-time buyer into a promoter who will return on a regular basis requires identification and nurturing tailored to their micro persona. The organic foods company could realize that a buyer identified initially as a Budget Bridget is actually driven to provide snacks that don't exacerbate her youngest child's soy allergy. Buying in bulk from the organic food company offers convenience and the ability to meet all her children's needs without causing a dangerous reaction. Through the progressive profiling efforts, this organization can provide sufficiently tailored marketing efforts to Bridget to convert her from someone who took advantage of a single sale to an individual who enthusiastically promotes the company's commitment to fun, soy-free snack foods.

By plugging a phrase such as "overnight shipping on soy protein" or "certified vegan snacks," the organic food eCommerce organization can quickly define which broad persona the lead likely fits. Truly defining and meeting each customer's needs and developing a sufficient relationship to lead to future purchases requires continued interactions that are shaped by the initial personas. Each interaction, which could include social media engagement, responding to a poll on a landing page, or completing a customer service survey, can funnel a customer into a more specified persona.

The bottom of the persona pyramid is filled with dedicated customers that you have built a trusting relationship with. You've sold to these customers on a regular basis over an extended period of time. They may engage with you on Facebook, recommend you to coworkers, or read each of your e-mails that promise savings. Make a point of progressive profiling to make sure you both benefit from every offer and interaction. By asking for a little information in return each time a customer visits a landing page or makes an additional purchase, you can further hone your marketing efforts and channel them into a more specific persona toward the bottom of the pyramid.

Personas are a powerful addition to your marketing strategy because they force you to recognize that it isn't all about you. Funneling website visitors and leads through the persona pyramid requires a largely customer-focused approach. Apply macro personas to your keyword research to produce content that will excite customers within your various categories. While specialized keywords are often SEO gold, avoid tailoring TOFU landing pages and blog content to fit highly specialized personas. Designing content and landing pages around keywords picked through the filter of macro personas can significantly lower bounce rate while increasing your leads. It is critical to develop well-rounded macro personas before doing keyword research, as imagining personas based on suggested or trending keywords will produce a lot less vibrant and effective images than ideas drawn from the real needs and pain points of your actual market.

Prior to applying the concept of buyer personas to their marketing plan, the organic food organization may have produced a lot of enthusiastic, high-quality content that yielded little customer engagement. Their search engine rankings steadily improved due to the frequency and quality of their content, which usually included generic keywords prevalent in their industry, such as "ethical meat" or "organic groceries." Their blog fulfilled many critical components of effective inbound marketing, including photos of their staff weeding a local community garden tagged with plenty of ALT text. However, their bounce rate was just too high, and the percentage of traffic converted to leads wasn't improving sufficiently. Maintaining the company blog wasn't offering a satisfactory ROI for the energy their staff dedicated. The failure to tailor TOFU content to personas—and the accompanying inevitable failure of return on employee blogging brain damage—is one of the most common reasons businesses abandon blogging as a traffic generation tactic.

The organic food company applied their four macro personas to keyword research. They drafted a list of the needs and priorities of each of the four personas before performing additional keyword research to make a list of posts for their content calendar. Edgar prioritizes having his organic groceries arrive quickly, while Allergic Allie cannot run the health risk of accidentally consuming gluten products. With the filter of macro personas applied to trending, specific keywords, the organic foods organization significantly improved the relevance of their content. While their content never lacked in quality or enthusiasm prior to adopting buyer personas, the new approach significantly improved the value that such content could bring to their customers.

While performing keyword research, the organic foods organization develops terms that succinctly summarize the needs of each major buyer persona. These terms are likely to be typed into a major search engine immediately prior to each of the persona's initial site visit. For Edgar, they find the perfect combination of keywords with the term "fast shipping on organic supplements." To meet the need of Allergic Allie, they work to identify which search term addressing "certified gluten-free bulk snacks" has the highest potential for SEO.

Once a series of high-potential keywords is developed, your organization should move toward tailoring blog posts and landing pages to include these salient keywords. Buyer personas are invaluable to keyword research because they increase the value of your content to customers. Writing blog entries to drive keyword optimization without enthusiasm or attention paid to the priorities and needs of your customer base never results in engagement or an improved crawl rate. Ensure that content written around the keywords developed through the filter of personas offers sufficient value to each of these groups.

In the case of the organic foods company, developing content to convert initial site visitors into dedicated customers would change the nature of their content. Gone are the generic blog entries about basic topics. The marketing director at the company had never considered that some customers prioritize convenience over cost-effectiveness and quality in their grocery shopping experience, but was able to develop a list of terms to attract macro personas similar to Edgar. To convert Budget Bridgets visiting the page, the organization could consider her affinity for researching how to save money without sacrificing health, and developed a landing page built around keywords and an offer she simply couldn't resist. To convert Bridgets from a customer to a lead, an e-book could be written detailing ways she can provide her kids with healthy snacks for less than $1.00 a day, including the cost of eco-friendly packaging.

A creative way to apply personas to drive business within the eCommerce realm is through guest and sponsored posts on independently run blogs. Identify which of your macro personas likely maintain active RSS feeds, and research blogs that are likely to be among their favorites. Out of the four personas developed by the organic food organization, Budget Bridget and Vegan Vic have the most time to dedicate to reading blogs. By offering a product or gift certificate giveaway through a blog run by a budget-minded, healthy mother of many children, the company can introduce themselves to a series of new leads. Writing an informative, intelligent guest post on ways that consumers can unintentionally consume animal by-products for a vegan lifestyle blog can gain the attention of Vegan Vics. Guest posts also offer the additional SEO benefit of inbound links.

Developing and maintaining repeat customers is critical in eCommerce business. Repeat customers are significantly cheaper than driving a continual, fresh supply of leads, particularly for organizations that offer highly specialized products. Repeat customers are also likely to be promoters of your company. These dedicated buyers are most likely to offer invaluable word-of-mouth recommendations, social media engagement, and testimonials. While consistency and solid customer service are key to maintaining positive relationships with repeat customers, using micro personas can significantly streamline efforts to upsell and resell. The more you get to know each customer, the more tailored your efforts to reach out to them can become. Since few organizations have the budget and staffing to personally e-mail customers with offers, apply the concept of the persona pyramid to ensure offers are increasingly targeted and relevant. Through progressive profiling, ensure your most dedicated promoters inhabit a highly specialized subpersona at the bottom of the pyramid.

The organic food company initially pegged a customer as an Allergic Allie because she was initially converted to a lead when she downloaded their e-book of gluten-free freezer meals. Convenience and money-saving seemed to matter to this buyer. Through progressive profiling, the company gradually found that the customer additionally prioritized humanitarian efforts and eco-friendly packaging. E-mailing this customer following the launch of a program to donate a percentage of profits to a charitable organization or to promote the addition of a new product, reusable lunch bags, is likely to bring her back to the website. While this customer may not have planned to purchase snack items in that particular week, progressive profiling efforts can drive these dedicated customers back to the site.

Out of their macro personas, the organic food organization may find that Budget Bridgets, Allergic Allies, and Vegan Vics are most likely to engage on social media following an initial sale. Using specialized personas as link bait is among the most effective way to drive a satisfied customer back to the web page through social media efforts. Link bait can also inspire social media shares, which are inbound marketing gold. To advertise their annual summer sale, which offers free shipping on large orders, the organic food organization could develop a series of social media descriptions that will tempt several types of customers that were initially under the category of Budget Bridgets. By posting the same link over the series of several days, the organization can tailor the description of their summer sale as an opportunity to save big on allergy-friendly snacks for the school year, vegetarian baby foods, and even early Christmas presents. These secondary priorities of school snacks, vegetarian items, and year-round bargain hunting target the micro personas developed through progressive profiling.

Buyer personas aren't just a powerful way to tailor your marketing plan, landing pages, and lead nurturing efforts. Buyer personas can pack a lot of punch when applied to every level of your business's operations, especially customer service and support. Bring your customer service representatives into the loop on your initial buyer personas, allowing them access to the pain points and priorities of each model so that they are able to provide top-notch customer service. Integrating buyer personas into your business model can allow your representatives to thoroughly address objections and provide solutions of real value.

At the organic foods company, one of the most commonly received complaints from initial buyers was perceived excessive packaging on their orders. By being provided with a profile of Vegan Vic, the customer service representatives were able to illustrate the organization's commitment to green practices at each level of operations in their response.

By knowing that this buyer persona prioritizes environmentally friendly practices and a minimal footprint, the customer service team will be able to pack a lot more punch in their e-mail response. Rather than simply addressing the customer's objection to how the product is packaged for shipping by discussing the percentage of recycled paper in the box, the customer service representative can address Vic's need for affordability. The e-mailed response can hit a home run by touching on both environmentally friendly practices and the consumer's need for products that fit his budget. Similarly, when receiving questions about the fact that soy protein powder is out of stock from a customer who seems to resemble Executive Edgar, the customer service representatives are able to offer a solution of preordering the product that best fits his busy lifestyle.

By bringing your customer service team into the loop on buyer personas, you can also use the information gleaned from their interactions with repeat buyers to funnel customers through the persona pyramid. They could discover that an Allergic Allie not only eats a gluten-free diet but is trying to eliminate animal products as well. Her questions on whether their organic body care products are tested on animals can significantly hone future marketing efforts to this customer. Treat each interaction with repeat buyers, whether it is through social media or questions e-mailed to your customer service representatives, as a real way to tailor marketing efforts to make these customers feel valued.

Buyer personas have long been a proprietary secret of the B2B realm. By building simple categories based on the real demographics and needs of their customer base, businesses have been able to attract the best kinds of buyers and efficiently address their pain points and objections during negotiations. Marketing, sales, and customer service efforts can be easily streamlined to provide a personalized approach by simply implementing buyer personas in the business model. Harness some of the power of buyer personas by applying the process to your own business model. Applying buyer personas is admittedly more difficult without the information gleaned about leads over an initial, in-person conversation, though it isn't impossible.

Sit down with your customer service team to figure out the main objections and pain points of your customer base, and apply this information to demographics you've gained from prior sales. Build vibrant profiles of your customers, and really dedicate some time to envisioning exactly why they came to your website in the first place. Tailor your progressive profiling efforts to make sure that each interaction with your customers acts to funnel them through the persona pyramid, leading to more efficient and personalized interactions. While designing and naming profiles of your customers can seem initially frivolous, buyer personas hold the potential for eCommerce businesses to create and maintain dedicated promoters of their products and nurture long-term relationships to improve the LTV side of their economic equation.

# Chapter 3:

## The Unit Economics of the eCommerce Marketing Funnel

Before any type of marketing operation can be planned, you must first define what your existing business funnel looks like and identify the points at which marketing can apply leverage. Funnel analysis, the beginning of this process, is quite simply the aggregation and expression of how your marketing efforts are currently performing. An accurate funnel is horizontally divided into three distinct segments and vertically segmented by traffic source.

The three horizontal segments of the marketing funnel are conveniently called the top of the funnel (TOFU), the middle of the funnel (MOFU), and the bottom of the funnel (BOFU). These segments refer to the progression of a consumer through the various phases of the buying cycle and form a funnel because, by nature, some consumers are lost as they progress through each phase. For example, many consumers visit a given website (TOFU), but only a small percentage reach the bottom and complete a purchase (BOFU). Funnel optimization, then, is understanding where and how consumers are exiting the funnel and pivoting marketing efforts accordingly to reduce funnel churn.

Defining the Internet marketing funnel and analyzing what marketing steps can be taken to optimize it is often referred to as TLC analysis. T, or "traffic," refers to the ability at the top of the funnel to drive adequate website visitors. L, or "leads," refers to the ability to convert customers during the research phase of the buying cycle. eCommerce companies that deal with very large e-mail databases typically refer to these as contacts instead of leads, but since "contacts" can be used interchangeably for consumers who have converted on a purchase at least once as well as those who haven't—and to maintain our "TLC" metaphor of "tender loving care" as consumers move down the marketing funnel—we'll continue to refer to them as leads. Finally, the

C refers to "customers," or the ability to convert contacts into customers who complete a purchase.

Rarely defined in the classic B2B marketing funnel, but equally valuable for eCommerce marketers to consider, would be V—or LTV (long-term value) if you prefer. In its most complete conceptualization, the eCommerce marketing funnel actually looks more like an eCommerce marketing *tuba*, where the bottom of the funnel forms an infinite loop with the middle of the funnel as consumers make multiple purchases from the same site. As discussed in chapter 1, increasing the LTV of individual customer contacts is one of the most important duties of modern eCommerce marketing professionals today, as this allows us to create a competitive economic model against long-tail eCommerce firms that operate on lower margins.

The key funnel metrics to quantify, then, are visits, visit-to-lead conversion rate, leads, lead-to-customer conversion rate, and individual customer value.

Now that you've quantified the horizontal segments of your marketing funnel (TLCV), the next step is to leverage the corresponding marketing tactic to improve the performance of the various phases. The rest of this book will delve further into how you can apply specific marketing tactics to influence the funnel, but some are fairly self-evident.

For example, to widen the top of the funnel and drive traffic, you can focus on social media optimization, search engine optimization, paid traffic sources, or offline marketing. To increase the visit-to-lead conversion rate, a marketer would have to focus on the web elements of calls to action (optimizing to increase the click-through rate) and landing pages (optimizing to increase the visit-to-submission rate) as well as marketing elements such as nontransactional offers (e-books, guides, and other forms of downloadable premium content). To improve the number of nontransactional contacts who complete a purchase, MOFU optimization would primarily consist of contact nurturing (i.e., e-mail automation and personalization, social media interaction, and other customer communication mediums). Similarly, to improve the value of individual customer contacts, you can leverage and optimize the same MOFU tactics to drive transactions and contact engagement as well as leverage business operations tools such as the average price of goods (either higher to increase per-order value or lower to influence velocity).

Finally, in addition to horizontally segmenting the marketing funnel, you need to vertically segment it by traffic source. Traffic from various sources performs differently and should be invested in and considered accordingly. For example, just because your site's overall visit-to-lead conversion rate is 10 percent doesn't mean that traffic from pay-per-click (PPC) sources will have the same rate. And since they have a different cost, this can significantly influence the overall economics of your site's performance.

If your PPC traffic only converts at 2 percent, then your cost of lead acquisition will be significantly higher even though you might be inclined to invest more based on the high level numbers. Social media traffic, on the other hand, already has some brand exposure to your site, which may make the conversion rate higher (because consumers already know and trust your site and content) or lower (because they may revisit more frequently without completing a conversion on each visit). Breaking down the funnel vertically by traffic source allows you to make smart decisions about what traffic sources to invest in and what cost-per-visit your model can sustain.

Within the funnel itself, there's some industry debate between conversion attribution to "first touch" (i.e., the source from which a consumer first finds your site) and "last touch" (i.e., the last source a consumer visits before coming to your site) sources. This debate is somewhat misguided, since each touch indicates something unique.

For the purposes of TOFU funnel analysis and optimization, first-touch attribution is the most useful. First touch indicates what inbound marketing elements are attracting visitors to your website to begin with. To "fill" or widen the top of the funnel, you'll want to focus on analyzing and investing in the traffic sources that are originally bringing traffic to your site. Otherwise, you may end up overinvesting in, for example, driving traffic from product or branded terms in PPC and organic optimization when what's really driving initial funnel value (and what you should be increasing investment in) may be research-phase-oriented keywords that are entirely different.

In addition to first-touch versus last-touch analysis, eCommerce marketers should also analyze "assisting" events within the funnel. These are events that have a high correlation to people completing purchases. We frequently analyze product and category detail pages and their correlation to conversion, but, in addition, we can analyze things like content engagement (such as downloading content or reading a blog article) or even social engagement (such as following or clicking from brand-account tweets).

In addition to helping us identify areas of potential improvement, assisting events also empower us to optimize where we are driving traffic to. If there's an e-book, for example, that has a high correlation to someone completing a transaction, then it makes sense to incorporate that into our MOFU nurturing automation. It may also make sense to do paid promotion of highly converting content offers if the math makes sense. In addition to allowing you to intelligently promote the types and pieces of content that drive the most business value, knowing what content is good at influencing visitors to become customers can also help drive the content creation strategy itself. Simply, you should create more content of the types and on the topics that have a high correlation to conversion.

There's an important distinction here between raw data and correlated data. Just because an e-book may generate a large number of leads or customers doesn't mean that it's the content that you should promote in MOFU nurturing automation. You want to promote content that, for every contact who touches it, has the highest probability of influencing a conversion. For example, if your e-book *The Ultimate Consumer's Guide to Televisions* has ten thousand downloads and has generated sixty customers, it shouldn't necessarily be promoted over your e-book *The Sports Fanatic's Guide to TV Feature Jargon*, which has only a thousand downloads but has influenced fifty purchases. The relative impact of these two content offers (with some tweaking for statistical significance) is different enough that promoting the latter offer gives a higher chance of influencing a purchase conversion.

Since the marketing funnel begins at the top, and attracting traffic is a function of creating content that consumers find appealing, it's also important that you create one of these funnels for each distinct buyer persona. We'll discuss buyer personas later in the book, but for the time being understand that these personas allow you to create content and messaging to attract and convert distinct types of visitors. Defining which buyer personas have the greatest probability of becoming customers and having high customer value will allow you to focus on investing in content that attracts them and web elements and products that convert them.

At the end of the day, you end up with multiple funnels (as many as you have buyer macro personas, which we'll explain later) that are horizontally segmented into TOFU, MOFU, and BOFU, as well as vertically segmented by traffic source.

One of the most critical and beneficial advancements of eCommerce marketing in the last decade has been the enhanced technologies that provide the ability to define, measure, track, and utilize key performance indicators that contribute to the true bottom-line economics of an eCommerce business. One of the most significant and defining differences between marketers of the new millennium and marketers of past decades is their ability to directly measure their impact on the overall economics of the business and make recommendations on where to invest marketing budget to get the maximum return. In the modern era, a good eCommerce marketing department will be able to say, at the end of the month, "Here's how much we invested in each individual buyer persona, broken down by expenditure on each individual marketing channel; here's the ROI from each channel; here are the trends based on how the experiments were performed within the channels; and here's how we plan to modify expenditure allocation and our tactics to improve the ROI in the future." Marketing departments in decades past would say simply, "Here so much money we spend; don't you feel good about yourself?" This kind of laissez-faire attitude taken by marketing departments in past decades is part of what drove many CEOs to view their marketing departments as a budgetary black hole and drove the perception that marketing teams didn't have a positive impact on the bottom line of the company. For marketers to be able to combat this perception and streamline their impact on the overall value of the business, they must first define the metrics by which they measure their success.

As discussed in chapter 1 where Matt Lauzon's point about learning lessons from SaaS economics, two of the most important metrics that eCommerce marketing teams can influence are the cost of customer acquisition (COCA) and lifetime value (LTV) of individual customer contacts. These are two of the most important enterprise-level metrics for business planning and also two of the metrics that marketing can most directly influence. The obvious goal is for marketing departments to lower the cost of customer acquisition and create methods to influence increasing the lifetime value of customers. The result should be the ability to say "for every dollar that the business put in the marketing within channel X, the business got Y dollars in return." In addition, the ability to express the COCA:LTV ratio for individual buyer personas allows CMOs and marketing teams to intelligently design content that attracts the *types* of traffic and converts the types of customers that provide the most economic value for the business.

The COCA is the aggregate of the expenditures made within each individual channel that results in the eventual acquisition of a new customer. COCA should factor in the cost of marketing software, media exposure, content creation, marketer compensation, and any other costs incurred by your business for marketing within a specific channel. This metric is entirely controlled by the marketing department at eCommerce companies where there's no "sales" influence on COCA (since there's typically no sales *team* at B2C eCommerce companies), and lowering the COCA is one of the easiest and most immediate priorities for marketing teams. Since eCommerce companies frequently operate at a greater scale and higher velocity of customer acquisition than sales-team-driven B2B sales organizations, influencing the cost of customer acquisition can significantly impact the overall economics of the business.

The beginning factor of COCA when measuring the performance of web-based eCommerce sites is COVA—the net cost of visit acquisition. Not an entirely new concept to those who have invested in pay-per-click marketing in the past, marketers should also model the COVA from other channels such as social media and search engines. Factor in the cost of employee time and software to engage in driving traffic from these sources and divide by the number of visits from each channel to determine the COVA by channel. For example, if you're paying a social media marketer $20 an hour to execute on the best practices described previously in this book for 40 hours per week and also paying $500 per month for various social media analytics and publishing software subscriptions, your marketing investment in social media is $3,700 per month. If you're driving 5,000 visits per month from social media, your COVA for social media is approximately $1.35. This is an important starting point when calculating the COCA from social media and determining which social media networks are worth investing more in.

The second step of analyzing the unit economics of the funnel is the COLA. This is the cost that goes into acquiring a single nontransactional prospect lead, sometimes even just a first name and e-mail address. Once you've defined and tracked COVA, it factors into COLA based on the number of visits that you're able to successfully convert into a contact record or prospect. Again, you should segment this metric by traffic source to help make intelligent adjustments and decisions about investing marketing budget. For example, if your visit-to-lead conversion rate for traffic coming from social media in general (although you should break it down further by individual social media network) is 10 percent, using the numbers above your COLA is $13.50. COLA is also the point at which you can track and retroactively segment the funnel economics by buyer persona since it's here that you'll begin to capture qualifying information. If your conversion offer is compelling enough (such as an interesting e-book, checklist, or guide), contacts will share some of the information that will help you bucket them into buyer macro personas.

For example, on your conversion landing page, you might ask for their date of birth (perhaps with the value proposition of getting discounts on their birthday) if age is one of the leading indicators for you of their buyer persona. You could also ask further qualifying questions such as (if you sell HD televisions) what their "ideal TV experience" includes (with options such as watching movies, watching sports, or playing video games) if knowing their primary intended use helps you segment the lead into a buyer persona.

When retroactively attributing the COLA to the COVA, you'll want to use analytics software that provides for "first-touch" attribution—or from what source that contact originally visited your website. The reason for using first-touch attribution instead of the popular last-touch attribution (i.e., from what source did a contact visit your site *last* before converting) is that the purpose of modeling the funnel by source is to know what types of content to create and what types of channels to engage in to fill the top of the funnel with visitors that you're "attracting." With inbound marketing, it's about making intelligent decisions about what content to create to attract specific buyer personas. By breaking the unit economics down by buyer persona (which starts with knowing from what channel they came to your website in the first place) you can better make intelligent decisions about what types of content you want to create to attract and convert what types of leads. In addition, the nontransactional offers (such as e-books) that are the value proposition for visitors to convert into leads and give you their contact information will, by definition, influence and convert different types of buyer personas. If Gary the Gamer is a valuable buyer persona for you (perhaps because of all the accessories and games that you can also sell him and the fact that gamers tend to actively refer opinions on technology to others within their community), then creating nontransactional offers such as *The Gaming Guru's Guide to Gadgets* will obviously attract and convert more of those types of leads than an offer unrelated to Gary's values and pain points such as one about child safety and parental controls on your televisions. Of course, if Paula the Parent is a valuable lead for you based on the modeling of the funnel, you'll do the opposite—create content that attracts and offers that convert *her* into a lead. It's all about modeling the funnel unit economics of individual buyer personas so that you know what types of content to create to attract more of the types of customers most valuable to your business into your overall marketing funnel.

Finally, you can calculate the end COCA for each buyer persona broken down by each channel by taking the COLA and analyzing your lead-to-customer conversion rate for each persona and by each channel. For example, if your lead-to-customer conversion rate from social media for Gary the Gamer leads is 10 percent, then using the previously identified COLA of $13.50 your end COCA for Gary the Gamer customers from a first-touch attributed source of social media is $135.

However, COCA is only half of the equation when analyzing the business value of the inbound marketing funnel. eCommerce marketers are fairly used to modeling the value of marketing ROI from the limited-point perspective of an individual transaction. However, as discussed in chapter 1, the great potential comes from the fundamental shift of measuring and modeling longer-term customer value and holding *that* as the other half of the ROI equation. Instead of measuring and expressing our marketing efforts using COCA:ASP (ASP being the average sale price) as has been the traditional ROI model for eCommerce, we can start to think of customer contacts as long-term units of value and expressing our unit economics using COCA:LTV (lifetime value). Once someone purchases from an eCommerce website, the marketer should focus on recycling them through the eCommerce marketing tuba and measuring their success against the ability to extract value on a long-term basis.

This fundamentally changes the way that we perceive the cost structure of marketing investments. If customer contact Mike Ewing costs us $135 to acquire but only spends $80 on his first purchase, traditional eCommerce marketing doctrine would consider that an investment of negative value. However, if we can use e-mail automation and social media nurturing to increase both his ASP per transaction (by intelligently targeting using micro personas) as well as cross-sell, resell, and upsell him on complementary items and get him to spend $80 five more times, his total LTV then becomes $480, and his COCA:LTV becomes roughly 1:3.6—which is an investment of *positive* value. By considering the unit economics from a broader, longer-term perspective you're able to outspend competitors in acquiring customers and still have a profitable, effective business model.

## Pipeline Revenue as a Marketing Metric and Objective

Part of the issue with LTV is that it's a difficult metric to forecast and therefore a difficult metric upon which to measure the ongoing success of marketing campaigns. Because LTV is an infinite metric that doesn't necessarily have an upper limit, it's hard to forecast how what you're doing for marketing is going to influence that. It's also hard to forecast how likely someone is to repurchase from your website based on the engagements that your MOFU nurturing efforts are driving.

In the world of SaaS marketing in lead-oriented, sales-driven organizations, the marketing team is primarily measured not just by the *volume* of the leads that they generate but by the predictive metric of how likely those leads are to actually turn into customers and how valuable those customers are. Each type of lead is assigned a dollar value, and the marketing team's goal is to generate enough in pipeline revenue (i.e., revenue that, based on historic performance, is likely to result from the leads generated) to meet the sales goals of the organization. For example, if the average customer LTV is $1,000 and the probability that someone who downloads an e-book will turn into a customer (the lead-to-customer conversion rate) is 5 percent, then every e-book download is worth (in theory) $50. If, however, the probability that someone who downloads a *Buyer's Guide* (which is a type of content consumed by someone further down the buying cycle) is *15 percent*, the predictive forecastable value of someone downloading a *Buyer's Guide* is $150.

SaaS, being a recurring revenue model, is also significantly influenced by the number of people that churn (or cancel their subscriptions) each month. SaaS companies can use a predictive metric called customer happiness index (CHI) to predict whether a person will or will not eventually cancel their subscription. The assumption with SaaS is that if people aren't using your software—or not using the features that have a high correlation to someone not cancelling—they're likely to cancel their subscription. Essentially, SaaS companies do a correlation coefficient analysis of users who don't use specific features and those who cancel their subscriptions. eCommerce companies can use a similar methodology of tracking marketing engagements with the brand (such as reading a blog article, viewing a product detail page, or following the brand's Twitter account) to create a predictive model for *repurchasing* (since, for our consideration, someone *not* repurchasing from our site is essentially our equivalent of them "churning").

Although these methods of measuring the performance of the middle of the funnel has rarely—if ever—been applied to eCommerce, it's interesting as we draw parallels between SaaS and eCommerce and try to shift our understanding of the unit economics to a longer term view of COCA:LTV to consider the ways in which we could use similar methods to measure the effectiveness of our marketing efforts and give our marketing teams specific, measurable, attainable, relevant, and timely goals.

# Chapter 4:
## Optimizing Product Detail Pages

Product detail pages are the backbone of eCommerce stores. These are the pages that host the products that consumers purchase and ultimately generate revenue for eCommerce businesses. The successfulness of a product detail page can literally make or break an eCommerce business. Most often these pages become the most important focus to marketers and can very likely take top priority for optimization.

Product detail pages are in fact so important that we suggest that you start optimizing these pages before engaging in any other marketing activities. The content, design, and search engine optimization of a product detail page should take priority to social media, blogging, e-mail marketing, paid search, or any other marketing activities. Your marketing efforts could be world-class, state-of-the-art, and best-there-is, but if they are all focused on promoting ineffective product pages, well, your efforts may be for naught.

Some eCommerce stores we have seen have no product detail pages but only category pages that host many products. Hosting all products on a category page can be a great disadvantage for several reasons. First, there is no way for a category page to adequately tell search engines all the products that are hosted on the page. Search engines rely on several core elements of a page to determine the page's relevance. One of the most important of these elements is the page title. A category page hosting ten different products cannot possibly fit all ten product names into the page title. Even if this were possible, search engines would be confused as to the specificity of the page, and the page would likely have a difficult time ranking well.

A second negative reason to host several products on a category page instead of creating individual product detail pages is that you are limited in the way that you promote your products. A common tactic that we suggest is to implement a curated collection of products on a page with a theme of a "buyer's guide" or "lookbook." For instance, a clothing retailer may create a "Fall Essentials Lookbook" that features a collection of its best fall clothes for men, women, and children. A sporting goods store may create a "2012 Baseball Essentials Buyer's Guide" featuring recommended products for different age groups. These pages will best perform when clicking on a product actually takes a consumer to the product detail page, not to a category page with lots of products.

Don't worry if you currently don't have product detail pages. This chapter will give you a great understanding of how to make them great from the start. In fact, this chapter is written with both beginner eCommerce marketers and advanced eCommerce marketers in mind. It is our goal to give every reader actionable advice to implement for increased eCommerce success.

## What Does a Good Product Detail Page Look Like?

A consumer can walk into a brick-and-mortar store and try on a pair of shoes, know that they fit right, look good, and be happy with making a purchase with little risk of not enjoying the product. An online store has the incredibly difficult challenge of matching or exceeding this level of interaction. An online shopper cannot pick up a product, feel it, use it. Technology simply has not caught up to this level of interaction, so an eCommerce store must turn its product detail pages into highly effective ones that get the consumer to picture owning the item and its intended use.

A highly effective product detail page will be optimized for search engines while consisting of content and design that is targeted to buyer personas. (You did read the buyer persona chapter and identify your macro and micro buyer personas, right? If not, stop reading this and go do that. Buyer personas are going to play a large role in the optimization of product detail pages and really do need to be defined. Ad copy, images, videos, and basically any content on your product detail pages have to be aligned with your buyer personas.) Product detail pages should have unique page titles, URL structure, and ad copy. Ideally these elements will include target keywords and be written in a unique way that is geared toward a buyer persona. Skip on ahead to the On-Page SEO section of the book if you want to dive deep into optimization.

Effective product detail pages consist of visual and textual elements and are geared toward a target persona. Minimally, the content consists of the text describing the product (ad copy), product images, product videos, shipping details, consumer reviews, and social sharing options. The product descriptions should be written in a unique way that appeals to the demographic and buyer personas. The product images and videos showcasing the product should also be geared toward buyer personas. The design, look, feel, and content of the product detail page should be aligned with your buyer personas.

## Buyer Persona Product Detail Pages

eCommerce marketers are often given product titles, descriptions, and images directly from the manufacturer to use on their websites to promote and sell the products. These product descriptions and images representing the product will be sent to every other eCommerce marketer who is selling the same product. What inevitably happens is that all of the stores use the same manufacturer information to sell the product on their websites. Thus, many website pages will be created with the exact same title, description, and images given from the manufacturer. This creates a case of widespread duplicate content that confuses search engines. A search engine will have to decide which of the pages with the exact same content to rank highest, oftentimes giving preference to the websites that have the highest authority and/or were first to publish the product pages with the exact same content as every other eCommerce store selling the product. An established eCommerce store with high-ranking authority and early access to new products may be able to use the exact title, description, and images from the manufacturer and still see success. However, we would advise even the established eCommerce store to look for an edge to continue to outrank and outsell their competition. Newly established eCommerce stores that are in competition with large and established companies should absolutely be looking for the edge to outrank and outsell their competitors as well.

This edge is going to be found in unique buyer persona–focused product titles, descriptions, and images. Both search engines and consumers will benefit from individualized product detail pages. Search engines seek such valuable content, and consumers are more attracted to words and images that they relate to. Hence, unique buyer persona–centric titles, descriptions, and images are needed.

You, as an eCommerce marketer reading this book, may have several buyer personas for your store. You will need to make a decision on which buyer persona is the ideal choice for each product or category. This will be the base persona use for the majority of your product detail pages. It should be on the macro level and should encompass the majority of your target visitors. We will be discussing later in this chapter how to use dynamic content to target multiple buyer personas on your product detail page. However, you will still need a base buyer persona to show visitors whom you have zero information on.

Once you have decided on your base persona it'll be time to start crafting unique product titles and descriptions for your product detail pages. This can be a challenge and is not a simple task to accomplish. Crafting, creating, and developing unique titles, descriptions and product images can be a very time-consuming task. However, the investment will be worthwhile.

## Crafting Buyer Persona Product Titles

Developing unique product titles is perhaps the most challenging aspect of creating content for your site. For example, an auto-parts eCommerce store will likely be stocking a large number of parts from multiple manufactures. Looking at a spreadsheet of thousands of different parts and trying to change those product titles into unique ones focused on buyer personas is a daunting challenge. Keep in mind though that even slightly changing the title from the manufacturer into an individualized one that potentially references a buyer persona can be an effective tactic. Let's look at a few examples and demonstrate how to take a generic title and craft it into a unique one focused on a buyer persona.

### *Example One*

Buyer Persona: Truck Drivers

Generic Title: "Four-Inch Round Red LED Light"

Unique Buyer Persona Title: "'Durable 4' Red Round LED Light Bright and Perfect for Trucks"

The unique buyer persona title is more specific and even includes a target audience, truck owners. Although a four-inch round red LED light may have many uses beyond those of a truck owner, the auto-parts store should focus on the ideal buyer for the product by mentioning the use in the product title. The base buyer persona for these lights may be truck owners and should be marketed as such—for both search engine optimization and consumer relevance. When the base buyer persona, a truck owner, conducts a search for this product, he may use the phrase, "'red 4' round LED lights for trucks." The eCommerce store using the unique buyer persona title will have a much higher chance of winning a top-rank placement over the eCommerce store using the generic title used from the manufacturer.

## *Example Two*

Buyer Persona: Competitive Squash Player

Generic Title: "Dunlop G-Force 10 Squash Racket"

Unique Buyer Persona Title: "New Dunlop G-Force 10 Squash Racket Made for Winners"

This example uses a descriptive product title that you will likely want to optimize for. In this case we want to make our description stand out among the competition on the search results page. When a consumer conducts a search for the phrase "Dunlop G-Force 10 Squash Racket," they are likely going to see many results for stores selling the racket. The unique buyer persona title will stand out among the rest and will have an edge in getting clicks over the competitors using the generic title provided from the manufacturer.

## *Example Three*

Buyer Persona: Consumers Upgrading Kitchen Supplies

Generic Title: "Stainless Steel Kitchen Tongs"

Unique Buyer Persona Title: "Stainless Steel Kitchen Tongs 100% Durable and Long Lasting"

This example again uses a title that you want to optimize for. Putting the description "100% durable and long lasting" at the end of the product title makes this unique while mentioning a value proposition important to the buyer persona. It is a slight but effective difference adding a value proposition important to the buyer persona into the product title.

Use tactics from the examples above to craft your own buyer persona titles from the generic ones supplied to you by manufacturers. Be specific and descriptive, use the ideal consumer, and describe value propositions in the product title. These tactics will help you take generic manufacturer titles and transform them into descriptive and unique buyer persona titles—giving you the edge to success.

## Crafting Buyer Persona Product Descriptions

Just like product titles, effective product descriptions need to be unique and written to a base buyer persona. The way you describe a product can have an influence on a consumer's purchase. Relying solely on the manufacturer to describe the product could mean the difference in your page ranking and consumers completing their purchase.

Good product descriptions will place emphasis on value propositions while being written in a style and tone that resonates with the base buyer persona. Knowing your audience and speaking in their language will create a more comfortable atmosphere for the shopper, reducing some friction that may unconsciously occur in their buying decision. For example, outdoor clothing and gear retailer Moosejaw does an excellent job of this by crafting their content to their buyer personas.

Moosejaw sells items in categories for hiking and camping, yoga, skiing, footwear, jackets, and clothing, to name a few. In these categories they stock and sell many popular brands such as The North Face and Patagonia. The items that they sell are sold by literally hundreds of other retailers, so Moosejaw must differentiate their consumer experience to stand out from their competitors and earn repeat and loyal customers.

Moosejaw's target consumers and base buyer personas are those of a younger, hipper generation that likes witty and humorous content. To appeal to these buyer personas, Moosejaw invests in crafting the description of a product from the manufacturer into one that would be enjoyable for their buyer persona to read. For instance, all of their product descriptions at the time of this writing start with the phrase: "DECENT FEATURES of [Product Name]." They could just use the phrase "Features of [Product Name]" but instead make their product detail page a bit more interesting simply by adding the adjective "DECENT" in all caps.

Staying on one of Moosejaw's product page for a few moments elicits a popup chat option where a consumer can connect with a representative to answer questions. Moosejaw customizes the chat widget to their buyer persona as well. The chat box reads:

QUESTIONS?

Chat with smartest person at Moosejaw

Baby Jeffie: 'Sup

Baby Jeffie: I'm ready to help

Baby Jeffie: And your hair looks stunning.

CHAT WITH US NOW

This chat box is witty and engaging—perfectly crafted to their buyer persona.

Identify your base persona and write your product description in their language.

## Utilizing Buyer Persona Product Images and Videos

High-quality product images represent one of the most critical elements to a successful product detail page. The product image will be one of, if not *the*, first elements examined by the consumer and will result in either a positive or negative first impression.

A product image that is of high quality, shown from multiple angles, and fully representative of the nature of the product will be the most effective. The more a product page can help the consumer picture the product in action, the more likely they are to see themselves using the product, and the more likely they are to be influenced to purchase.

One way to ensure that a product detail page is maximizing the use of product images is by not solely relying on stock photography from the manufacturer. Stock photography from a manufacturer can be of high quality and can be used when the images provided clearly represent the nature of the product in action and include multiple images from various angles. However, it is unlikely the case that a manufacturer provides such quality images.

If the manufacturer's stock photography is not adequate, an online retailer should invest in the photography of their own products. Invest in models that represent the target demographic of your online store as well as a photographer to photograph these models using your products in action. Product images will be more effective when including a model of a target demographic using the product as desired.

This is especially true for clothing manufacturers. An online retailer selling high-end clothing should invest in the photography of models that represent their buyer personas. Again, Moosejaw is a prime case study. In a webiar co-hosted with HubSpot titled "Consistent eCommerce Branding for Increased Customer Loyalty", Eoin Comerford, VP of Marketing and Technology, & Gary Wohlfeill, Creative Director of Moosejaw said "we create a brand experience that is engaging and compelling and is consistent across all customer touch points. If it's not notable and engaging we just won't do it." In this webinar Eoin and Gary discuss taking pride in developing their brand and image by hiring their own models for all of their product images and advertisement of Moosejaw clothing. Models are shown wearing Moosejaw clothing in the environment that would appeal to the target demographic. For instance, Moosejaw uses product images of twenty to thirty year olds wearing Moosejaw clothing hiking, mountain climbing, kayaking, and other outdoor activities popular with their target demographic. A consumer in Moosejaw's target demographic visiting a product detail page will feel comfortable with the product because she can imagine herself in place of the model in the picture. This visual reinforcement of a desire helps create a positive first impression and encourages an impulse to buy.

Multiple high-quality product images, from various angles and views taken with the buyer persona in mind will be most effective. Invest in the photography of your products and ensure that they are appealing to your buyer personas.

Product videos, although not applicable to every product, can be a great vehicle for showcasing a product and it's intended use. Video of a product allows consumers to not only visualize using the product but also to also confirm in their minds what the product will look like when it arrives. This in turn helps to remove anxiety and make them more comfortable and confident in making a purchase. REI, an outdoor gear and clothing retailer, has heavily invested in videos of their products in action, for example, in their Outdoor Video category of their website (http://www.rei.com/video) where users can watch videos on categories like cycling, hiking, kayaking and even snowshowing. These videos showcase target buyer demographics having fun using products that REI sell in a creative way. For instance, the video titled "Moment of Zen – Acoustic Campfire" shows young 20-30 males and females having a good time camping while listening to a sing along song by "their man Ethan Stone as he plays his original song 'See you in the dark.'" Another video highlights Paddleboarding where REI members paddle on Lake Mead. These videos help give the consumer a glimpse into the fun they could have if they only had these REI products. REI completes their optimization of videos by giving consumers quick links to purchase the products that they watched in the video description:

### REI Summer Adventures - Paddleboarding

Take part in the fastest growing water sport in the world, stand up paddleboarding, as some REI members paddle a glassy day on beautiful Lake Mead. Check out the featured gear that gets us out there below. #REIGearUp bit.ly Carve Board shorts bit.ly Patogonia Wavefarer Board Short Blue/black Fitz Stripe bit.ly Surftech Universal Bamboo Stand Up Paddleboard - 10' 6" bit.ly Surftech B-1 Stand Up Paddleboard bit.ly with Kialoa Pupu Paddle in Green bit.ly"

Reference: http://youtu.be/5zShusvnLQA 11/28/2012

REI even showcases their products by having employees with expert knowledge demonstrate their products as if the consumer was in a store speaking with a sales associate. One instance is their video on "How To Choose Downhill Skis" (http://bit.ly/V13qg3) which highlights an employee describing all the information a consumer would need to make an informed decision to purchase downhill skis. These videos by REI help make the consumer feel informed, knowledge and comfortable enough to make an online purchase.

Effective product videos can be shot in a number of ways, but should, when possible, include people in the target demographic of the retailer using the product as it is intended to be used. Consumers visualizing themselves using the product will be more likely influenced by video, which can lead to a purchasing decision.

In addition to demonstrating how a product works or would be used by the consumer, a product video can also be used to enhance search visibility in video search engines like YouTube. According to YouTube Press Statistics, YouTube had more than 1 trillion views or around 140 views for every person on earth in 2011. In fact, at the time of this writing 500 years of YouTube video are watched every day on Facebook, and over 700 YouTube videos are shared on Twitter each minute. A smart online retailer will take advantage of this massive viewership by having their business and most popular products present on YouTube. Once uploaded to the site, a product video should be embedded on a product detail page. This gives the video added exposure on the YouTube channel as well as a more interactive experience to the product detail page.

An example of an effective product video that went viral is that of Blendtec. Blendtec is a manufacturer of blenders, claiming to have the most durable blender on the market. To differentiate themselves from other blender manufactures and to show the effectiveness of their product, Blendtec launched a campaign and website called Willitblend.com. Willitblend.com features many product videos of the blender blending very durable yet unexpected items. The most memorable video is that of the blender blending up an iPhone. The video caught on with consumers and was shared throughout many social networks garnering more than 10 million YouTube views as of the time of this writing. Blendtec ensured that it would maximize the value of these viewers by including a few seconds at the end of the video advertising the link a consumer could go to purchase the blender.

Blendtec may or may not have been successful as a company without the Willitblend campaign, but there is absolutely no question that the product videos of that campaign massively contributed to their success. Unfortunately Blendtec's success is the exception, not the norm, with most product videos. However, there are still great lessons to learn from their success. First, an engaging video that appeals to the target audience will likely be well received and shared among consumers. Brainstorm creative ways to showcase your products in action. Second, the takeaway from Blendtec's success is to demonstrate the product in action with a narrative that explains the primary value propositions in a fun and creative way. This will help reinforce a visual understanding of the product in use, which will contribute to a positive experience and potentially influence a consumer to make a purchase. Third, the call to action at the end of the product video pushes consumers to the main site. A few seconds at the end of the video should advertise the product or store with a link that a consumer can type in to go directly to the store and purchase the item. Even better, include a link in the description of the video on YouTube that links consumers directly to the product, category, or store home page.

## Conversion-Focused Design and Structure

A product page description and layout should be focused on buyer personas that echo an understanding of the target user. Although the actual design of a high-quality product detail page will vary depending on the target audience, several core elements remain a constant. A high-quality product page should be optimized for SEO, draw immediate attention to conversion buttons (e.g., add to cart, watch video, download buyer guide, etc.) while highlighting the elements most important to the targeted user. User-centric product images, descriptions, key benefits, pricing, and customer reviews are all elements that work together to make powerful product pages.

A clean URL structure for a product detail page will help search engines better identify the product page, giving it a better chance of showing in non-paid search engine results, considered "organic results". A clean URL structure will include the product name and stock-keeping unit (SKU) number while staying as close to the root URL as possible.

Optimal URL structure: https://www.mysite.com/category/product-name-SKU-number.aspx

Poor structure: http://www.mysite.com/98745/bin/category/aj/4ft-1237310.aspx

Ensure that product page URLs are optimized for search by including product name and SKU number.

The actual design of the product page should focus on simplicity, engagement, anticipation, and social reinforcement. When used in combination, these elements can be an incredibly powerful and persuasive set of tools that will enable a consumer to establish an ease of usability, comfort, and trust of a retailer and product. The absence of these elements may pose a serious problem to the usability, and hence, conversion rate of a product detail page. Designing product pages for conversions starts with designing for usability.

**Simplicity.** A clean design that focuses on highlighting the value of the product in a structured, appealing way to the target demographic will enhance usability and should be the first area of concern when either designing or redesigning a product detail page. Consumers feel at ease and are comforted when a task is easy to do or understand. Consumers get frustrated and leave when a task is hard to do or understand. Consumers simply don't want to work or think more than they have to when shopping online. This means that an online retailer has the job of making the product detail page simple and for a consumer to feel at ease, understand the value of the product, and know exactly how to access the information or perform the task that they wish to take on the product detail page—all without overwhelming the consumer with too much information or actions to take. This can be a tough task, but is more easily accomplished when the focus of design is on simple usability instead of on product information. Provide only the information and features that a consumer really needs to understand— the value that the product is offering—and strip away any information or elements that contribute to misunderstanding or ambiguous actions that a consumer should take. It is better to show consumers a little bit of information and let them choose if they want more details or to take further action. An unfocused, cluttered, and overly complicated product detail page will yield lower conversion rates. Consider redesigning your product detail page if you feel that it lacks the focus and simplicity that your consumers desire.

**Engagement.** Consumers will only look at information or read so much text on a product page before losing interest. The advent of the Internet has made our society less focused than ever before, making it more difficult for online retailers to capture and retain the attention of a visitor who has vast options for distractions available at the click of a mouse or stroke of a key. Consumers' attention spans are generally low, which means that retailers must make their product detail pages optimized not only for conversion but also for engagement as well. Grabbing and holding onto the attention of consumers, and not distracting them with unnecessary information or elements that do not influence conversions, is important to retaining their engagement. Highlighting the visual representation of the product using high-quality images and videos, utilizing contrasting colors for conversion buttons, larger fonts for important text, and product descriptions that are easily scannable with headers, bullet points, and short blocks of text will go a long way in the design of an engaging product page. Combat consumers' low attention spans with a simple design that highlights engaging product images, videos, and descriptions that are easily read.

**Anticipation.** If a retailer can get a consumer to commit to a small action, even as small as downloading a buyer's guide or signing up for a free coupon, then that retailer is much more likely to get the consumer to commit to a larger action such as purchasing a product. An online retailer should be anticipating the information and desires of their target demographic. Are there many options of products available in a particular category that could satisfy a consumer's needs? If so, a buyer's guide would be a great anticipation of the consumer's desire for more information about the options available to satisfy their needs. Are the majority of your items impulse buys? If so, the advertisement of a coupon could help anticipate the desired value from the consumer and encourage a purchase. Anticipate all the hesitations a consumer may have when making a purchasing decision and match those hesitations to solutions that you can offer on a product detail page. Anticipate the actions of your consumers to anticipate a positive conversion rate.

**Social reinforcement.** Consumers inherently look to others for guidance on whether to purchase, especially if they are uncertain if they're getting the most value from a particular purchase. This is called social validation and is the reason why ratings and reviews are so powerful on product detail pages. Social networks such as Twitter and Facebook have made it easier than ever for consumers to achieve social validation before making a purchasing decision. Embrace social networks and the desire for social validation by bringing the networks into your product detail pages. Encourage consumers to upload and share photos of the products that they purchased not only to your product detail page but also to their Facebook wall as well. Simply advertising the fact that you will give away a certain amount of store credit for an amazing photo or video of your products in use will likely encourage fans of your products to engage with your brand. Another successful tactic for the encouragement of social validation is allowing visitors to leave comments on Facebook directly from your product detail page. There are several Facebook plugins that enable this functionality. Facebook even has one freely available in their Social Plugins page of their Developers subdomain. You can access it by visiting this link:
https://developers.facebook.com/docs/reference/plugins/comments/

Enable social comments with your storefront and integrate it into your product detail pages. Encouraging social reinforcement will only help to increase the conversion rate of new and returning visitors with real consumer reviews, images, and videos generated by your consumers themselves.

A customer review can be more effective than even the best user-centric ad copy or enticing photos and videos. In fact, a study conducted in February 2010 revealed that consumer reviews are significantly more trusted – nearly 12 times more – than descriptions that come from manufacturers. This is according to a survey of US mom Internet users by online video review site EXPO. A consumer will only give a marketer so much trust, likely a fraction of trust compared to that of a trusted source or an unknown reviewer of a product. Consumer surveys consistently show that buyers prefer shopping on sites that feature customer reviews because it reduces their risk of purchasing a bad product. Even negative reviews are important because they will show transparency and honesty. According to a Social Trends Review conducted in June 2012 by Bazaarvoice, over half of Millennials (consumers aged 18 to 34) trust the opinions of strangers online over those of friends and family.

Prominently feature and encourage product feedback. Consider sending a follow up e-mail encouraging consumers to review their product sometime after a purchase has been delivered.

# Using Consumer-Centric Psychology to Enhance eCommerce Product Detail Pages

Understanding how to influence buying decisions using the application of consumer-centric psychology to marketing can be an incredibly powerful tool in a marketer's belt. Consumer-centric psychology is the study of consumer behavior and the power to learn, and even help manipulate, how consumers make purchasing decisions. Utilizing the word *you*, contrasting colors on primary and secondary call-to-action buttons, adhering to common layout patterns, and emphasizing visual ad copy are just a few of the common and easily implemented applications of consumer-centric psychology that can have a significant impact on the conversion rates of your product pages.

## The Power of *You*

Even the most selfless human beings are incredibly narcissistic when making purchasing decisions. We buy products to help resolve an internal emotion, need, pain, or conflict within ourselves. Consumers do not make a purchase because they like your products; they buy products from you because they desire the resolution of their internal emotion, need, pain, or conflict that your product helps them solve. Even when a purchase is made because they like your brand or product, the consumer is really buying from you so they can enjoy the use of it. The brand affinity for your company simply helps them make the decision to buy from your store.

Consumers buy with their emotions as much or more than they buy with the logical side of their brain. This makes the left brain–right brain dichotomy incredibly interesting and important to online marketers. Win the hearts of the consumer and their money will follow. The most effective product pages are not focused on the product; they are focused on empowering the consumer to feel comfortable, important, and relieved that their purchase satisfies their emotional conflict.

Consumers like to feel important and special. Imagine going into a clothing store and being greeted by an associate that takes a personal interest in you. The associate may want to show you clothing that he or she thinks will look good on you, based on your interest and tastes of course. The associate may even be particularly skilled and will take a personal interest in you, making you feel appreciated and important, even special, as a consumer. The best associates will tell their potential consumers things like "that suit fits *you* really well" or "this blouse brings out *your* eyes" or "*you* really wear this well." These phrases appeal to the self-centric emotion of consumers, helping resolve their emotional conflict while having confidence that the product is perfect for them.

Although we as eCommerce marketers do not have the ability to use a physical associate who can give compliments to online store browsers, we do have control of the text and visual elements that potential consumers will read and view to help them come closer to a purchasing decision.

Use of the words *you* or *your* in product ad copy and including images of people using or interacting with products is a good first step in appealing to consumer-centric needs through product pages and will make your store appeal to the subconscious narcissism that exists within nearly all consumers.

## The Power of Contrast

The power of contrast should be used to make important design elements of a web page stand out from other elements on the page, such as call-to-action buttons. Large buttons, strong colors, and stark contrasts help ensure the visitor doesn't have to work too hard to read or find what they are looking for and what you want them to click on. Make it easy for visitors to click on important elements of a page and they will in turn have a more positive experience while giving your site an increase in click-through and conversion rates in the process.

Two powerful contrasting methods to use are size and color. For example, a large button in a contrasting color to the background of the site will immediately draw user attention and will likely yield higher click through rates than elements on the page that blend in with the structure and color scheme of the website page. The size of an element relative to its surroundings indicates the importance of that element. The larger the element, the more important it is. Similarly, the more contrasting an element is, the more likely it is to be read and clicked on.

Another important element of size and color contrast is that it gives a site focus. Too many similarly styled elements will lead to too many choices and indecision by a visitor. Use the power of contrast to lead a visitor to the most important elements of your page. For example, if your site is primarily made up of black text on a light-blue background, then a small light-blue call-to-action button will not be very effective because it does not contrast. A proportionately large red or green button on a light-blue background will contrast and should be used instead.

## The Power of Familiarity

We like familiarity as much as we like contrast. Website visitors like patterns and familiar elements because they understand and feel comfortable with these elements. Essentially the visitor does not have to assess the structure and "likeness" of a page because they already understand the lay of the land and feel comfortable. Patterns and familiarity make consumers feel safe.

Use a site structure and page layout similar to major online retailers to adhere to a common pattern while making it easier for consumers to feel comfortable shopping. The structure and layout does not have to be exactly the same but should not be so different that visitors feel disoriented and have to work to find what they are looking for. Amazon.com is a great example to learn from. Amazon currently controls a large percentage of the eCommerce market share and is a likely destination for online consumers. Use this to your advantage and make site structure and page layouts similar to the online commerce behemoth.

Another way to harness the power of familiarity is to include images of faces on your website pages. A smiling face, especially one that is attractive or appealing to a target demographic, will help visitors subconsciously feel more comfortable.

However, there is a right and a wrong way to including images on important pages. Including cheesy stock photographs, like businessmen shaking hands in suits, can actually have a negative impact because users will not trust them. Images of faces should be real and honest. Use images of people from your company instead. Include an image of a real support rep or maybe even the CEO on the checkout page with some text below telling the consumer that you take customer support seriously and can assist with any of their problems. Be honest, not cheesy, to maximize the value of familiarity.

## The Power of Numbers

You already know about the importance of the word *you*, contrast, and familiarity, but what about the power of numbers in consumer psychology? At the end of the day it is, after all, the bottom line those business owners are concerned with. That bottom line is comprised of numbers, so it's important to understand the power they have over the consumer.

One of the first instincts of advertisers is to compare their lower price to the higher price of a competitor. It seems to make sense that consumers would automatically go for the lower-priced product if all other factors of the item were the same. Unfortunately, this is never a reliable marketing method and can affect a consumer's perception in more than one way. First, the customer may perceive the lower-priced item as more of a risk and gravitate toward the higher-priced item. Conversely, they may simply purchase nothing at all.

The difference can be found in implicit versus explicit comparisons. When a customer compares two or more items using nothing more than his or her own initiative, it is referred to as an *implicit* comparison. If the comparison is suggested in any way by the advertiser, it is considered an *explicit* comparison.

Studies of the two types of comparisons have found that explicit comparisons cause adverse reaction in buyers. Buyers become much more cautious when specifically asked to compare prices because they felt they were being tricked in some way. Comparative pricing can be a very powerful selling tool, but it is not without its risks. A better option may be to highlight the unique strengths of an item you are trying to sell.

One of the best examples of the use of numbers comes with the number 9. Using the number 9 in pricing will not only influence people's perceptions of prices, but boosts their buying as well. Rutgers University professor Robert Schindler and his colleagues did a real-life test with a women's clothing catalog. The clothing line normally advertised items ending in 88 cents. For the experiment, the researchers divided the 90,000 customers into three groups. One group got catalogs with traditional prices, one got prices ending in .00 and one got prices ending in .99.

The 99-cent catalog significantly outperformed the .00 one, Dr Schindler said, reporting 8 percent higher sales even through the average price decrease was only three-hundredths of a percent.

Manoj Thomas, a Cornell University business professor, has conducted experiments with graduate students showing that the biggest impact of 99 cent pricing comes when it changes the leftmost digit in the price - $19.99 vs. $20 for instance as opposed to $3.49 vs. $3.50.

"Generally, it can be said that this happens because we read from left to right," Dr. Thomas said, and we place extra importance on the first number we see.

A 99-cent ending "makes the price 'feel' less," Dr. Schindler said, "and goes deeper than just appearances. If you give people two ads for a blouse, one priced at $22 and one at $21.99, people are more likely to judge the $21.99 item as being on sale.

But while utilizing 99-cent pricing has shown to be effective in increasing sales, Schindler has found that it can also work against retailers.

"On the other side, it can give the image that an item is of low or questionable quality." Schindler says most people are more concerned about quality over price when buying luxury products, services or making risky purchases.

"Retailers don't want those items to come across as cheap. For example, if you're going to do some work on a person's house, you wouldn't want your price to reflect that you might do a poor job. In that case, the customer is concerned about quality and I would suggest not using 99-cent endings. It's better to be straightforward when selling that kind of product."

The major takeaway for retailers is that you should generally use 99-cent endings for your products, with the exception of items that you want portrayed as high-end retail.

Another point to remember is that priming is just as essential as context. Once you've gotten the consumer to commit to a purchase, they are more likely to purchase something that costs more if it is anchored next to an even more expensive item. If you want your customers to spend an average of $50.00 on an item, place that item next to items that cost $100.00.

It's also important for marketers to be aware of a consumer's perception of a stimulus (a.k.a. an advertisement). Perception is an individual's approximation of reality and is heavily influenced by exposure and interpretation. How do you get a consumer to notice your stimulus? The stimulus must be relevant and surprising to really grab attention. Weber's Law suggests that an individual's ability to detect changes in stimuli is related to the intensity of that stimulus from the onset. For example, if you are consistently advertising "20 percent Off!" all of your merchandise, consumers aren't likely to notice when you have a "Big Sale! 25 percent Off!" If you want to draw consumers in greater volume, use your stimuli wisely.

# Chapter 5:

## Blogging and SEO

There are very few things can be said with absolute certainty; one of them, however, is that it is difficult to be successful—almost impossible to be successful—at inbound eCommerce without blogging. Blogging in content creation is the linchpin for driving "organic" traffic from search engines. Of the many factors affecting organic traffic, blogging is one of the most critical to master. Since organic traffic frequently has the lowest cost of customer acquisition, it is inherently some of the most valuable. The strongest signals for a search engine to determine the relevance of the website domain or specific page to a keyword query is the freshness, frequency, and relevance of content being created on the target domain. There simply isn't an easier or more effective way of creating a high velocity of quality keyword-relevant content than blogging.

## Why Should an ECommerce Site Blog?

A great benefit of blogging is that it offers the type of web content in which it is natural to have a high velocity of topically oriented content creation. Unlike product detail pages, service detail pages, general information pages, or—really—any other type of web pages, blogs are expected to frequently discuss the same issues—or variable takes on the same issues or group of issues—without reaching a level of excess. It would be unnatural to repeatedly create new product detail pages or general, descriptive web pages all about the same product, whereas a blog discussing uses, opinions, features, and other issues relating to the product is an area where high-velocity content seems very natural. Since Google and other search engines are frequently making the freshness, quality, and the social amplification of content ever stronger for keyword relevance, the nature of blogs and their high velocity of content that is fresh, relevant, and frequently socially amplified, makes blogs the most valuable tool for driving organic search traffic.

# What Is a Business Blog?

A business blog article is a long-term marketing asset that will bring traffic and leads to your business. It introduces you as a thought leader in your space and allows you to earn people's trust. A successful business blog focuses on a specific keyword-oriented subject relevant to a business while following the best tactical and technical applications for driving targeted, valuable, consumer search traffic to a website. High-priority elements for optimization of a blog post include the title, the image, the keywords, the amount of copy, effective call to action, and social sharing features.

Magdalena Georgieva from HubSpot defines a blog further in her Ebook "An Introduction To Business Blogging":

> "A blog is a long-term marketing asset that will bring traffic and leads to your business. It introduces you as a thought leader in your space and allows you to earn people's trust."

In addition to establishing you as a thought leader, a business blog allows you to create an audience of readers for a specific type of buyer personas outside of the normal transactional context of your website. It allows you to create content that will attract specific types of consumers to your website and provide them with a non-transactional call-to-action to help you generate leads.

## Blog Title Best Practices

All search engines consider the title of the page to be extremely relevant to what that page is supposedly about. Similar to how you might choose what articles to read first in your morning paper or e-mail by looking at the headline or subject lines, search engines use the title of the page or blog as a strong indicator of what that page or blog is about. The title of the blog article should be housed in the URL slug (the extension coming at the end of the article URL) as well as in the H1 tag on the page. The title should also be reflected in the HTML header element title. Aligning these three elements with the blog article title will reinforce to the search engine that this blog article is about this specific long-tail search query and any relevant keywords that the search engine associates with the keywords in the title. Therefore, it's extremely important that you put a level of strategic and tactical application of SEO thought into crafting your blog headlines.

The title of a blog article is one of the most important elements for a business blog for its value as a mechanism of search engine optimization. The title should be keyword oriented, often using a specifically targeted long-tail keyword phrase (keyword phrase of three to five words) and focus on a single topic or subject. For example, a bad blog keyword title is one that is not descriptive of the topic and does not use relevant keywords. A common pitfall—especially for new business bloggers who are extremely knowledgeable within their industry or product vertical—is to create blog article titles that are artsy and imaginative. While you might be tempted to call a blog article about LASIK surgery "The Eyes Are a Window to the Soul," that is not an effective blog article title. Artsy titles, devoid of targeted keyword phrases, are competing for search engine relevance and placement with content that has absolutely nothing to do with the primary product or service. The example "The Eyes Are a Window to the Soul" as a blog article title will be competing with angsty teen blogs about unrequited love—most likely not an area a LASIK company will want to compete with. Furthermore, the search engine traffic driven by such a title would not be relevant to people seeking LASIK surgery at all. A better title for that blog article would be "What Questions Should I Ask before Having LASIK Surgery?" This title has several advantages over the first. The primary advantage is that the title is actually relevant to the type of traffic that a LASIK business would want drive—consumers who are interested in LASIK surgery. The title targets a short-tail primary keyword—"LASIK surgery"—that any LASIK surgeon would want to rank highly for. LASIK surgery as a short-tail keyword is a very competitive keyword, yet this title has the advantage of falling into what is likely a common long-tail keyword query. "What questions should I ask before having LASIK surgery" is the long-tail keyword phrase that a consumer considering LASIK surgery would likely search for. That is, it's entirely probable that somebody might google that exact phrase, making it an optimal title for a business blog article optimized for search traffic.

## Blog Image Best Practices

Although not frequently considered a critical part of a well-crafted blog article, articles with images perform better. In fact, a 2011 study by content production firm Skyword found that "total views increased by 94% if a published article contained a relevant photograph or infographic when compared to articles without an image in the same category".

Typically, an image that either refers to or directly graphically conveys the general subject matter of a blog article oriented in the upper right-hand corner of the article with the first paragraph text wrapped around it is the general standard and a best practice. Images serve to break up a blog article text while preventing the text from overwhelming to the reader.

Images also help to give context to the blog article. However, since search engines only see pictures as an image filename and alt tag, in blogging, a picture is not worth much. Thus a properly optimized article should use images to supplement article copy with graphical representations of the topics. The key factor of using images for search engine optimization is the proper application of the image filename and alt attribute. Frequently forgotten or neglected, the image filename and alt attribute are the only elements currently being textually indexed by search engines. Therefore, it's an additional signal to a search engine crawling a page that a specific page is relevant to a specific keyword if the indexable attributes of the images on that page are also relevant. Also, assigning the images' attributes that are searchable by search engines allows them to show up in image searches, such as those from Google images.

## Blog Copy Best Practices

As a general rule, a blog article should have no less than 600 words. Fewer than 600 words rarely gives a search engine enough context to determine that a body of copy is relevant to a specific keyword query. There is some debate over whether a blog article can have so much copy that it's better off being split into two articles with a smaller word count. Since the content will be indexed again as fresh, keyword-relevant content, it may gain a greater boost than one long article. Also, from a user-experience perspective, blog articles should be short, concise, and valuable. Readers may lose interest if a blog article is too long, and if they lose interest they're unlikely to click the calls to action spread throughout the website.

One of the most significant reasons that marketers used to have a "cap" on the amount of copy on any given web page or blog article was that Google used to only index about 100 kilobytes on any given page – meaning that articles with too much copy would not get it all indexed. However, according to Matt Cutts who runs the Google webspam team, Google is now indexing far more than 100 kilobytes, so many marketers are focusing much more heavily on the value of the blog content and less on capping the copy.

For the most part, to optimize blog copy should marketers ignore advice around a specific density or frequency of keywords in your copy and just write naturally. If you're writing naturally, the keywords a marketer is trying to optimize for should appear in a natural way throughout the article. The general rule of thumb is that if you were smart enough to game Google, you'd be working at Google. Instead of trying to stuff keywords into your copy to make your article seem more relevant to a specific keyword than it actually is, just write the copy that comes naturally based on your topic.

## Blog Call-to-Action Best Practices

One of the great values of business blog articles is the fact that they can be optimized to be found organically and socially for long-tail keyword phrases. They provide the opportunity for a marketer to create indexable pages while exploring the many different permutations of the keyword phrases that they're trying to optimize for. Properly optimized articles will frequently generate possible leads or prospective customers. Therefore, business articles should include a primary and a secondary call to action on the actual blog article page. We'll discuss later in the book the differences and tactical applications of primary versus secondary calls to action, but in general, primary calls to action—such as buy now or request a demo—goes "above the fold" (meaning above the point on a page where a website visitor would have to scroll) and to the right of the article in the secondary call to action—such as "download the ultimate guide to a topic relating to the article you just read" goes at the end of the article copy. The presence of effective calls to action in the blog article page allows you to capture real value from the organic search traffic to whom that blog article page is their first touch.

## Blog Keyword Best Practices

One of the greatest challenges that most marketers have to overcome is discovering and implementing the topics and titles that drive high-velocity, keyword-relevant blog content. The first step, after identifying the buyer persona that the article is designed to attract, in writing an effective blog article is selecting the keyword or keyword phrase around which the blog article is intended to drive traffic. This keyword or keyword phrase should be relevant to the business or industry while also providing the business an opportunity to rank higher in organic search results.

Analyze your website for keyword search ranking placements using analytic tools. Good keyword analytic tools should, at a minimum, show a business where they are currently ranking for a keyword and the associated traffic that the keyword or phrase is driving. Proper use of an analytic tool will help define and put structure to keyword optimization. Avoid focusing blog articles on keyword phrases that are already ranking very highly, unless there is a strong need to protect the ranking achieved. Instead focus on keywords that are not in the top 10 search result spots but rank in the top 100. This can be an effective discovery tool to develop a keyword list to derive relevant and opportunistic keyword topics.

Also avoid targeting keywords with an extremely high level of difficulty. A high level of difficulty is determined by the current ranking of a keyword, the competition for that keyword, and the search traffic associated.

## Blog Problem-Oriented Optimization Best Practices

Blog article titles are a good place to exercise problem-oriented optimization (POO). Instead of focusing on writing articles about what a product or service does, focus on writing articles that explore or address the problems that consumers face. These topics will likely contain long-tail combinations of keywords designed to drive specific, targeted traffic.

Problem-oriented topics can also be general problems that are relevant to a specific customer base. For example, a company specializing in small-business debt mitigation will certainly want to optimize for keywords relating to small-business debt. This business should create blog content around problems relating to small businesses and finance. By writing articles that help small businesses address how to work with credit, how to raise capital, and other critical small-business finance issues, this blog will become a valuable resource for prospective customers as well as bring in high-quality search traffic and prospects who—although they may not fit their immediate exact targeting parameters—are also potential customers.

## Blog Idea Generation Best Practices

A good source of ideas for blog articles are your frontline employees (e.g., salespeople and customer-service representatives). Your frontline employees are those who respond to customer and prospect questions every day and may also witness customer issues each day that could make for rich and valuable problem-oriented blog content. Support staff, similarly, likely receive a high volume of queries that could easily be turned into rich and valuable blog content. Ensure that the lines of communication are open between frontline, support staff and marketing teams for optimal blog content.

When considering what to write blog articles about, the place to start is with your buyer personas. Whatever blog articles you write are going to attract more of whatever types of buyer personas find that piece of content interesting. If you've done your funnel analysis properly and you know what types of buyer personas you want to attract or avoid, you can go to your persona analysis and find out what their pain points are, what their level of sophistication is, what their key-use cases are, what their general-but-related concerns, issues, and interests are, and all of the other valuable aspects of the psychographic analysis that you've done. Even the tone and personality of the content will help you attract the types of readers—and therefore the types of future customers—that are valuable to your eCommerce business.

## Blog Audience-Targeting Best Practices

A good business blog should always consider the audience members for whom they are writing. The first audience members—and the most important—are the search engines themselves. Like any audience member, search engines have their own preferences and unique elements that they value. Search engines primarily care about the structure and density of the keywords on the page as well as the number of other web pages that are linking to it. As stated before, to write effectively for your search engine audience, you should ensure that your blog article has the fundamental elements of search engine optimization. Also, considering search engines as a unique audience member reminds us that blog articles should be written with a specific keyword in mind.

The second type of audience member to target is the sharer or influencer persona—those blog readers who read your blog for the express purpose of sharing it in social media. Sharers and influencers share content because they believe it will add value to their social network. Frequently reading only the headline or simply skimming article content, sharers and influencers are concerned with whether the members of their social network will be interested in your article—and whether sharing your article will increase their reach and authority within their social network. Although the amplification of sharers and influencers is often considered a primary goal of blogging, it's not as important as you may think to intentionally craft content for this specific persona. Interesting keyword relevant headlines and remarkable topics or viewpoints will naturally gravitate shares and influencers to your content as it will satisfy their primary benefits for amplifying content.

Equally important is paying attention to the types of content that garner the most social shares as a key performance indicator of content—not necessarily because of the direct benefits of being amplified into social networks, but more so because social sharing has increasingly becoming a strong signal to search engines for the relevance, quality, and authority of web content. One of the most notable trends of 2011— a year of far-reaching implications for the future of search engine optimization—is the increasing reliance of search engines on social signals. In fact, a 2012 study by SearchMetrics found a higher correlation between Facebook shares and Google search rankings than inbound links.

Since search engines aim to serve the most interesting and relevant content to their users, it's only logical that they will weigh heavily the positive opinion of real humans who consumed a piece of content and then amplify intentionally into their social network. No matter how good Google's algorithm gets, it will always be difficult for them to compete with the collective wisdom of more than 10 percent of the world's population using real lives and real opinions to judge how remarkable and how authoritative a piece of content is.

The third and arguably most important audience for business blog content are readers, subscribers, prospects, and customers. A goal, and primary value, of business blogging is that consumers will find a relevant blog article from a search query and click through to a website. From there, calls to action and website-user interface can direct consumers through the buying cycle of a business. However, since a blog article may be a consumer's first impression of your website, it's important that the content be useful and remarkable to the reader. Primarily, this audience cares about the brevity and usefulness of your content. This audience is why numbered lists, bulleted lists, and other easily digestible content performs very well. Summations, takeaways, and conclusions also serve this audience well.

Most marketers' initial reaction is that frequent readers of their blog are their most valuable readers, since they are frequently most engaged. However, they should remember that one of the primary purposes of a business blog is to drive new traffic and create conversion opportunities. A great fear of most business owners and marketers is that the blog will reach a level that begins to bore their regular readers. However, if a reader has been reading a business blog for an extended period of time and has not converted on an offer or become a customer, then the value is somewhat diminished from a strategic blogging perspective. Frequent readers of your blog certainly have value—with great potential to amplify content and the possibility of becoming a future customer—but it's not as important to be consistently creating content interesting to frequent readers as it is to be creating content that helps you rank higher in search engines and provide interesting content to new prospects.

## Blog Publishing Frequency Best Practices

Both marketers and business owners frequently ask how often they should blog. There is a simple, yet incredibly effective, metaphor for the inbound marketing philosophy that answers this question. Blogging is like jogging. If you've ever tried to lose weight, you know that cardiovascular activities such as jogging are an extremely important part of the equation. You also know that it has to be done frequently, consistently, and that it takes some time to see results. There is an interesting and convenient correlation between the number of times you should jog if you're looking to get in shape and lose weight and the number of times you should blog if you're looking to drive more traffic and improve your search optimization. There are some general minimums, such as two to three times a week, which interestingly parallel minimum number of times a person should jog per week if you'd like to see weight loss. However, jogging two to three times a week for only one month will not show the same results as jogging two to three times a week for ninety or more days. Just like jogging, a business blog should keep a consistent blogging strategy of two to three times a week for ninety or more days to see significant results.

The "blogging is like jogging" metaphor has another great parallel: If you want to lose weight, it's far more important to get out there and start jogging *today* than it is to make sure you have perfect form before you begin. It takes a great deal of practice jogging to get the breathing, stride, arm swing, and other factors of form perfected. If you wait until you have a perfect understanding of the theory and application of jogging to start jogging, it will be that much longer until you receive the results of weight loss that you're looking for. Similarly, it's far more important that you start blogging today than it is that your blog adhere to all of the criteria set forth in this book.

A healthy business blog will be publishing articles consistently, frequently, and with the understanding that it will take some time to see results. Organic search traffic is one of the most valuable traffic sources in terms of its overall quality and cost of customer acquisition. Although it's tempting to focus on sexy topics such as search optimization and link building, there is simply no substitute for the effective strategic application of a high velocity of "pretty good" blog content.

## Unique Content Creation Ideas

One of the many benefits of content creation is the increased likelihood that someone will find your content interesting and link to your website. Simply put, no one finds your About Us page to be compelling content that's going to generate inbound links. Google's algorithm is fundamentally predicated on the concept that that content interacts with each other. Websites that have other websites linking to it are considered more interesting and authoritative, since another website owner took the time to include a link to you on their website. Also, Matt Cutts and the Google webspam team have made it clear that linking out to multiple websites dilutes the authority of each individual link, that website owner think you're important enough to deserve some of their PageRank.

This has led to the rise of "link-baiting"—or creating content that's specifically designed to incite inbound links. The general psychology behind link-baiting and share-baiting is similar. Content that's disruptive, controversial, visually compelling, or especially unique is going to be generally more compelling than the bread-and-butter blog content that will power your strategy. You should note that bread-and-butter, text-oriented content that's keyword relevant and useful to prospective and existing customers should form the basis of your strategy, but you can gain exceptional traction from mixing in disruptive and compelling content.

You should understand, particularly, the interests of the people who typically link to your website or your competitor's website. Do they find breaking industry or product news compelling? Do they find unique testimonials interesting? Do they find silly content the most unique and worthy of links? Knowing this can help get you started, and you'll want to analyze on an ongoing basis what kinds of content are generating the most inbound links to your website.

Let's discuss some particularly valuable types of link-baiting and share-baiting content:

# Infographics

Infographics are probably the most commonly thought-of link-bait content. An infographic is a visual representation of data, a story, or a process that fits within a blog article column. Visual content can be particularly impactful because it's easily digestible and understandable, which makes it particularly effective for explaining complex concepts or the significance of data within a process. Infographics can help explain complex relationships, processes, or other ideas by leveraging the human ability to comprehend patterns and trends faster through visual information than text.

Because of this, infographics are frequently linked to by other websites, especially pundits and bloggers who are commenting on the topics or conclusions that your infographic covers. Because it allows you to clearly and succinctly explain complex concepts, it can allow you to share particularly compelling stories with data or show interesting processes. Good infographics should tell a story, bringing the reader to a compelling conclusion based on the information you're sharing.

eCommerce companies can use infographics to explain the lifecycle of product development and testing, for example. What may seem complex and uninteresting to your company may, in fact, help your customers understand the complexity and care involved in bringing the product they're purchasing to market. In addition to personifying the product by showing how people are involved in the process, it can increase their understanding of the product's quality (which can increase their trust in the product and willingness to buy) as well as give them insight into the factors of cost in your product, which may actually make them less price-sensitive. An infographic showing the development of your industry or product over time could also garner a large number of inbound links if it shows the long journey that your industry has taken to date, and particularly because bloggers and pundits (who are part of your industry no matter how annoying you may find them) will be emotionally influenced by the article describing the industry they work within.

In addition to publishing the infographic on your website and hoping that people link to your article, you should also make it easy to embed the infographic on other websites. While it may sound counterintuitive to freely give away a piece of content that took so much time and effort to assemble, the fact is that many people will find it easier to share your infographic with their audience accompanied by a snippet of commentary rather than create an entire article referencing your infographic. Given this, it's likely that bloggers will repost this content anyway. By creating an easily embeddable option on your article, you can, however, control the way that it's embedded and make sure that you get a keyword-oriented text link back to your website.

You can even take this concept of helping bloggers create an interesting content a step further and create infographics specifically for them. Because infographics are such useful and interesting—and difficult to create—pieces of content, they're likely to be well-received by blogs and websites that might reject other guest-blogging advances. You can create unique infographics for influential websites or just offer other websites the option to publish your infographic exclusively before you do.

## Lists and Stats

Similar to the way in which infographics are easily digestible and useful pieces of content, lists and statistics articles are simple, easily digestible, and useful pieces of content that can inspire websites to link to you for attribution or reference. If your list is the source of discovery by a person for a statistic or piece of specific information (especially detailed, long-tail keywords that are easy to rank for), that person will typically link back to your website as the reference source if they're following attribution rules properly (if they're not there's not much you can do about it).

Lists also make handy pieces of content that people like to keep for reference, and because of this they're inherently interesting and shareable. Cheat sheets, one-liners, glossaries, and checklists are good examples of listable content that other websites will find useful to cite, share, and discuss. Articles with particularly high numbers also tend to perform well in social media (since they're disruptive in scope), and since it's hard to write a comprehensive article with 100+ topics or points, lists offer a valuable substitute.

## News

Breaking news is some of the most compelling and disruptive content on the Internet. Although it's highly improbable that your marketing organization has the resources to conduct actual journalism, you can certainly offer a unique perspective on news that affects your industry. Again, the key here is to craft an opinion that's interesting enough to warrant attribution, so the point that you make will have to be insightful enough that it can be commented or expanded upon. If there's a key piece of legislation or news affecting your industry, don't respond with the simple and dry mouth-piece content that your public relations firm is pushing on you—get your CEO out there with a strong and unique opinion and factual piece that's worth talking about.

You can also share company news—if you have something interesting to say. Absolutely no one is going to find it interesting that your office will be closed for Memorial Day (don't laugh, there are companies who have published that exact article to their marketing blog). However, if you're releasing a particularly interesting product, announcing a surprising or interesting partnership, or have some other news that will be interesting to someone that doesn't work at your company, then you can create a compelling piece of content around it. Part of the mission of bloggers and industry journalists is to cover exactly that—interesting news from the players and influencers.

If you're going to share news that's just part of your corporate narrative, it's important to frame it from a perspective that's exceptionally compelling. If you acquire a competitor or other company, publish an article about the significant value that this brings to your company's mission. Dry content rarely gets links, so try to craft a narrative that journalists will find compelling and readers will find inspiring.

# How-To's and Guides

One of those easiest pieces of content that you've never thought to create are the simple how-to articles that are typically relegated to support and documentation PDFs. However, "how do I" questions are often asked *during* the sales process, not after. Because of this, it makes sense to create product-oriented how-to content for your marketing blog. Although it may seem elementary and obvious to you, the particular-use cases and applications of your products may not be immediately evident to prospective customers.

In addition to your product-oriented content, problem-oriented content can be extremely beneficial to your sales cycle. Because online shoppers tend to have a significant research phase of their sales cycle where they're searching for and consuming information about their particular use case or problems, controlling this content can enable you to generate leads early in their sales cycle. Since one of the significant causes of shoppers not buying online is shipping costs to get products as fast as they need them (or indeed, whether or not it's physically possible at all to get the products there as fast as they need them), capturing eCommerce prospects while they're in the research phase of the buying cycle can increase your sales by introducing your website as a potential vendor for the product they're looking for early enough that the shipping process won't be a barrier.

For example, if you're a website that sells bicycles, you can create how-to content such as "The Commuter's Guide to Bicycles" or "The City-Dwellers Guide to Getting Around." You can also create content around how to plan your bike route to work, how to bike safely in morning traffic, etc. Although the prospects that see this content may not buy immediately, they're much more likely to find your website useful and become eventual customers.

Also, because how-to content is so inherently useful to readers and consumers, they're much more likely to get linked to by writers within your industry. Remember that the key purpose for authoritative websites that will link to you is sharing interesting and useful content within the industry they cover. If you can create guides or how-to articles that have enough significance that someone could write an article *about* it that has a unique angle or value, you're much more likely to get inbound links.

# Controversial Content

An extremely dangerous yet potentially highly effective form of bait content is a controversial stance or opinion about a topic affecting your consumers or your industry. We won't give any examples here and instead allow you to use your own imagination and discretion. Just keep in mind that any controversial content will, by definition, upset or even offend some segment of people. The backlash can be severe, but polarization can have particularly beneficial side effects if the audience that you're alienating isn't an audience that you ever intend to target or that has any value for you. For example, if your product is particularly disruptive within your industry, you can create content talking about existing trends and solutions that will be extremely controversial but only alienate those who wouldn't be adopters of your disruptive solution anyway.

Another effective way of mitigating damage to your website's brand from controversial content is to emphasize that a person is creating this content and possibly even facilitate a dissenting opinion side-by-side with the controversial stance. Essentially, if you're the venue for both sides of a controversial argument, then your site will reap the rewards of buzz without potential fallout of partisanship.

## Odd and Unusual Content

Odd and unusual content is particularly useful, and can be a factor of any of the above types of unique content. If your content can't be useful or particularly compelling, there's some value in just being strange. Especially useful for share-baiting, disruptive content is a very easy way of being interesting enough to incite social sharing and linking. Especially useful if you have visually striking examples, odd or unusual content will perform well on social sharing sites like Pinterest as well as amplification-heavy sites like Twitter. For example, an online make-up retailer could create an article such as "15 Bizarre Make-Up Styles," which would certainly garner a significant number of social shares and possibly some inbound links if there's a niche trend within the bizarre examples that people want to discuss.

The basic psychology of people make odd content particularly compelling because it's often the most disruptive and shareable. Entire museums, books, and blogs are dedicated to weird facts and examples—leverage this to add some variety to your content creation that will keep your readership engaged and influence some social-sharing and link-building.

## Understanding the Elements of On-Page Search Engine Optimization

On-page search engine optimization (SEO) is the process of optimizing elements of a web page to improve the crawl and readability of search engines to improve the chances for achieving high-ranking placements on search engine result pages (SERPs) for desired keyword(s). The primary elements of a web page that an eCommerce marketer should ensure are optimized for targeted keyword phrases are the URL, page title, H1 tag (also known as header tag), body text, anchor text, images files names, and alt text. Let's take a look at each element and how to optimize for maximum search engine exposure.

# URL

Keyword relevance in the URL of a web page is a ranking factor used by search engines to determine the ranking of a page. An optimized website page URL should be short in length while including the primary target keyword phrases as early in the URL as possible. The closer the primary keyword phrases are to the domain name, the better. Extensive domain research for primary keyword phrases in the URL should be examined if launching a new website. Any nonroot-level page name should be optimized with useful and descriptive phrases for optimal results. The part of a URL that comes after the subdirectory designation is commonly referred to as the "URL slug," and this is the area where many people ignore the use of keywords. Do not make this mistake by ensuring you have targeted keywords in your URL slug.

An optimal structure for a product page example:

http://www.mysite.com/category/product-name

An optimal structure for a blog page hosted in a subdirectory:

http://www.mysite.com/blog/descriptive-keyword-focused-title

# Page Title

The page title, also known as the title tag, is easily one of the most important elements of on-page SEO as it appears in three primary locations: window title bars, search result pages, and bookmark lists. Properly optimized title tags will include a primary keyword phrase close to the start of the title tag, be under 70 characters in length and be unique across all website pages while being descriptive and relevant to the content of the webpage. A page title should be under 70 characters because that is the limit that Google displays in their search results.

When writing a page title, think of being very descriptive to the content on the page. If the page you are optimizing contains content about a specific product within a category, the page title should be structured as "Product Name | Product Category" using a pipe bar to separate the product name and category. If you notice that a lot of other websites are advertising the same product, you may want to be more descriptive of the product in your page title. For example, "Extremely Durable Product Name | Product Category." This distinction makes your page title slightly different than the other websites that would have the exact same as yours, enabling you to differentiate and rank if a searcher does type in the prefix "durable product name."

## H1 Tag

Each website page should have one heading tag that incorporates the primary target keyword and aligns with the page title and the URL. The header tags represent the beginning of a new section or area of content on a web page and alerts search engine spiders of the relevancy of the content following. Limit the length of heading tags by avoiding words that are not relevant to the web page content.

Typically, the H1 tag will align with the Page Title and the URL slug to give a keyword consistency to the primary on-page SEO elements. When all three of the elements are aligned with their keywords, then the page is likely to be considered heavily relevant to the referenced keywords.

## Keywords in Product Descriptions

Primary keyword phrases should be used two to three times on short web pages and four to six times on longer ones, but never in a context that doesn't make sense with the copy. Don't force keywords into ad copy; use them naturally. Search engines attempt to detect when a keyword is being used with an unnatural frequency and may penalize websites for that. Be aware of the fact that you are optimizing a page for a group of keywords and use those keywords as they naturally come up in the descriptions of a product to avoid keyword penalties.

Think of keyword body text optimization as a method to better highlight the topic of a web page and thus keep the reader interested. Keep the body text focused on the topic of the page and develop new pages for topics that are not directly related to the main topic of the page. The more pages available to optimize (referred to as the number of "indexable pages"), the greater the opportunity for a website to rank for a keyword phrase in search engines.

## Anchor Text

Descriptive keyword phrases should be used as the "anchor text" for internal links on website pages. Anchor text is the visible text of a hyperlink. Search engines heavily weight SERPs toward the anchor text of links to a page. Optimized anchor text will reflect the content the link is linking *to* and ideally help the page is linked from as well. A good example of anchor text is "fire-engine red t-shirt sale" linking to a category page of fire-engine red t-shirts on sale. A bad example of anchor is "click here to view the sale" linking to the same category page.

## Image Filename and Alt-Text

Optimizing for target keyword phrases in the image file name and alt-text is important for eCommerce stores because image search results, which are separate from organic search results, tend to drive significant traffic for products. To start optimizing images, you first need to save your product image as the product name, including the model number when applicable. Avoid uploading images titled "23fr.jpg" as that has no keyword relevance. Instead, rename the image as "productname-modelnumber.jpg."

You have the option of adding alternative text (alt-text) to an image once the image file is uploaded to a web page. A search engine can't actually see an image; it can only see what we describe the image as using proper filename and alt-text. Alt-text is also useful from a user-experience perspective because it frequently appears as the text shown when someone hovers over an image. Use of descriptive alt-text in combination with an optimized file name can help to show product images higher in the image search results as well as contribute to a search engine's understanding of the keyword context of a page.

An optimized web page should contain targeted primary keyword phrases in all of the elements of on-page SEO mentioned above. However, it is also important for a highly optimized page to provide unique content about a given subject while being extremely specific to a topic, usually to a product or single keyword phrase. If a given web page contains multiple topics or products, a webmaster should consider creating new pages about those given topics or products. This will allow for more robust optimization while making it easier for search engines to know what a given web page is really about.

# Using Keyword Phrases to Optimize for SEO

There are three types of keyword phrases that searchers will use in search engines to find a given web page. The three types are branded keywords, jargon keywords, and nonbranded, nonjargon keywords. You should use a variety of each type depending on the goal of the page you are optimizing.

## Branded Keywords

Branded keywords coincide with a company brand or product name. Branded keyword phrases are typically used when a search query is performed for an exact company, brand, or product name. These searches are generally associated with either end-of-sales cycle searches or for company research. Since most sites will rank well for branded keywords naturally, often the homepage website is the only web page where a website would focus on branded keywords.

- Homepage example: "Company X | Product X"

## Jargon Keywords

Jargon keyword phrases are keywords that are product specific but do not include brand or company names. These keyword phrases are used by searchers who understand what they want, just not the brand or where to buy from. Jargon keyword phrases are typically associated with the middle-sales cycle it should be included on product or blog pages when applicable.

- Blog title example: "5 Amazing Digital Cameras with 10x Zoom and HD Video"

- Product title example: "Leather shoes with cushioned sole and heel support"

### Nonbranded, Nonjargon Keywords

Nonbranded, nonjargon keywords are associated with natural language searches. These phrases are typically research-based and are an indication of top-of-the-buying cycle searches. Blog articles serve as a great vehicle for promoting nonbranded, nonjargon keywords.

- Blog title example: "Best forest-green jackets for windy climates"
- Product title example: "Stainless Steel Tongs Used for Grilling"

# Optimize On-Page eCommerce SEO in 10 Easy Steps

1. Choose SEO-Friendly eCommerce software

Most eCommerce software includes functionality such as the ability to create category and product pages, the ability to securely accept payments online, and some even offer the ability to build any types of pages using a CMS. From an SEO prospective, a cart should also include the ability to automatically generate and manipulate page titles, meta tags, alt text, and URLs of every page, easily customize page content, and integrate social media promotional buttons on every page. Avoid software that does not offer this functionality. Also avoid software that does not allow the ability to turn off automatic settings like the inclusion of a business name in the page title of every page and software that uses query string parameters to display all products through a single page.

Software that hinders on-page SEO will make it difficult to achieve and sustain a high volume of prospects landing on your store pages. Your eCommerce software solution should enable, not hinder, your product and category pages' ability to attract valuable targeted traffic from search engines. As you probably already know, more traffic to your store will likely yield more sales, especially if your pages are optimized for conversions as well as searching. Like any other business, eCommerce is a numbers game. Get more visitors to optimized pages and get more sales. Simple as that.

## 2. Optimize URLs and Page Titles of Product and Category Pages with Natural Language Keyword Phrases

An optimized URL structure is important to maintain for high search engine placements. Both product and category pages should include keyword phrases that describe the page as best as possible with natural language. This is almost always accomplished with user-friendly keyword phrases; that is, the URL and page title of a product/category page should include the words that would be used when describing it to someone who knows little about your products or services. A seller of auto parts would not describe all of their auto lights as simply "lights," but would instead break down the lights into various categories with specific names, such as "Round Red Stop Lights" or "Oblong Amber Turning Signals." These words more accurately describe a category and should be included in the URL and page title of the category pages.

The same concept applies to product pages. Instead of naming a product "Red Stop Light," a smart auto seller would name this product more specifically in natural language. "Red 4-Inch Round Stop Light with 3-Prong Fitting" is a better name than "Red Stop Light" because it more accurately describes the product. Updating your URL and page titles to include natural-language search will have a positive influence on your search rankings.

## 3. Create Unique Product Descriptions

Unique product descriptions should be used to avoid having a store's product pages include the exact same content as other merchants. Google generally frowns upon duplicate content, so it should be avoided when possible. That being said, most of us know that product descriptions are inherently and necessarily not unique and that they can be difficult to make unique. Simply rewriting or spinning a description into something slightly different from the original will not always cut it and may not yield higher product-page placement in search engines. Google has gotten much smarter about rewritten content and can detect it better than most users think. Content that is 20–40 percent unique is sometimes not enough. Unique content varies in length, theme, and style—elements that can and are being detected and used in the ranking algorithm.

Developing high-quality and unique content for product/category pages is a better investment than simply copying the manufacturer's description or even slightly modifying or rewriting the description. The process of creating these product pages will take time but will be a better use of your time than trying to slightly modify the descriptions of 10,000 pages at once.

The best way to create unique product descriptions is to pick a handful of best-selling or high-margin products and create the absolute best page about them on the web. Do research on the product and include that research on the page. Write a personal story about the usage of the product. Write a humorous and witty description similar to those of Groupon deals. Invest in high-quality images from multiple angles of the product. Shoot a video of the product in use. Be creative and dominate the search results by having high-quality content that both search engines and your customers will love. Repeat this process one product or category at a time, really investing in the quality of the content.

## 4. Shorten and Reorder Page Titles

Long page titles can have a damaging effect on the impact of search-ranking placements and can also lead to lower click-through rates on organic search because searchers tend to skim results. A common mistake that leads to long page titles is including the company name and/or slogan in the page title of every page. A business will inherently rank well for their company name, especially if it is in the URL, so it is most likely not necessary to include in every single page title. Simply removing the company name will help to shorten the title.

Another common mistake is including a tag line in every page. A bad example of a tag line and company name being used on every page may make a product page title look something like "Engineering Greatness Since 1945 | Widget Supplier Warehouse | Round Blue Widgets | Super Bouncy Blue Widget Ball." Notice how the tag line and company name came before the category and product names and makes this page title so long that it is unlikely for the product name to even display in an organic search result page. The product name should, at the very least, be at the beginning of the page title. A better page title would include the product name followed by the category name. An example would be "Super Bouncy Blue Widget Ball | Round Blue Widgets." This format puts the most important keywords up front and will likely help increase search click-through rates.

## 5. Use Internal Linking for Product Pages

Product pages can be some of the more difficult, yet important, pages to obtain high rankings in organic search engine placements. This scenario is likely true for several reasons. Product pages, especially those without unique and high-quality content, rarely get linked to from external sites. An inbound link to a product page, even from a mildly authoritative site, can have a positive influence on the search-result ranking for that page. Second, product pages may not get PageRank passed from high value pages, like the homepage, because they are buried too deep within the site's architecture and may not look to be important by search robots. Search robots may even decide that the page is so unimportant that it may be unlikely to display the product page in search results at all.

Internal linking within an eCommerce site to product pages can help to offset these negative scenarios and even help improve the number of pages visited per user. Two easy ways to implement internal cross linking among product pages is by using recommended products links and linking to products from blog pages. Linking to product pages from within a product page using a recommended-products section will help to keep visitors engaged on-site and create a new record of an internal link for the search robot to see. Including product links on a blog page can help increase the number of pages that a visitor clicks to per visit. A visitor may find your blog post through a social media site like Twitter or Facebook and click through to your store using a product link from the blog page. This has the double benefit of increasing the pages-per-visit average as well as increasing site traffic to a particular product page—both very positive influences on higher search rankings.

It is important to note that although an internal link will not have as much SEO value as an external link, these internal links will still send signals to search engine robots that the page is important and should be indexed.

## 6. Optimize Internal Anchor Text

Internal linking should only be done with optimized anchor text. Anchor text comprise the keywords that are linking to the website page. For example, "click here" is a typical anchor text keyword phrase used to link to another page. However, "click here" is a terrible use of keyword optimized anchor text. The anchor text of a link is used by search engine robots to help notate what the page behind the anchor text is about. So if the keywords "click here" are used as anchor text linking to a product detail page, a search robot may think that the page is about "click here" when in actuality the page is about the product. Instead of using "click here," use the product name associated with the page title of the product or a variation of the page title of the product.

The same is true for internal linking of category pages. Use a descriptive keyword phrase to link to the category page, preferably a phrase that you are trying to get that category page to rank for. If you want a category page to rank better for the phrase "round blue widgets," the anchor text for a link to that page should be "round blue widgets," not "click here." Essentially the internal anchor text used should emulate a keyword strategy, and the keyword strategy should follow common usage. Use anchor text that is specific and can be understood very clearly.


## 7. Add Direct Product Links to the Homepage

Most eCommerce sites have hundreds to tens of thousands of website pages, making it nearly impossible to have a flat architecture. A flat architecture means that there are fewer clicks to get to a specified page from the root domain. Pages closer to the root-level domain typically rank higher in search results, which can be a problem for product pages because they intrinsically have a deep architecture due to the category and subcategory pages used to catalog them. In fact, most product pages will naturally end up having a hierarchical structure of 3+ levels deep within a site—which is fine, if the architecture makes it clear to both visitors and search robots, but that deep level may leave critical product pages with little ranking power.

One solution to help flatten the architecture of important product pages is to link directly to them from the homepage. Linking directly from the home page effectively flattens the architecture and even gives a bit of link juice via an internal link to the product page. A popular tactic for adding direct product links to the homepage is to use a "Featured Products" section or "Best Seller" section or list. Including links to your most important product pages on your homepage is a good strategy and should be used for your best-selling products.

## 8. Remove Links from the Homepage

The value of a link can be altered by the number of links on a page. For example, if a website page has only one link on it, that link will get 100 percent link-value credit. If a website page has two links, each will get 50 percent credit. If a website page has three links, each will get 33 percent credit. And so on. Thus, a homepage with fifty links on it is giving each link about 1/50 of credit. There is a lot of splitting of credit happening there!

Often, homepages will include links that never get clicked on or are not important to the user experience. These links should be removed to allow more credit to go to the links that are more important. Avoid the temptation of linking to every single page on your site as often as possible. This is a common mistake made by many new online merchants and should be corrected if already implemented. There is an old saying, "When everything is a priority, nothing is a priority." Don't let this be the case for your store's internal linking. Focus your efforts on boosting the most important pages by removing low-value links from your homepage.

## 9. Encourage User-Generated Content

According to a report by *Bazaarvoice's Report* (www.bazaarvoice.com, 2011), "Talking to Strangers: Millennials Trust People over Brands," over half (51 percent) of Millennial users, also known as Generation Y, trust user-generated content more than information presented on a company website and trust advertising even less about a company at about a 6 percent rate. In fact, user-generated content on a company website is more likely to influence a Millennial shopper's opinion than the advice of family and friends. Bazaarvoice's research also revealed that almost two-thirds (65 percent) feel that user-generated content is a more trustworthy source of information than any other online, and 86 percent believe it gives a better idea of a brand or retailer's quality of service and products. But why are Millennial shoppers so important to pay attention to? According to Bazaarvoice, their demographic will have more purchasing power than any other by 2017. That alone is reason enough to be actively encouraging user-generated content as much as possible!

eCommerce sites typically get user-generated content developed on product pages. The most common user-generated content for a product page comes in the form of comments, testimonials, photos, and videos. (Pretty self-explanatory really.) Unfortunately, *obtaining* user-generated content is not so self-explanatory.

The first step to generating user content is by simply allowing users to add it to a product page. The next step is in making it easy from them to do so. Start by allowing comments, reviews, and testimonials on your product pages. This should be relatively easy and should not include much coding. A nice second step is to allow users to upload photos and videos of themselves using the product. Consumers love to show off what they bought ... encourage them to do so! Run a monthly contest for the best photo or video submission or develop a reward system that gives credit toward store purchases for uploaded content. Don't just assume that consumers are going to e-mail you photos of themselves using your product; they very likely will not. Instead make it easy and encourage them to do so on your product pages.

## 10. Improve Page Loading Speed by Optimizing Images

Page loading speed has become a significant factor in Google's algorithm, so it is critical (from a search engine and usability perspective) to make sure that product pages and images are loading relatively fast. A simple way to improve page load speed is by optimizing images used on website pages. Ensure that pages do not include very large image files that are resized to look smaller on a page. For example, do not use a $3700 \times 3700$ dimension image with a size of 3.2 MB on a website page. Resize this picture to the size you wish to use on the page, say, $350 \times 350$, and then add it to your page. This will take less time to process and speed up how quickly a website page responds to a web request.

A more advanced way to improve page loading speed with images is by hosting images on subdomains of a server and referencing the subdomains on the website page. This way a page that would normally be loading, say, thirty-two images, could actually be loading images from three different subdomains, making the root domain load much faster. Examples of subdomains that could be used are "images1.mysite.com," "images2.mysite.com," "images3.mysite.com," and so on. This advanced tactic can be a bit complicated for novice merchants but can have significant impact on page loading speed.

# White Hat SEO for ECommerce

SEO techniques are most commonly classified into two categories: techniques that search engines recommend and techniques that search engines do not approve. Search engines attempt to minimize the effect of the latter by delisting websites that are in violation of their guidelines and promote with greater visibility websites that are active in activities that search engines recommend. The SEO community has classified these methods as either "white hat SEO" or "black hat SEO." White hat SEO is commonly defined as techniques that conform to the search engines' guidelines and involve no deception. White hat SEO tends to produce results that last a long time. Black hat SEO pushes or breaks the boundaries of the guidelines and typically results in being banned either temporarily or permanently once the search engines discover what they are doing.

White hat SEO advice is best summed up as creating content optimized for the user and their on-site experience and then making that content easily accessible to the search engine spiders, rather than attempting to trick the search algorithm from its intended purpose. Two effective tactics of white hat SEO for eCommerce are found in conversion-focused optimization as well as guest blogging. Conversion-focused optimization can help ensure that your website pages are structured in a way that your most profitable keywords and pages are highlighted to search engines. Guest blogging helps to generate quality inbound links, enhances exposure, and maintains consistent velocity in content publication—all factors needed to rank high in organic search.

# Conversion-Focused SEO

Conversion SEO keyword research and implementation is a method of optimizing both paid and organic search traffic for maximum monetary conversions. One of the most important elements of conversion SEO resides in first-touch attribution, or in layman's terms, how a visitor found your website for the first time.

The world of eCommerce is highly competitive, so to get ahead of the curve you need to focus your attention on narrowing down the keywords that will make your site the most money. Putting in the time, effort, and research will produce results that will help you plan a strategy, implement it, and use conversion-rich keywords to generate new revenue. Most analytic packages use last-touch attribution to determine how conversions are allocated to the most recent source of a visit for that visitor. Conversion-focused SEO is interested in first-touch attribution to identify and attribute the keyword phrases that initially attracted the most conversions and revenue.

A converting keyword phrase is one that was used by a visitor to find a website for the first visit and is also called the first touch. The visitor then made a purchase and subsequently became a customer. Using these converting keyword phrases generates revenue for the website. Analytics tools or an analytics platform must be used to collect these phrases and then identify them.

Using first-touch attribution analytics allows you to organize your database of keyword phrases and list them in order from the most valuable keyword phrases down to the least valuable phrases. This is an invaluable way to find out which keyword phrases are generating the most monetary conversions as well as visitor interest, ensuring that your website will get more hits and make more money.

There is a difference between high-quality and high-quantity conversion keyword phrases. Using a high-quality keyword conversion phrase will generate a high amount of revenue over one business quarter; a high-quantity conversion keyword phrase ensures higher revenue per order. Keep these two separated in your mind; they are quite different and, used as they should be, will impact your business in two different ways.

Big ticket B2B eCommerce websites may want to look specifically at high-quality conversion keywords as their focus. This will ensure that higher revenue will produce more impressive quarterly results. Smaller-ticket B2C companies should place their focus on high-quantity phrases to gain higher revenues per customer order for best results.

It will be time to create a roadmap of implementation of conversion keyword phrases into your existing website content once you have identified, classified, and prioritized high-quality and high-quantity phrases for your website. Use those phrases to optimize on-page SEO elements like the page title, header, and anchor text of your target pages. Optimizing these keyword phrases gives your pages an edge and an instant boost when it comes to conversion-focused SEO keywords.

Implementing the keywords is the start of success when it comes to keyword optimization and conversion.

Take a look at your homepage. You'll need to adjust the links there with conversion-focused, keyword-rich anchor text, as this will likely be the most highly ranked page of your website, thus gaining the most attention for search engines. The homepage is the highest-valued page of a store's website and should be used to promote the most successful pages with the addition of conversion keyword phrases.

Update and optimize the internal links and the navigational menu to include conversion keywords and phrases linking to different category pages throughout the site. Don't neglect hidden spots where you can add conversion keyword phrases such as photo captions or even in the link to your actual page. Use internal conversion-focused keyword linking everywhere you can on your site; some places include navigational links, breadcrumbs (the URL path at the top of a page that designates the directory flow that brought you to this page), and embedded links that click to keyword-rich anchor text on relevant pages.

An important note is to not overdo the same keyword phrases in all of your internal linking; feel free to sprinkle in various words and phrases all over the page to add interest and keep the visitor engaged in the content.

Create content that's based around your conversion keyword phrases, and use that content to build inbound links. Take this opportunity to create a blog for eCommerce. A blogging platform will allow you to create unique, original content that you can add lots of keyword-rich conversion phrases and SEO keywords to. This will drive more visitors to your site. You will want to add photos, videos, or other content and use your conversion-focused keywords when naming and uploading. Upload videos of yourself speaking about your products, talking about how-to's, or showcasing a particular item. Be sure to include targeted keyword phrases in the name of the video.

Another great way to drive conversions is to optimize product feeds to comparison-shopping engines. Use keyword optimization and conversion-rich keyword phrases in your product titles sent to marketplace websites such as eBay and Amazon and search engines such as Google Products. These shopping search engines, such as TheFind.com, may not lead potential customers directly to your website, but they will drive conversions that will ensure higher potential for revenue in the end.

The last item on your to-do list for conversion-focused SEO and keywords is to build paid search campaigns from your conversion keyword phrases. Paid traffic is a nice way to get a leg up on competitors and increase traffic to your site. However, this can come at a cost to the customer. Paid traffic has the highest overall cost of customer acquisition. A way to negate this cost is to narrow your focus to optimizing for specific keywords that you know for a fact will generate the revenue you need. Go through your keywords and eliminate any that aren't bringing in revenue, focusing narrowly and heavily on the ones that do.

Do an experiment with finding high-conversion keywords that produce very little traffic. Use these keywords to tap into a gold mine of lots of original, unique content that was created to generate organic search traffic and therefore bring in the revenue you expect and desire.

# Guest Blogging

Guest blogging, which is dually defined as either allowing others to write blogs for your website or you writing blogs for other websites, is one of the most underutilized tactics for eCommerce blogging and content creation. Guest blogging on other websites can allow you to effectively artificially build inbound links in a safe and acceptable way as well as expose your brand and links to your website audiences that may not otherwise have discovered you. Allowing others to guest blog on your website can help you sustain your significant velocity of quality content creation and enable you to leverage the promotional and social amplification resources of your guest bloggers. Guest blogging can be so effective that many successful bloggers go as far as setting the goal of having a guest blog post published to every five posted on their own site.

Guest blogging builds credibility and makes it easy for people to trust you. Imagine yourself as a product and the guest blog posts as promoting your product and selling it to the public. Seeing your name repeatedly on big blogs or having big-name companies on your blog will help people trust you and take you seriously. They'll be more willing to make an investment in your brand name. The more people are exposed to your name, the more comfortable they will be with your brand.

One of the top benefits of guest blogging on other sites is generating new inbound links with keyword-rich anchor text to your site. The anchor text is the text displayed to the reader that when clicked links them to a website page. When you post a blog on another site, you will want to ensure that you have at least one keyword-rich anchor text linking back to a page on your site that you are wanting to gain exposure and higher search-ranking placements for. The more popular the guest blog post becomes, the more valuable the inbound link to your site. An optimized inbound link with keyword-rich anchor text can drive more traffic to your website as well as help to increase the organic ranking of that particular keyword phrase for the website page it is pointed to.

Gaining traffic is the next top benefit and reason that successful bloggers engage in guest blogging. Having your blog content featured in a particular niche you've chosen will build up traffic and will likely be the best avenue to gaining additional exposure. The more blog posts you publish on other blog sites, the more followers you are likely to gain, which can result in subscribers that keep reading what you write. You are advertising your expertise, ideas, and value of your own blog when publishing content to members of another blog's community. This can result in a larger readership for your own blog and can be a great jump start to an increase in traffic and social shares of your future blogs.

Another reason to start guest blogging is that posting your content on other influential websites will help to build up your brand. Building a niche for yourself means writing on several particular topics that you specialize in. It is a good idea to build your brand around the type of blogs you will write. The more guest blog content you have published, the more your guest content will display in search results when your company name is searched with topics relevant to the articles. Make sure to use the most relevant keywords when titling your guest blog posts and also in the blog copy to ensure as many hits as possible through search results.

A key benefit to allowing others to guest blog on your website is that most people heavily promote content that they write in their social networks. This allows you significant reach into an audience that may not otherwise be reachable through your existing social media marketing. Also, the social connections of regular guest bloggers will frequently augment your blog subscriber base to stay up-to-date with the product or industry if it interests them as well.

Allowing others to guest blog on your website can also help provide fresh and unique perspectives on your topics and keywords. All eCommerce marketers can eventually become stuck in a rut of content creation and unable to create unique perspectives and valuable content. Guest bloggers, however, are coming in with their own unique perspectives, which can help you keep your blog interesting and fresh.

## How to Start Guest Blogging

When it comes to guest blogging, creativity is welcome, but there are some rules that must be followed to ensure optimum results. Don't just sit down and pound out your guest blog; prepare for the task before you start typing. Having goals will set you up for success and help you produce the results you desire. Here are a few key things to have in mind before you blog.

**Research**: Submitting guest blogs without doing research lessens your chances of doing your best work. Thoroughly read each blog you want to submit a guest blog post to. This will ensure you're going to be contributing something worthwhile to their blog. Check out the last few pages of blogs posted, as well as readers' comments to be informed of the tone of writing, topics readers may want to engage in, and what kinds of blogs are already on the site. Research means being prepared, so do all the homework before you begin blogging.

You should create a prospecting spreadsheet of relevant websites with significant domain authority from which you could benefit guest blogging on. The targeted websites should be relevant, that is, having topics, traffic, and keywords similar to yours. This gives the inbound link to your website additional context when being indexed by search engines and helps increase your overall domain authority for those keywords and topics. In terms of significant domain authority, websites that have been regularly producing content have a significant number of relevant and valuable inbound links that will provide you with links of greater value back to your website when you guest blog.

When creating your prospecting spreadsheet of websites where you can benefit from guest blogging on, you obviously want to avoid direct competitors. Not only will they probably not allow you to guest blog on their website, but remember that one of the key factors search engine optimization is a consistent velocity of new keyword-relevant content creation. Therefore, guest blogging on a competitor's website with enhanced their domain authority from new indexed content far more than yours with the inbound link.

Use whichever common search engine you like to find the types of blogs you want to write for. Specific search terms can be typed to find the right blogs for the types of content you want to write. This can be accomplished by typing in some of the following phrases when you search (replace "your niche" with your main niche):

Your niche + submit guest post

Your niche + write for us

Your niche + contribute

Your niche + submit post

Your niche + guest blogging

Your niche + submit your post

Your niche + submit an article

Your niche "submit post"

Your niche "write for us"

Your niche "guest blogging"

Your niche "guest posting"

Your niche "submit an article"

These terms can be modified to produce more varied results if needed.

**Writing**: Raise your writing standards when you guest post. Doing your highest quality writing ensures that your guest post will stand out among others. Research effectively and ensure that every guest post is unique, detailed, presentable, and informative. Think about how difficult it is to read posts that contain grammar or spelling errors, and strive to make no mistakes in your posts. Back facts up with sources, if necessary.

You should always remember to include at least one keyword-rich anchor text link back to your site in the writing of the guest blog post. The anchor text gives further context to search engines that understand that the website to which that link is pointing is related to the anchor text defined on the website. Give your anchor text actionable language—essentially a textual call to action for the readers—to not only provide search engine context but also potential to provide referral traffic from the website back to your website. However, since it is not your website, you cannot always control the anchor text factors in the guest blog post. Some webmasters will not allow any anchor text links in the ad copy of the blog post and will instead require that the linked keywords be included in the byline of the article. While it doesn't hurt to ask to include anchor text links in the ad copy, there is still value in byline hyperlinks back to your website.

**Proofreading**: Submitting a guest post without proofreading is a guaranteed way to fail. Proofreading shows professionalism and that you care about how you present your work. Even if you are using a spell checker, it may not catch every word or abbreviation. Read through each post you are going to submit at least three times before submitting to ensure you have made no mistakes. Mistakes show you can't be taken seriously, and you may not be asked to write a guest post for that particular website again.

**Submitting**: Some people believe in pitching blog ideas before writing posts, but the reverse may be more helpful. Sending your full post will allow the webmaster to assess it and tell if it's right for the blog. Be polite and courteous when corresponding with webmasters. Good manners can go a long way, and webmasters appreciate the courtesy. Pitch relevant, interesting content to blogs that you think will appreciate your style, tone, and topics. Don't waste anyone's time submitting irrelevant material.

Manufacturers, reviewers, influencers, bloggers, and anyone else whose website is discussing your industry or products would make valuable guest blogging partners. These websites are often incentivized to allow you to guest blog on their website for the same reason that you allow others to guest blog on your website—it helps them sustain a significant velocity of quality content creation. Approaching them using their contact forms or engaging them in social media and asking if they'd be interested in having you guest blog is the most direct—and one of the most effective—ways of finding guest blogging opportunities.

Your work isn't done when you submit your blog post. Check your posts and respond to readers. This shows you care about your work and you're relatable, which will lead to more subscribers. People feel like you're not invested in your writing if you don't follow up and respond to questions or comments.

# Google Algorithm Updates

Google and the other major search engines are consistently releasing public updates to their algorithms to improve search results. In addition to the publicized updates, the search engines are constantly making more minor changes to their algorithms that are almost impossible to keep up with.

There are some major updates, such as Google's 2012 Penguin update, which fundamentally changed the way that we view SEO. However, for the most part, all of the search engine updates are designed to move them closer to their goals: providing relevant, valuable results to search engine users. High quality, authoritative content is the goal for search engine results pages. They're trying to make it so that fewer and fewer of the results are irrelevant, and the way that they do that is through an increasingly draconian policy of deterrence. The search engines, especially Google, have become such an integral part of the ability of websites to make money online that most websites could not function without traffic from organic sources. The search engine algorithm updates are being accompanied more frequently by changes to the ways that search engines are punishing websites that violate or abuse the intent of their systems. While there are instances of websites that are unfairly penalized by these updates that weren't actually abusing or violating the intent of the system, for the most part websites that are suffering from these updates are doing so because they attempted to artificially influence their position in search engine results outside of the intended spirit of the system.

For example, one of the results to come from Google's Penguin update was that if there was a disproportionate number of inbound links with the same anchor text, Google was going to penalize the site to which they were linking. There's some potential for competitive abuse here, but for the most part Google's assumption was that a high percentage of inbound links having the same anchor text was a result of past transgressions of the target website trying to follow what were—even at the time—considered gray hat SEO tactics.

The moral of this story is that the spirit and intent of the search engine algorithms are clear: they want to provide accurate, relevant, useful, authoritative results to searchers based on as clear an understanding of the intent and context of their search query as possible. Since the clear intent is quality content results, the "right way" to improve your search engine rankings and drive traffic from organic search results is to create a significant inventory of high-quality content. This is the only method of search engine optimization that is guaranteed to never suddenly be the target of a devastating penalty, whereas your investment in SEO consultants, artificial link building, and overoptimization of your pages may very likely result in the loss of those investments as well as potentially disastrous future penalties.

# Chapter 6:

## eCommerce Marketing Using Facebook

Any business owner, from the Fortune 500 CEO to the mom-and-pop online retailer, has heard about the tremendous potential of social media when it comes to Internet marketing on either a local or worldwide scale. However, while most people with a website are aware of the general benefits social media can provide when implemented correctly, few are as familiar with the specific, practical marketing applications that can really draw an audience.

## Facebook

### What Is Facebook?

First on our list is Facebook (www.facebook.com), the 800-pound gorilla in the social media marketing world. The brainchild of Mark Zuckerberg, Facebook has surpassed 850 million users as of February 2012 (or about 10 percent of the population of the entire planet) and has created a worldwide phenomenon of unprecedented scope and scale. Hundreds of millions of people spend sizable segments of their daily lives on this one site interacting with friends, sharing content, playing games, and scheduling or organizing their social lives. It's become a venue for collective action, knowledge, and an incredibly detail-rich (if personally detached) social environment. Users willingly share an incredible amount of personal information and tend to greatly trust product and service recommendations made by members within their network.

The excellence of Facebook's off-site integration options is another terrific boon to the social media marketing world. Although many other social media sites, such as Twitter, Digg, and Pinterest, have buttons that allow you to share content from other pages, Facebook has created a new and unique phenomenon with their social media plugins. The ubiquity of Facebook around the world makes it easy for a huge number of people worldwide to share and comment on the posts, photos, and other items you might add these plugins to. Sharing specific products, updates, or insights that you might have on one's site or blog is now doable with just a few clicks of the mouse, making these easy-to-use plugins a simple and phenomenally effective way to drive web traffic your way. Scan the QR code below to access Facebook's developers guide, which is probably the best and most comprehensive way to learn about the options these social media plugins have. Basic installation directions are included in the developers guide as well.

## Like me!

The best-known of these social plugins is the Facebook "Like" button. Whereas Facebook used to give users the option to become "fans" of something, be it a brand or company or person, they can now "Like" something with a single click. The button is easy to install on any web page and operates on a simple iFrame. When used properly, this button allows the owner of the page to publish updates into the news feeds of users who "Like" their page. This is incredibly valuable from a marketing standpoint, as it makes it easy to turn a single visitor into a returning one without having to capture an e-mail address. Whereas e-mail marketing has long been the predominant means of capturing personal information for most websites, gathering "likes" is quickly gaining in importance. The Facebook "Like" button should be on every page of your website (or on every individual product that you offer, if possible), and you should use the attention of the users who "Like" these things to create sticky traffic by consistently publishing relevant and interesting updates into their news feeds.

Facebook also has an incredibly useful comments module that allows people to leave comments on your web page while logged into Facebook. Since there's a probability that some of your visitors may not have Facebook accounts, we strongly recommend that you create a back-up comment module. This useful Facebook comment widget allows your users to carry the conversation about your products or brand in general back to their network of Facebook friends, since their comments will post back to their profile by default. Essentially, commenters now have the power to share your products, brand, and content far beyond just your own page visitors and into each of the commenter's social networks.

Add a Facebook "Like" button and comment widget to every product page on your site and decide on the relevant content you would like to share with those that click it. Google and Bing have both released statements admitting that the number of Facebook "Likes" an item has is now part of these search giants' respective algorithms when determining SEO rankings. In fact, as cited earlier, a 2012 study by United Kingdom–based search marketing firm "Searchmetrics" found that Facebook "likes" have a *higher* correlation to search engine rankings than inbound links. This is a staggering development, since building inbound links has been a core strategy of businesses since the dawn of the search engine.

However, it shouldn't disrupt the SEO efforts of marketers who are doing it right and following the spirit of social media and search engines—creating valuable, engaging content worth sharing. The fundamental psychology of engaging content as an incentive for sharing is the same as for linking, but with some very useful advantages. First, it has expanded the sample size of the Internet-using population that gets to "vote" or contribute to search engine rankings. With inbound links as a primary metric of quality and value online, only webmasters or those who maintained websites really had the ability to influence search engine rankings. Because of this, the "link bait" content actually had to be tailored to the interests and values of webmasters and site owners—not the business's actual consumers. This focus made it more difficult for marketers to craft content that would boost search optimization while simultaneously influencing the buying cycle of their consumers. With social media sharing and engagement becoming a more influential metric, marketers can focus on creating buyer persona–oriented content that doesn't include webmasters (unless, of course, you're selling products to them!).

Another benefit of the increased emphasis on social sharing as a key metric for search engine relevance is the greater amount of difficulty involved in gaming or spamming social media. A popular black-hat tactic of buying links from link-farm websites or building websites to link back to your site was mostly driven by the fact that the Internet doesn't, in any way, try to police the creation of websites created for the sole purpose of building links. Google and other search engines have done well in trying to detect and deter marketers using this tactic, but it's made a very small impact on the industry as a whole. Social media networks, for all of their vulnerabilities to account for automation and spam, are at least actively trying to identify and disable spam accounts. This now makes it fairer for marketers while simultaneously increasing the value of content that consumers find when using search engines.

Implementing "Like" buttons on your site can be an easy way to boost your visibility on the web, and the CTR (click-through rate) of Facebook "Like" campaigns can be quite good when targeted appropriately to a specific audience.

## Easy Logins

There is a great deal of value in having users be able to easily login and register at your site. User logins create unique accounts and individualized experiences for each visitor to your site, offering you valuable insight into customer behavior.The need to identify one user from another is as fundamental to the long-term success of any other site as it is to Facebook itself. Many sites, such as Formspring (www.formspring.me) for example, allow you to register on their site with a single click instead of the arduous, old-school registration process of entering your name, age, state, zip, e-mail, gender, et cetera. The average user will appreciate the convenience!

Remember that Internet marketing is much like electricity. Users will take the path of least resistance, but the more resistance (i.e., steps) involved in any process, the more people that you'll lose along the way—whether it be user registrations or primary conversions. By making it simple to register an account on your site by using Facebook's one-click login system, you've instantly created a format that's easy to use with low resistance. Also, by integrating Facebook login options wherein users can revoke certain access and permissions, you can make people feel more comfortable than they otherwise might have been when giving you their personal or contact information.

Keep in mind that not everyone has Facebook, so you should have other, non–social media account-registration options on your site as well.

*Decide* if there is any reason to have a visitor register with your site. If yes, make Facebook a one-click option. It should be noted here that users who register on various sites via existing social media accounts tend to stay on these external sites about 50 percent longer than they otherwise would—and tend to visit twice as many pages within a site while they are there.

## Personal Information

Facebook's history is fraught with concerns of privacy violations and what they're willing to share with marketers. As a marketer who spends a lot of time trying to squeeze demographic data out of Facebook, I can assure you that gathering your personal information isn't as easy as it sounds.

However, Facebook does allow sites and applications to request "extended permissions" to access additional personal information, such as e-mail addresses, birthdays, pictures, and more. Facebook users can revoke these permissions, but for the most part, Facebook users tend to be very willing to grant extended permissions to various applications. Again though, you may want to build both basic and extended applications that are designed to collect different levels of personal information. That way, users who are nervous about granting extended permissions to an app can still register on your site.

Is there any information you'd like to gather? Birthdays? E-mails? Locations?

Since several popular external Facebook games and apps (such as Farmville and other Zynga products) have abused the personal data they have gathered on their users, it is always a good idea to pledge that you will keep your users' information safe and secure at all times and refrain from selling this information to unrelated third parties. Make sure that you are consistent and truthful when making this pledge, and you will gain a stellar reputation for good company etiquette over time, which can convince many wary Facebook users that your company is indeed worthy of their trust. Simply stating the truth of the matter up front—that you have no intent to abuse the privilege of the personal information you have been given and that your social media login options are a matter of mutual convenience—can go a long way toward demonstrating your good faith in the candid world of the web.

## Facebook Pages for Brands

Facebook now allows users to "Like" specific brands (formerly called "fan pages"), which then connects the user to the brand page that the company in question has set up. These pages are the bread-and-butter of marketing on Facebook. They have both advantages and disadvantages.

Traditionally, the consensus has been that Facebook profiles are for people, and Facebook pages are for businesses. However, the functionality of Facebook has blurred those lines to a great extent because Facebook pages and profiles each have their own unique features.

On a page, users can simply "Like" the item, and the information that you can gather about the individual user is very limited, as is the potential for individual connection. Facebook pages share some of the same features as profiles, such as the ability to share pictures, post status updates, and share links. Pages also have some unique advantages as well, including a fairly robust reporting system that provides interesting information on user demographics. Additionally, the options for customization on Facebook pages are quite broad, even with the recent retirement of the FBML (Facebook markup language) code. Nowadays, if you wish to create vivid and unique landing pages to capture e-mail addresses, show off special offers, and anything else you can imagine, you can simply use JavaScript SDK or Facebook's social plugins, as detailed on the Facebook developers page.

It's important to note that Facebook is continually updating their user interface on both their web and mobile-based systems—especially now that they've completed their (admittedly painful and awkward) initial public offering. Facebook recently altered their structure of both profiles and pages to a format called "timeline," which has been modified from the previous iteration to place a greater emphasis on the chronological lifecycle of the page. This modification also had some inhibiting factors, such as making it harder to display CTAs. However, in general, most brands have actually seen a higher engagement since Facebook migrated everyone to timeline.

Along with timeline also came an interesting new algorithmic development called "EdgeRank." Facebook had struggled with their original "live feed" version, which some users found great value in but others found overwhelming. The get past this, Facebook restricted the live feed to the upper right-hand corner and made the primary news feed a function of their new EdgeRank algorithm.

The EdgeRank algorithm is somewhat akin to Google's algorithm for ranking websites - fundamentally it's based upon showing the best results or posts based on the types of content that a given user typically engages with. Instead of allowing pages to insert all of their posts into a user's feed (which had become unmanageable for users), Facebook analyzes which pages typically get engagement with their posts. The more engagement a page receives, the easier it becomes for that page to be seen by their fans in their news feed. Although Facebook's exact parameters for EdgeRank are proprietary and unknown, it's likely that Facebook analyzes the types of content that a user typically engages with as well as the similarity of their behavioral profile to others who like a given page. Facebook's objectives is to fill the timeline with as much content as possible that a given user will find valuable and engaging. This has made an emphasis on engaging content even more crucial to eCommerce businesses on Facebook. Quite simply, it's improbable that users who like a page will find product detail pages interesting or engaging. Because of this, sharing a high volume of product detail pages will inevitably lower your EdgeRank and make it more difficult for *any* posts to be seen.

As EdgeRank becomes a greater focus for social media marketers, analyzing the times and types of postings that get the most engagement becomes more important as well. For example, Facebook has recently done a much better job of emphasizing images in the user experience as a response to the fantastic success of websites such as Pinterest. Images tend to have a higher clickthrough rate as well as a higher engagement rate. Since "surfing" Facebook tends to be a fairly fast-paced process and users give individual posts a short period of evaluation before either engaging or moving on, being able to communicate meaning quickly becomes more important. You may have heard the common claim that humans process images up to 60,000 times faster than text (we haven't been able to verify this study, but suffice it to say that it's axiomatic that we process images faster than sentences even if we can't quantify the degree). This makes leveraging rich and engaging images on Facebook even more useful since they tend to receive a higher level of engagement on Facebook, which will subsequently increase your EdgeRank.

# Facebook Profiles for Brands

There are some cases in which Facebook profiles could be very appropriate to use for certain brands, such as personal or celebrity brands. Profiles provide the unique ability to invite users to events, organize these users into convenient lists, tag them in posts and photos, and interact on a very personalized level by commenting on the posts, links, walls, etc. of your users. However, we must be mindful of the fact that many consumers still resent the intrusion of marketers into social media. Many of them find it bothersome enough that we have paid ads and pages on their social networks, and the fact that we'd intrude into their lives with profiles of our own may offend some.

Also, there are issues of scale, ethics, and potential accusations of spamming/abuse when choosing between pages and profiles to represent your brand. Facebook does not intend for profiles to be used when marketing businesses, and they reserve the right to prevent you from making excessive friend requests. This can severely limit the potential reach of your Facebook marketing efforts, so if you have big dreams of brand expansion, this option is probably better left by the wayside. However, if you have a small business or recurring local event that you intend to keep small and exclusive, a Facebook profile might be your best bet. Again, tread cautiously here, lest you be accused of spamming or abusing the system by other Facebook users.

However, most eCommerce ventures would more likely be better served with either a Facebook brand page or company page. There are a few subtle differences between the two, so it pays to do some research on this ahead of time.

For example, if you are building a personal brand, a simple website, or creating a certain product line that you hope to build a loyal following for, the brand page is probably your best option. The more specific your aim, the more likely it is that the Facebook brand page will provide you with the fun and super-specific categories you have in mind for marketing purposes.

However, if your eCommerce marketing plan involves a company with many different facets, a provider of services, or a local, physical storefront or franchise, the Facebook company pages are more likely to be suited to your purposes. The company pages offer the opportunity for a multifaceted marketing approach, whereas brand pages are, by their nature, typically limited to certain products, ideas, or industries. Additionally, a company page offers service providers a more professional front to the world, with much more room to expand if their scope or focus grows and shifts in the future; the broader categories of company pages on Facebook make it far more difficult to box one's self in.

## Facebook Ads

Facebook ads are one of the more underutilized and misunderstood paid-traffic mediums. They've had some bad press because of organizations that have used them improperly and seen a poor ROI. The primary point of failure has been organizations trying to use them the same way as they've used search engine PPC ads in the past—which is fundamentally flawed because traffic on social media websites is inherently different.

Whereas search engines allow you to target ads at users based on what they're actively interested in at the time, paid social ads target based on passive, static interests. That is, I can target you with ads because you specifically "like" eCommerce marketing. Facebook does also allow contextual advertising for people "talking about" or reading about a specific topic, but someone passively consuming content on Facebook still has a different psychological profile than someone who is actively searching for more information on a search engine.

Because of this difference, it becomes highly improbable that anyone will complete a primary or transactional conversion from clicking through on a Facebook ad. When you consider the phases of the consumer buying cycle, clicking through on a Facebook ad would have someone at a phase even higher than the awareness phase called "contextual curiosity." That is, they're being exposed to a concept that they had not been actively searching for a solution to based on the fact that they were consuming content that's related, in context, to the product or service being advertised. Because of this, they require an entirely different type of content to influence conversion. The further up the buying cycle a consumer is, the further they are from being ready to consider and evaluate a specific product purchase—which is the primary goal of product detail pages on eCommerce websites. Because contextual curiosity is as far as possible from actual purchase, in that the product being sold addresses a problem that the consumer had not yet developed an awareness that they have, the type of content that's going to influence a conversion is going to be high-level, educationally oriented content that's specifically aligned with the context that triggered the ad, such as a downloadable guide or e-book. A buyer's guide is too far down the cycle, being designed for those who are considering and comparing product solutions, and a product detail page is even further away from the consumer's area of interest. One of the major mistakes that firms make when leveraging Facebook ads is trying to drive traffic to an immediate transactional conversion point—which is almost certainly going to fail to deliver a tolerable return.

In addition to driving traffic from Facebook to an educational conversion on a landing page, you can also use Facebook ads to grow the fan base for your page. What you choose to do depends on the relative values (per the funnel analysis we discussed earlier in this book) of the transactional value of Facebook fans versus the conversion rate to and value of a contact from a landing page. Many eCommerce sites opt to use Facebook to grow their page's fan base because the long-term transactional value is often higher *and* because of the intangible benefits of network effect created when a consumer engages with your brand's page.

In addition to their web-based advertising, Facebook has recently invested a great deal in their mobile targeting ad displays. One of the primary drivers for Facebook's dramatic decline in stock price shortly after their 2012 IPO was their revised earnings estimates from mobile advertising, which they had previously done a very poor job of investing in. As Facebook continues to invest in improving the mobile advertising experience—and as more users in general shift the majority of their time on social media to mobile devices—the need for image-rich and educationally oriented content in the creative for ads will only become more important over time.

In addition, in June 2012 Facebook launched their first retargeting platform for advertisers which has, as of this book's writing, shown very impressive results. The retargeting option is *significantly* different from the advertisement options that we've discussed so far (the PPC model that most advertisers are familiar with, which is primarily a function of demand *generation* as opposed to demand *fulfillment*).

Essentially, Facebook's retargeting system allows you to use "cookies" (small files of data that websites can temporarily store on the computer of a person visiting their website) to target specific ads to Facebook users based on their behavior on a given website. This is fundamentally different—in fact, the mirror opposite—of their traditional ad model in that focusing on a primary conversion event here can be significantly more valuable since the consumer has already been exposed to your product and is further down the buying cycle. This may be the missing piece of the puzzle in Facebook's advertising service having value for eCommerce retailers, as it allows a much faster velocity of measurable return on investment.

## Facebook Apps

You may remember when Facebook first opened themselves up for third-party application development. For a while, many people checked every day to see what was new and what was the latest and greatest. Now, with countless apps being added every day, it's almost impossible to keep up with them all.

Facebook apps have an inherent and obvious value to app developers for monetizing their apps through advertising and in-app transactions, but they also provide a fascinating opportunity for marketers. If you can create an application that is useful to your target demographic, you can create your own marketing phenomenon to help put your brand in front of a massive audience of existing and potential customers alike. If you can create a tool, game, or other system that builds value relevant to your target consumer base, you can do amazing things.

If you decide to build an app of your own, first make sure that you have a specific purpose in mind that is designed to solve or alleviate a certain pain point that your customers typically face in your industry. You can also think of a fun game to play that might incorporate some of your products or ideas into the object of the game. Once you have a few concrete ideas regarding what you want your app to do, find a reputable developer that can create a smoothly running application for your business that will be easy and painless to integrate into the Facebook world. Any buggy or poorly designed apps will leave the users feeling uneasy about your brand and commitment to quality overall, so make sure that all user information gathered by this app is secure and that the app itself is unlikely to cause Facebook or a web browser to malfunction. Remember that these apps represent your business, so make sure that any such thing with your name on it puts forth the type of image you wish to project!

## Translating Social Login Options into Dollars and Cents

Abandoned carts can prove to be a major source of frustration for eCommerce retailers, and it behooves you greatly to minimize this issue as well as possible to maximize profits. This is where the benefits of offering social media login options at checkout can really help your business overall. In 2012, research aggregated by the eCommerce software company Monetate that customers who are offered the option to check out via their existing social media accounts, such as Facebook or Twitter, are more likely to complete their purchases. The same research showed that approximately four in ten social media users have expressed a firm preference for social media login use over creating new accounts with various online vendors at checkout, so any online enterprise ignores this significant market share at their own peril.

As of this writing, Facebook social media logins offer the lion's share of external checkout options used worldwide, although Google, Twitter, and Yahoo also make fairly significant showings in this field. Add at least one of these social login options to your site at checkout, and you should notice a significant increase in your sales figures overall. Check your web analytics to determine which social media sites your visitors come from most often, and implement your social login checkout options accordingly.

## Tips and Tricks to Try

Here's a neat trick to employ when using Facebook PPC for B2B eCommerce sales: If you're targeting a specific company, find out the city in which the company is headquartered. Then, target fans of that company's page who live in the same city as the company HQ. Odds are, most or many of their employees (including senior management) are fans of the company Facebook page. This gives you a unique opportunity to put your ad right in front of their faces, and you can even use this opportunity to create custom landing pages designed to capture their e-mails or phone numbers for follow-up campaigns.

Above all, make sure that any Facebook-based efforts that you create and promote on behalf of yourself or a brand or company you are affiliated with are completely truthful in their claims, ethical in their handling of personal user information, and able to provide a degree of fun and value to anyone who is interested in what you have to offer. These users should be happy to see what you have to post and should look forward to useful updates and insights on a fairly consistent basis.

Be careful not to overpost the same message to your Facebook page or profile, as this can easily annoy a good proportion of your user base as well as adversely impact your EdgeRank and make it more difficult for you to get into the news feeds of your fans. While there are general rules in terms of frequency, we'll add that you should always analyze and test these for yourself, as the frequency tolerance of your consumers for your brand may be orders of magnitude different than another.

# Chapter 7:

## eCommerce Marketing on Twitter

## Twitter

Twitter, the popular microblogging service, can present something of a conundrum for online marketers. Many companies and marketing professionals employed on their behalf have yet to really nail down the specific value that they can bring to consumers via Twitter, and understanding the methods that can be used to engage with potential customers without drifting into the realm of spam can present a sticky situation for many as well.

Here are a few tactics you can use to leverage the amazing user volume and openness of Twitter for your eCommerce marketing.

### Drive Traffic

One of the most fundamental and easily quantifiable benefits of being engaged on Twitter is the ability to drive qualified traffic from Twitter to your website. The valuable and important metrics of marketers on Twitter are the number of clicks that their tweets generate—being able to drive traffic to your website to generate nontransactional secondary conversions that build your list and start people in the nurturing process as well as being able to drive traffic to your site that may even convert on purchases of your products. The basic concept is extremely simple: tweeting links that your followers see means that they have the opportunity to click the link.

However, there are a few factors to consider when leveraging Twitter for traffic generation.

The most directly correlated factor when driving traffic from Twitter is the composition of the tweet copy itself. Typically, having the link be closer to the beginning of the tweet tends to increase the click-through rate. Adding a personal commentary or endorsement also increases the chances that a follower—who is, after all, following you because you have at least some mindshare on the topics you're sharing—will click-through by giving the link that you're tweeting context. The positioning of the three primary elements of a traffic-generation tweet, {{content title}}, {{content URL}}, and {{commentary}}, are something that you should test yourself to see which gets the most clicks.

An important thing to remember about links is that they typically show up shortened by Twitter's URL shortening service, t.co, although the link will display as the original in the tweet copy. The problem is that URL shortening services don't show the end destination URL, and the enormous omnipresence of spam and viruses on Twitter have made people a little nervous about clicking shortened links. This makes it important to avoid features that are typically used by spammers, such as poor grammar ("hey this user are writing shocking things that are about you" is a common virus currently travelling around Twitter) or providing little or no context for the link (e.g., "click this it's cool"). As social media users become more savvy about protecting themselves from spam and viruses on Twitter, it's becoming more important that marketers differentiate ourselves from the tactics common to spammers.

You may assume that people following you know that you're not a spammer or are sending them any viruses through shortened links, and to an extent this is somewhat true. However, it's actually not that uncommon that Twitter profiles—even those of legitimate brands—get compromised and hijacked to distribute viruses, so to make users positive that the link is coming from you try to adhere to a consistent style and tone differentiating you from spammer tactics. Be careful what links you click when signed into Twitter, and make sure that any page asking for your Twitter login credentials is legitimately Twitter. If you find out that your account has been compromised, either through yourself or through feedback from your followers, you should immediately change your Twitter password *and* go into your Twitter settings to make sure that any third-party applications connected to your account are applications that *you* added. When a Twitter account is compromised, it's not uncommon for spammers to use Open Authentication (OAuth) options to grant access to your account to third-party Twitter publishing application that will allow them to post from your account even if your password is changed.

In addition to Tweet composition, the mixture and composition of your tweets in general can help raise or lower the number of clicks and overall follower engagement with your clicks. In general, if you do nothing but promote your own content, Twitter followers won't find that interesting or engaging. If Twitter followers wanted to see an endless stream of your product detail page links, they could go to your website and browse or create an RSS feed of a page. Twitter provides a chance for retailers to build context and personify their brand and product by doing more than just self-promoting. You can test the exact mixture of tweets for your own brand, but investing only a third of your tweets promoting your own content, a third in promoting the content of others, and a third engaging (asking questions, answering questions, and making observational commentary) can actually *increase* the number of net clicks that you're able to drive through Twitter by making your account more interesting and engaging.

A great deal of study and data analysis has gone into determining the best times of day and days of the week to post tweets to maximize the number of clicks, but of all the factors of driving traffic through Twitter, timing is the least generalized. The times and days that your followers and consumers are on Twitter can vary wildly from any generalized study. You should make *no* assumptions on this topic and instead experiment yourself with different days of the week and times of day. For example, just because you're selling a B2B product doesn't mean that you shouldn't tweet on the weekends. In fact, some B2B eCommerce organizations get *greater* engagement from Twitter on the weekends because people have more time on the weekends to monitor and engage with their social networks. Keep in mind that, although you may consider being on Twitter to be a marketing activity, some employers have even blocked Twitter and other social networks from being accessed from their offices, which makes being engaging during nonwork hours and days more important.

Geography and buyer persona are two additional influencing factors in tweet timing. If you have an international audience, scheduling tweets to go out during the night when your audience overseas is likely to be awake and engaged with Twitter is a better idea than scheduling it to go out when you're awake and engaging with Twitter. Also, keep in mind that different buyer personas use Twitter for different types of content consumption. You should build timing and frequency of social media use into the psychographic dimensions of your buyer personas, and try to experiment with those times to optimize clicks.

In addition to the frequency with which your audience uses Twitter, the frequency with which you tweet can also impact the number of clicks that you're able to drive. However, the issues with frequency aren't usually overposting, as many marketers assume. Again, the posting frequency that your consumers and followers will tolerate can vary wildly from generalized studies, but few organizations have consumers so sensitive that they unfollow or don't click if there are too many posts. In the grand scheme of things, if you get an average of thirty clicks per tweet if you tweet once an hour, and increasing your posting frequency to two per hour and your click-through rate falls a staggering 33 percent, you're still getting forty clicks/hour instead of thirty. There is probably some marginal impact on click-through rate by tweeting frequently, but more important is if you can give the followers the tweets of content that they're going to *want* to click. Of course, there's certainly a reductio ad absurdum argument that can be made that posting fifty times an hour will impact the click-through rate of your tweets (in addition to probably creating a massive follower churn problem), but in general most marketers suffer from a lack of ambition in Twitter post frequency, not an excess.

Amplification of links that you tweet by your followers will also significantly enhance your ability to drive clicks. Your followers have the option to use the native functionality in Twitter to retweet your posts, which literally inserts your tweet into the feeds of their followers as though they had been following you, or they can use the classic method of retweeting where the tweet is copied and "RT @Username" is added either to the beginning or end. Because of the continued prevalence of the classic method for retweeting, you should do your best to make sure that your tweets leave enough room for users to add your username without having to heavily modify the tweet.

Because follower amplification of tweets is such an important part of gaining penetration into the networks of your followers and increasing your ability to drive clicks, a great deal of research has gone into how you can compose your tweets to maximize the probability that they'll be retweeted. For example, Dan Zarrella of HubSpot frequently encourages marketers to add "Please RT" or "Plz RT" to their tweets, since it may not occur to all of your followers that they'd be giving you great value by helping amplify your content. This works well, especially if you're in a consumer-enthusiast vertical where you have a significant amount of consumer passion and social capital. We caution against overusing this tactic though, since making frequent withdrawals from your "bank account of social capital" can damage or diminish your ability to leverage that action from your following in the future.

## Create Enthusiast Vertical Accounts

Most eCommerce marketers have inventories that are too large to simply set up an RSS feed that can broadcast products on Twitter—nor is there any real value in that approach. Instead of managing one account that broadcasts every product in your inventory, you can create separate accounts that focus on different aspects of your business, such as @MyStoreTelevisions and @MyStoreApparel, for example. Use each one of these accounts for a balance of individual user engagement and product tweets.

To get more advanced, create accounts that are based on the buyer macro personas discussed earlier. Although you may consider consumers to be vertically oriented by product category, consumers consider themselves horizontally segmented by buyer persona. Also, since social media is inherently about creating relationships, and it's difficult to build a relationship around a single point of shared interest, aligning around buyer personas can increase the width and depth of content and engagement that you'll be able to share and therefore increase the depth and meaning of a given follower's connection with your brand's Twitter account.

For example, if you're an eCommerce store selling televisions and associated electronics and accessories, you can do @MyStoreTelevisions as previously suggested, but that will limit your content to issues directly affecting televisions—which are products and not in and of themselves an enthusiast vertical. However, if you created @MyStoreGamerz (substituting the "z" for the "s" to speak to buyer personas of the metaplasmus-heavy Millennials who tend to be the frequent gamers), you'd have the ability to share content and engage with followers along the massive variety of issues affecting gamers (game releases, hacks, accessories, culture, etc.). It's far easier to create a sustainable community around a persona-oriented topic like gaming than it is around a product-oriented topic like televisions.

Many eCommerce companies focus on acquiring huge numbers of followers, which is a completely misused metric. While the number of followers you have on Twitter is not an *entirely* meaningless metric, its value is limited most to the ability to gain more followers (i.e., people are more inclined to follow an account with lots of followers) as well as the credibility that it lends you (i.e., people assume that an account with a large number of followers is not likely to be a spammy or disreputable account as well as assuming that it's likely a subject-matter expert).

Better metrics for Twitter are follower churn, click-through rate, tweet engagement (i.e., responses), and tweet amplification (i.e., ReTweets). These metrics are more closely aligned with the actual enterprise value that your organization is deriving from being engaged on Twitter and therefore should be more heavily weighted than the net number of followers that a given account has.

In addition, a large number of diverse followers makes it inherently difficult to be highly engaging since each buyer persona has different concerns and considerations. It's far better to have a targeted network of engaged followers, such as @MyStoreGamerz and @MyStoreMoviegoers, than a large and chaotic network of followers of a generic account such as @MyStore where followers have no particular attachment to or use for the content that you have to share. Segmentation is more likely to create an engaged community that drives enterprise value than size. It's not the size that counts; it's how you use it!

## Run Contests

Contests are a tool typically used either far too often or far too infrequently by marketers on Twitter. They're very good at getting a response out of a stale base of followers or to incentivize excitement, but it can be dangerous to make contests the only value proposition for engaging with your account. While you may gain followers and increase key engagement metrics such as clicks and mentions, you're primarily speaking to the extremely price-sensitive customers who, at the end of the day, are going to be more susceptible to the cost-minimizing, long-tail firms like Amazon.com.

However, Twitter users do love contests and discounts {{DATA POINT NEEDED}}. In almost all self-reporting data, consumers say that one of their main reasons for following brands on Twitter are to get discounts and promotions. However, as is the case with most survey data, consumers typically aren't surveyed on (nor would they probably accurately know if asked since most consumers like to think of themselves as immune to marketing) how true content and engagement influences their buying cycle.

It's also critical to emphasize here that the prizes of any contest in any social media venue should be related to your industry. There was a big trend when Apple first released the iPad to use that as a contest incentive because of the tablet's huge popularity among consumers and the massive buzz it had created. However, even though social media contests offering iPad prizes did generate huge numbers of consumers engaging with them, they were *Apple's* consumers—not necessarily consumers of the brands offering the prize. For example, several companies in the cigar industry offered iPads as prizes for social media contests and saw the expected response of massive engagement and social media reach growth. However, a very small number of those who participated in the contest were actually cigar smokers at all, which means that the growth in reach didn't equal a significant growth in the value of the social media presence for the brand. What the contest did was to dilute the overall value of the individual brands' social connections, which the brands failed to recalculate and thus continued to overinvest in. Because the cigar companies were assuming that the value of individual social connections would remain static with growth, their marketing teams continued to invest in iPad contests until senior management noticed that there was no growth in traffic or revenue from social media.

A better idea would have been to give away something related to their industry, for example, a box of cigars! Because the only people who would enter or participate in such a contest would be potential consumers of that product, they'd grow their following (you'd be surprised what people will do for a free box of cigars) without diluting the value of their individual social connections. Whatever your industry, make sure that any social promotions or contests that you run attract consumers who will actually be valuable social connections for you.

Now that we've established that contests can be valuable but are not a substitute for sharing content on Twitter, there are a few key characteristics of Twitter to consider when designing and implementing a campaign.

First, Twitter users consume a significantly higher velocity of content on average than users of other social networks, and the half-life (the amount of time it takes for a particular tweet to get half the amount of engagement that it's ever going to get) of posts tends to be shorter for Twitter than for networks such as LinkedIn or Facebook. Because of this, Twitter users are more highly responsive to time-sensitive promotions.

One of the most basic types of Twitter contests is the "Follow" contest, which is exactly what it sounds like. The brand offers a prize based on their growth of followers. You can make it a regular contest, such as once a week (or at another interval that makes sense) you'll select a random follower to receive a prize. Threshold contests are also straightforward, such as "Once we reach X followers, we'll select a follower to receive a prize." Threshold contests are particularly effective because they directly incentivize the follower base to actively ask others to follow your account. However, frequent use of this tactic by itself will cause the follower base to become less responsive since their engagement dilutes their chances of winning by adding more potential winners to the pool. In fact, brands that already have large followings on Twitter will often find this tactic less effective since the chances of winning become so small that followers aren't willing to invest the marginal effort in diluting their own chances of winning. This tactic is much more useful for narrower, persona-centric accounts that are trying to increase their reach within a niche social market.

"ReTweet" contests ("ReTweet this for a chance to win X product!") are also very popular with Twitter users. ReTweet contests have the added benefit of not being explicitly against Twitter's terms of service like such contests are against Facebook's. ReTweet contests are one of the easiest types to design and deploy and have the added advantage over other contest types of requiring participants to amplify your content to enter—which allows you immediate access to their network effect and can create a critical mass of growth much faster. ReTweet contests are excellent for marketers who are simply trying to get additional exposure because of the inherent nature of the contest forcing participants to share the tweet with their followers. The copy should include "ReTweet this for a chance to win" so that when it *is* retweeted, their followers also know that they can enter by retweeting it.

ReTweet contests are best when combined with a follow requirement— and the plausible pretense is fairly easy since following is required for the brand to be able to send a direct message notifying winners and gathering e-mail addresses for follow up. Instead of just making it ReTweet oriented, you can make it "ReTweet and follow us." This way you can guarantee that the increased exposure will lead to an increase in social media reach.

Engagement contests require a little more forethought but can be more effective at increasing the depth of relationships with the existing follower base. Engagement contests typically include asking for a response on Twitter from the follower base, such as asking them to complete a sentence, answer a question (or the *Jeopardy* version of having them come up with the question in response to your answer), or tweet some other kind of response @you. Because this requires a greater investment of brain power than simply clicking "ReTweet" or "Follow," these types of contests don't always have as large a number of participants and rarely lead to significant growth.

Another contributing factor to engagement-oriented Twitter contests having a lower impact on aggregate social media reach is the simple fact that most people reply to such types of contests with the @Username at the beginning of their response. When a user starts a tweet with @Username, only those of their followers that already follow the user at whom the reply is directed will see the tweet in their feeds, as opposed to ReTweets which will be shared with their entire follower list. Because of this, engagement-oriented contests should not be used with the intention of increasing net follower reach but rather with the objective of improving the engagement with the existing follower base.

Content contests are similar to engagement contests with the notable exception that they involve content created and shared outside of Twitter. Photo contests are one of the more popular types of content contests, where followers are asked to take a photo or create a graphic and submit it for a chance to win. It's important to note that this is a valuable opportunity for you to "crowd source" (i.e., get large numbers of people to assist in) the development of visual content, which is an increasingly important type of content on other networks such as Facebook, Google+, and Pinterest. Because of this, it's again important to make sure that the contest is oriented around your industry and the topic of interest that connects your followers together. For example, it wouldn't make sense for the aforementioned cigar retailers to have a photo contest of, say, skyscrapers (unless there was a person in front of it smoking a cigar). Be sure to make it clear that you retain the publishing rights to all photos that are submitted to avoid any potential confusion, especially because even content that doesn't "win" the contest can be of value to your marketing organization.

Content contests are particularly valuable because in addition to the inherent value of increasing engagement with the contest participants, they help marketing organizations overcome the significant marketing challenge of creating content that reflects the interests and values of their consumer audience. When the consumer audience is creating the content for you, it creates a valuable symbiosis that helps the site itself have a greater volume of high persona-oriented content.

Another popular method of contests are voting contests, where contest participants are judged based upon how many others they can get to "vote" for their piece of content. You can do this on Twitter using favorites or ReTweets as a contest metric. Favorites are more likely to get engagement from participant's networks since it doesn't require amplification into their connection's networks. ReTweets, obviously, have more value for the brand precisely because they require the participant to encourage others to amplify the content, which increases your brand's exposure. Voting contests are most effective when paired with content-oriented contests that allow users to submit pieces of content that, instead of winners being randomly selected or selected by your organization, entrants are required to leverage their social capital to win, and in doing so increase your exposure to their network. Particularly because this method typically requires entrants to solicit action from their network multiple times, as opposed to ReTweet contests that only require them to expose your brand to their network once, this can improve the penetration of the brand into the entrant's social network.

Charitable contests are a variation that can be applied to any of these types of contests. Simply, instead of offering a prize to a participant, you allow entrants to nominate or vote for selected charitable organizations to whom you'll make a donation if they win. These are paired frequently with the voting contest type, where entrants (and often the organizations themselves) will promote the contest to their followers to get the donation sent to the organization that they support. This particular type of contest is somewhat sensitive and delicate because of the emotional dimension of charities and the relatively cynical nature of tying the support of a business to a cold metric like votes. Although it's rarely backfired on organizations that try it, and it seems that consumers have been fairly accepting of this tactic, you should tread lightly because if there ever was a backlash it would likely be severe and damaging.

A safer, yet arguably also somewhat clinical and cynical, variation on charitable contests is to tie the amount of the donation to the engagements on Twitter. For example, "For every person who ReTweets this post, we'll give $X to Y charity." This is safer because it avoids pitting charitable organizations against each other and instead focuses on supporting a single charity. This can frequently have a significantly better return than giving prizes to contest entrants because people (even those within the networks of the entrants) are more prone to support charitable organizations than individuals. Charitable contests in general also have the additional benefit of the emotional appeal, which is frequently stronger at incentivizing low-investment actions such as ReTweets than direct value-oriented appeals. In addition, charitable contests generate a general goodwill and perception of social responsibility for the brand. Of course, there's also the added benefit that the "prize" for this particular type of contest is tax-deductible for your business!

Contests can be valuable when used in moderation. You don't want to make the primary value of engaging with your brand on Twitter the pursuit of discounts or prizes, but they can be useful tools to increase your social reach or to reenergize the engagement of a following.

## Consumer Support and Social Proof

According to a 2012 study conducted by Gartner, failure to respond to inquiries and complaints consumers make through social media channels can increase the churn rate of your customers by up to 15 percent. As marketers gain greater depth of penetration into social media, consumers have a growing expectation—rightfully so—that the connection should be a two-way street. Consumers in social media won't tolerate marketers that take and take by broadcasting content and pitching products but that don't *give back* to the social ecosystem by providing support. One of the greatest benefits of marketers engaging in social media is the ability to personify their brand, and consumers expect that people will have a greater depth to their existence than simply asking for investment from the social community. Brands that refuse to offer support through social media are asking for value from the social ecosystem without giving back when consumers need it most—when they have service issues or complaints.

Although most organizations have a method for contacting customer service on their website, such as a form or live chat, consumers are frequently more prone to share their feelings in social media, where many are more comfortable sharing their feelings and opinions more readily than directly with traditional customer-service mechanisms.

Again, you have to remember that consumers don't consider a purchase as an independent, isolated life experience. Instead, it's one of the many life experiences that people typically share in social media. People are programmed and comfortable with sharing their life experiences in social media—in fact, that's one of social media's most important benefits. Twitter, especially, holds enormous social value not because of the ability to develop deep, significant relationships horizontally aligned across a large number of interests but rather because Twitter empowers complete strangers to share experiences vertically aligned within specific topics. Because of this innate nature of Twitter coupled with the compulsory brevity on Twitter that lends itself to emotional venting with shallow details, Twitter is a natural place for consumers to share experiences with eCommerce retailers.

The good news is that consumers are willing to share positive experiences as well as negative experiences. Marketers should monitor Twitter for positive mentions of their brand or products and amplify them into their feed. Because these are public messages (unlike e-mails or chats through a website which have an expectation of privacy), marketers can use positive brand mentions for "social proofing"—that is, showing tweets on their website or marketing collateral to help influence other consumers by relaying the positive opinions of similar consumers. Due to the high volume, velocity, and diversity of consumer engagements on Twitter, it's easier for organizations to build a library of social proof through Twitter monitoring. This empowers marketers to use dynamic content to align social proof with the concerns, pain points, and values of others within a buyer persona.

For example, being able to use a tweet as social proof on your website for a buyer persona that needs to be reassured that your product is easy to use can be significantly more effective than you simply claiming that it's easy. You simply can't buy the kind of persuasive power involved in someone tweeting "Wow, Product X is actually really easy."

However, most brands fail to monitor positive brand mentions, and those that do at best tweet back a thank-you. If you're not using positive brand mentions on Twitter for social proof in your other marketing collateral, you may be missing out on a valuable opportunity to capitalize on the most persuasive messaging there is: happy customers.

Of course, there's always the dark side of social media monitoring and engagement—dealing with unhappy customers and customer complaints. This was one of the earliest advantages identified of brands being engaged with social media, and yet it remains one of the most underused types of engagement. Social media engagements with consumers won't always be sunshine and rainbows, just like engagements through your website or in a physical retail location. Regardless of the quality of your product or service, all companies invariably experience customer difficulties. As discussed earlier, ignoring these messages from consumers can lead to a greater loss of recurring customer business—which is one of the key methods to improving customer LTV and competing against long-tail eCommerce firms as discussed earlier in the book. Also, failing to respond to negative sentiments on Twitter means that, if the customer continues complaining, their entire following will be exposed to damaging, negative messaging about your company, significantly reducing the probability that some of them will buy from you.

The best way to handle negative comments on Twitter is to respond as quickly as possible—freakishly fast if possible—and offer support. Follow the person and ask them to direct message you their e-mail address so that you (or one of your customer service representatives) can reach out to get the details of the issue. The quicker that you can get the conversation off of Twitter, the better. It's not productive to try to gather details of the issue through Twitter. First of all, Twitter's character limits make it unlikely that someone will be able to communicate enough detail to help you. Second, most customer-service discussions go through a process of back and forth before a resolution can be reached, which isn't always something that you want to happen publicly. Most consumers soften their position as soon as they realize that someone cares enough to listen and respond promptly and is willing to reasonably engage with a customer-service process.

There is, however, another category of complaints on Twitter that bears ignoring. Colloquially referred to as "trolls," there are those in social media (and the Internet in general) that like to complain or berate people and brands for little or no reason. "DON'T FEED THE TROLLS" is a common aphorism among social media marketing professionals, which essentially means that engaging with them has the exact opposite of engaging with a legitimate consumer—they become more aggressive and abusive because they're getting attention. This is one of the reasons that social managers must be, above *all* else, calm and level headed. Many of the largest scandals in social media marketing have been caused by social marketers who allowed themselves to become emotional and respond condescendingly or aggressively to trolls who then seize upon this response and amplify it into social media. Because the natural inclination of the Internet community is to side with consumers over brands, providing this kind of fodder can be damaging and counterproductive.

Trolls are typically fairly easy to identify by the excessive vitriol in their comments or their vague references. Frequently they're not even actual customers of your brand and therefore won't engage rationally when you ask them to direct-message you contact information so that you can resolve their issue. Trolls aren't interested in conflict resolution but instead are simply seeking attention. Therefore, if a plaintiff ignores your requests for contact or complaint details, simply ignore them and move on. Pressing the issue or continuing to engage with them won't help and will simply validate their attention-seeking behavior.

A good idea is to create a "crisis response" playbook for social media. Most large organizations have crisis-mitigation and customer-communication procedures in place for conventional mediums but fail to understand and appreciate that most of the negative messaging during a crisis will come through social media.

## Identifying and Nurturing Prospects

One of the earliest imagined marketing applications of Twitter was the ability to identify consumers with a need or interest in a given product or service and engage with them. While this hasn't panned out as marketers had dreamed, with hordes of people saying "I'd really like to buy this product if only the company would send me a tweet," consumers have demonstrated a significant propensity toward using Twitter to ask their community for information or express need or pain point for which there's a product solution. However, there's still a thin line between identifying and engaging prospects on Twitter and spamming. Some consumers still aren't entirely accepting of marketers intruding into social media, and still aren't entirely comfortable with the concept of social media monitoring. It's crucial that you approach prospecting on Twitter from the perspective of adding value to the social ecosystem instead of simply pitching your product. Regardless of whether or not you feel your product is the social cure to all the world's woes, consumers have been conditioned to be wary of—or ignore entirely—unsolicited engagements from marketers or brands.

You can identify potential prospects on Twitter through keyword monitoring using either Twitter's native search functionality or using a third-party application. Twitter's native app isn't ideal for marketers because it's ill-adapted to monitoring multiple keywords, instead being primarily intended for users to follow a specific thread of conversation (often a #hashtag that allows users to track and engage with a single ongoing topic). Third-party applications that allow you to sort specific keywords or groups of keywords into columns make it significantly easier to monitor and process what can, at times, be an extremely high velocity of content. Some companies have even implemented NORAD-like command centers with dark rooms filled with large monitors to make sure that they don't miss any possible mentions of their brand or of the keywords that are leading indicators of purchase interest in their product. This is a bit overkill for most organizations, where having a single person dedicated to social media monitoring or distributing the duties across a team of marketers is usually adequate.

The types of keywords you should monitor depend on your industry but usually expand beyond the obvious company and product branded keywords. For example, a pain reliever such as Tylenol would want to monitor their branded keywords and those of their competitors but also monitor keywords related to the early-phase indications of a need for their product such as "headache" or references to relevant topics such as injury, pain, or soreness. This can get particularly complex since the syntax of Twitter, with the compulsory brevity created by the character limits they impose, can often be varied in the use and spelling of words. "Health insurance" can be abbreviated "health ins" or "ins" or any number of additional variations that make it very difficult to create keyword monitoring schemas that capture them all. There are some pieces of social media monitoring software that have tried to combine contextual syntax analysis with keyword databases to expand the power of monitoring tools, but these technologies are still in their infancy in understanding how the uses of language are significantly shifting with the increasing adoption of digital media communications.

In addition to identifying prospects through keyword monitoring, you can also use your existing inbound marketing efforts that grow your contacts database to improve your Twitter prospecting abilities. Twitter's API has integrated with some third-party apps to allow you to determine, based on the e-mail addresses in your contacts database, the Twitter accounts of those who have completed a form on your website. If you can use dynamically updating list criteria to sort these based on the buying-cycle stage indicated by the conversion (such as differentiating between those who downloaded an e-book versus those who have requested a free sample of your product), you can intelligently categorize and monitor movement through the funnel.

If you've identified a prospect on Twitter who has already organically converted on one of your forms, you have a greater advantage because the prospect has had brand exposure and you're not making the approach cold. However, the ongoing battle for consumer information privacy has made consumers skittish about unexpected consequences from providing information online. Actions that depart from their expectations, such as being engaged on Twitter, may make the prospect feel uncomfortable with engaging with you further if handled improperly. Again, how prospects respond to social communications should be part of the psychographic profile of your buyer personas so that you can determine the level of aggressiveness that you can nurture contacts in social media. Also, if you intend to use this capability of Twitter's API heavily as an active outreach trigger instead of a passive monitoring method, it may be a good idea to emphasize on the landing page that you have a robust Twitter community.

When you're first making an approach to someone on Twitter, you can take a few different actions to "introduce" yourself. You can either simply follow them (they'll receive a notification that you've done so), you can "Favorite" the tweet that triggered your monitoring (or a tweet relevant to you if you identified them using the e-mail address), you can retweet one of their posts that's somewhat related to you, or you can take a more active approach and send them an @Username mention.

If you're using the latter method, it's absolutely critical that you provide them some kind of problem-oriented value that's not overly assertive. Sending them a link to a blog article if they've asked some kind of research phase–oriented question is a soft but effective way of making an approach on Twitter. If you don't have a relevant piece of content, an @Username mention that asks a qualifying question or provides an answer not directly pitching your product as a solution is a good, easy way to introduce yourself.

After you've made the initial approach, you can engage with the prospect further and later in the relationship offer discounts or e-book downloads or some other kind of value offer to get them to engage with some phase of your buying cycle. This process can take some time and you shouldn't think of Twitter nurturing as a method of accelerating the sales cycle but rather an augmentation to the normal buying cycle and a way of making sure that the prospect doesn't fall out of the funnel entirely. Also, the keyword monitoring can serve as a function of demand generation for you by simply exposing relevant consumers to your brand through Twitter interactions. Even if you simply favorite or retweet a post that's related to your industry or the pain point your product addresses, Twitter users typically take a bit of time to look into those who are interacting with them if they're not already familiar with you.

Another useful tactic is to remember that your product or service is typically only part of a holistic experience for the consumer. We've talked about how HD televisions could have micro personas concerned about gaming, movies, or sports, and the same basic understand of the diversity of applications for your product can be applied to Twitter engagement. For example, a major hair-cutting franchise has a person dedicated to monitoring branded keywords who reached out to author Sam Mallikarjunan when he tweeted "Just got my haircut at X Store for my speech at the #Inbound12 conference Tuesday." However, instead of reaching out with a simple thank-you or offering a coupon to schedule a return trip for a trim, the company sent Sam a tweet that said: "@Mallikarjunan Good haircuts boost confidence! Here's an article on building confidence before speaking in public: {{link}}." It was an incredible act of social media goodwill that created an instantly accepted connection on Twitter. Sam included the brand's name but didn't directly tag them on Twitter, so the approach was unsolicited, but they made an approach that provided Sam with a valuable piece of content that was the underlying pain point for purchasing their service. By doing this, the brand created a value-based social connection with Sam and can continue to nurture him using Twitter engagements with content at their leisure. Also, if they have a profile of the buyer persona into which Sam fits best, they may even be able to predict when he'll need a haircut in the future and actively reach out to him without seeming spammy or overly aggressive.

## Personification and Distributed Management

People have an inherent inclination to trust individuals more than faceless brands. By allowing your presence on Twitter to show some personality and personify your brand beyond simple promotion and classic marketing broadcasting, you can help consumers feel more comfortable with trusting you—and trust is a major factor with consumers when deciding to engage with an eCommerce retailer. If your brand can share content outside of its direct area of interest and engage with followers on issues outside of the immediate sphere of applications for their product, you can build a personified relationship where people feel connected to your brand as they would a normal social connection. Because people have a significant trust for recommendations made by social connections, if you can reclassify yourself in the minds of your consumers as such instead of being bucketed as a business, the personified relationship can increase your ability to execute traditional marketing actions but with the responsiveness that consumers typically reserve for personal friendships.

For example, if you're an E-mail Service Provider and someone that you've followed and exchanged a few messages with tweets "When @ConstantContact goes down my whole life is on hold" it's much easier to reply and remind them that you have an ESP that they might consider as an alternative. In fact, it even makes traditional rhetorical devices, such as paralipsis, even more effective by providing an extracommercial context for the engagement. For example, a marketer could reply "@PersonOnTwitter, it would be utterly shameless of me to suggest @MyCompany as an alternative ESP at a time like this, so I won't :)" (which is a classic example of the rhetorical device paralipsis) without sounding condescending or sarcastic. A personified relationship between the followers of a brand allows consumers to feel like they're doing business with a real person, which makes them more receptive to marketing messaging as well as creating a sense of personal connection that's easy to build brand loyalty from than a faceless corporation.

To encourage personification from a marketing-managed Twitter profile, you can leverage "distributed" management where multiple employees monitor and engage from the profile. These employees typically use "^FL" (the "^" separating the initials from the tweet copy and the F standing in for the first initial while the L stands in for the last). In author Sam Mallikarjunan's case, he might sign a tweet from an account with distributed management with ^SM. This helps create a context for the curated content on your Twitter account (the tweets that your account shares that aren't just from your website but are selected by employees) as well as allows for "personal" tweets from the account. Obviously, there's a level of responsibility that this maintains, and you don't want employees abusing the Twitter account or sharing controversial posts such as political opinions, religious views, or preferences between PC versus Mac (three very explosive topics), however, some personal tweeting from conferences, passages from industry-related books, and other "personal" thoughts and observations that are in some way related to the brand, the industry, or the pain points of the buyer persona can allow a single Twitter account to have multiple voices. It allows for a steady, diversified stream of content from the account that prevents it from being an ad nauseum rebroadcasting of the company content and allows it to be a voice of the employees who are highly engaged in the industry.

## Engaging with Influencers

Marketers tend to overemphasize the importance of identifying "influencers" on Twitter. First of all, "influencer" is an incredibly difficult metric to accurately identify. As previously discussed, for example, absolute numbers of followers is a very poor metric for measuring a person's influence on Twitter. The true measure of an influencer, which is obviously their ability to *influence* and encourage the actions of their followers (from a perception, preference, and purchase perspective) is almost impossible to measure because there's no feedback mechanism built into Twitter (or, really, any technology) that provides accurate reporting on this.

However, traditional measures of influence (follower count and the only-slightly-better metric of Klout—which is a company that attempts to truly classify Tweeters by their influence on specific topics) are effective at distinguishing the lower echelons of Twitter influence from the rest. That is, if someone has only twenty-five followers on Twitter, they're unlikely to be able to drive a significant network effect from their account. Similarly, Klout scores do a decent job of telling those with low influence but are far from perfect in identifying those with mediocre influence from those with more significant influence. Also, just because someone doesn't have a large following on Twitter doesn't mean they're not influential in other media. Your PR team probably has a wish list of those they wish they had connections to, and if you have a B2B eCommerce element, odds are you have a similar wish list of customers you wish you had so that you could use their logos and testimonials (and the accompanying influence and credibility). This is a good place to *start* when looking for influencers with whom you'd like to build a relationship.

When making an approach to an identified influencer, keep in mind that they have to deal with a significant velocity of unsolicited engagements (after all, you're not the only one that would benefit from their friendship). To break through the noise, you have to differentiate yourself from the crowd of solicitors and admirers that they already deal with. You can start by simply following them (an obvious gesture of respect that many marketers ignore) and retweeting some of their posts that you think your followers will find value in. There should be a significant number of their tweets that organically provide value to your account's followers. After all, if your purpose in networking with them is to gain some access to the influence they leverage in your industry, then they should have opinions, information, or content that consumers in your industry will find valuable.

There's a lot of goodwill that's created when you retweet someone; it's not an act that most people take without forethought, and it's a good way to begin to introduce yourself to an influencer. There are two ways to retweet someone: you can use Twitter's native ReTweet interface (the "ReTweet" option that you'll see when looking at a particular tweet), or you can copy and paste the tweet into a new tweet box and add "RT @Username" to the beginning. Twitter intends for us to use their native interface; however, ReTweets from the native interface show up in the "interactions" feed for a user that is also cluttered with favorites, follows, and public @mentions as well as ReTweets, which means that it's much more plausible that an influencer who receives many such interactions won't even see the ReTweets that you're investing in building that relationship. When you copy the tweet and add the "RT @Username" it shows up in the user's *mentions* feed, which mostly people (especially those with a significant velocity of interactions) tend to monitor more closely. In addition, modifying their tweet allows you to add an opinion or comment to either the beginning or end which can help add context to the influencer's engagement. For example, instead of using the native ReTweet functionality you can tweet "{{insert opinion here}} RT @Username {{original tweet copy}}" or "RT @Username "{{original tweet copy}}" {{insert opinion here}}." This will insert your ReTweet (which builds good will) into the mentions feed of a user (which gets the tweet seen) along with a comment (which builds context and incentivizes response). In terms of prospecting influencers, it's a much better method of getting noticed.

When you finally decide to ask for value from the relationship with an influencer, it should be aligned with his goals and values. For example, asking him to promote his book or blog by writing a guest blog article, coauthoring a buyer's guide or e-book, or participating in a webinar should align with his goals of increasing exposure while providing value content to the industry's consumers. You should *not*, however, simply ask him to tweet one of your product detail pages and expect him to comply. He may do this organically over time, but more likely the immediate benefit that you're going to get from engaging with an influencer will be content and social proof for your consumers. Once he's created content with you or for you, he's much more likely to tweet *that content* that will drive awareness and exposure of your brand into his channel of influence.

Similarly, you can use Twitter to find guest blogging and content-creation opportunities for your own marketing efforts. One of the few white-hat or proper ways to build inbound links is to write guest blog articles or content that gets posted on websites related to or affiliated with your industry. Influencers (especially second-tier influencers who have a hard time maintaining a significant velocity of keyword-rich content) are often fairly receptive to guest bloggers for the same reasons you are—free content plus penetration into another industry influencer's social channel.

## Gaining Search Authority

As previously discussed, Google and other search engines are increasingly considering the number of times a website, domain, or piece of content is shared on social media sites as part of their SEO rankings. They are monitoring this data and identifying strong signals of its quality and authority. Of all the social media sites at the time of this writing, Twitter lends itself most readily to rapid and frequent sharing of links, and the same study previously discussed that demonstrated a significant correlation between Facebook "likes" and keyword rankings in search engines showed a similar—though slightly lower—impact by Tweets to search engine rankings.

Again, one of the reasons that social media networks are useful for determining value and relevance is the fact that they actively try to curb spam and those attempting artificial influence or to abuse the system, unlike the Internet in general where people can create an unlimited number of websites and can create content to try to artificially influence the inbound linking algorithm that has historically governed the majority of influence on keyword rankings. Although Twitter has a reputation for being largely infiltrated by spam due to the openness of its API and the potential for scalable spam automation that that creates, Twitter also has one of the most active communities in terms of manually reporting spam outside of the e-mail consumer community. This is helpful to Twitter and lends greater credence to their having a strong influence on search rankings since identifying spam is something that's extremely difficult to create computer programs to do. In much the same vein that former US Supreme Court Justice Potter Stewart famously said that, although he could not create a specific set of rules and legal doctrine to define obscenity, "I know it when I see it," having a massive, active community of actual people that's helping Twitter to identify spammers is making the process more accurate and better at identifying spam, even if it's not now (nor will it ever be) a truly effective system for deterring those who would abuse the system.

However, influence and expertise in social media is not equal for everyone, and identifying who has expertise in specific industries is an ongoing priority of companies like Klout. Klout, for all of its weaknesses and faults, tries to identify *who* has influence in *what* categories. This is the logical continuation of the concept of social sharing influencing search engine rankings, since it's likely that author Sam Mallikarjunan tweeting a blog article about marketing is a better indicator of the content's quality or relevance than someone who has no expertise or experience in the industry tweeting it. This is likely to be an imperfect system, at least initially, but represents an interesting trend of providing more accurate results based on the feedback of the segments of the social community most qualified to comment on specific topics.

Perhaps it is for this reason that tactics for Twitter marketing have become known as some of the better methods for driving traffic to a website and gaining critical amplification of content. In terms of enhancing your search engine optimization via engagement on Twitter, share baiting—or creating content that is likely to be tweeted and shared—is one of the more effective tactics. The number of times an article or product page is tweeted should be one of the key performance indicators that you use to determine the effectiveness of various types and topics of content.

## How to Get More Followers on Twitter

We hope that you didn't skip right to this section of the chapter since, as we discuss several times during this chapter, the sheer number of followers that you have on Twitter is not an effective indicator of your influence or your marketing team's ability to drive enterprise value. Part of our rationale for putting this section at the end of the chapter is the fact that the overemphasis on number of followers as a vanity metric is far too distracting for most marketers. If you have "only" two hundred followers, but each of them tweets you once a day and are highly engaged and they amplify your content and provide you ample social proof, you may be achieving your marketing goals without the vanity metric of net followers on Twitter.

However, Twitter followers are a contributing factor to the social media marketing funnel, just like number of websites visitors are a leading indicator and contributing factor to the marketing funnel of your website itself. Net number of Twitter followers also has a positive impact on credibility, especially for eCommerce firms with less broad-spectrum brand recognition. Simply put, if you're competing within a niche vertical where repeat purchases are infrequent and a significant number of customers may not have done business with you before, enhancing your credibility with an engaged social following can help create a "safety in numbers" perception that will help people feel more comfortable doing business with you. Also, as you follow others, they're more likely to make positive snap judgments about the value of your tweets if they perceive that many others value your tweets.

The best way—and one of the only "right" ways—of getting more followers on Twitter is to create valuable content on your website (usually blogs) and the websites of others (usually guest blogs) and include a citation that directs people to your Twitter account. Adding "@Mallikarjunan" to the cover of this book helps expose the Twitter account of author Sam Mallikarjunan to anyone who sees the book at all, for example. When giving speeches, talks, or making presentations, including your @Username is a good way of exposing people to your account, and including the @Username (and perhaps even a link to the account) in the content that you create across the web helps amplify your reach even further. The prevalence of Twitter has made it so that "@Username" is widely—almost universally—understood to be a call to action to follow and engage with a Twitter account to the point where you don't necessarily even have to add additional call-to-action copy. Depending on the level of social media adoption and technical sophistication indicated by the psychographic profiling in your buyer persona, you may need to add some simple descriptive text such as "Follow us on Twitter @Username" or "Tweet us @Username" to add context and distinguish from the more popular and longer-standing usage of the @ symbol for e-mail. Many marketers fail to take advantage of the everyday exposure and opportunities to leverage their existing penetration into other media channels, such as print, television, guest blogging, etc., to incentivize or encourage engagement on Twitter. Since engagement on Twitter can be valuable in increasing the long-term value of customer contacts, or even helping to nurture and convert customer contacts to begin with, and given the fact that promoting a Twitter handle typically doesn't take up a lot of copy or creative space, it's usually a good idea to not miss out on opportunities to expose your Twitter account to your audience in other channels.

Within the Twitter channel, amplification by your existing followers is an effective way to gain penetration into their social networks. It can be useful if their followers share a similar consumer interest and make good potential customers, but also just to increase your number of followers. ReTweets have, as discussed earlier, the benefit of exposing your *content* to Twitter users who are not already connected with you. However, there's the added benefit of if the content they amplify is relevant to their followers and they find you interesting and relevant as an account, they might choose to directly follow you in addition to engaging with the content that was retweeted. Although one of the primary marketing applications of Twitter is the ability to drive traffic, not all of your tweets have to contain links. Since a retweet has an intrinsic value of exposing your *account* to the follower channels of your followers, text-only tweets that get retweeted can add value. Since a tweet with a link has the context of being connected to the piece of content to which it's linked, Twitter followers may be more inclined to retweet short, simple statements, ideas, or one-liners that don't require the investment of engaging with the link to determine its value. Data analysis by Dan Zarrella, the Social Media Scientist at marketing software giant HubSpot, on the number of ReTweets that include links indicate that tweets containing links tend to get more ReTweets than those that do not, but it's a factor that you should test and experiment for yourself to help you gain penetration into the follower channels of your existing followers.

In addition to those that already follow you on Twitter, participation in "hashtag" conversations on Twitter can help you get exposure to topically targeted followers. Hashtags use the # symbol to connect a tweet to a topic or idea, often an ongoing event or topic of conversation, such as #eCommerce or #marketing. It may not make sense to include a specific keyword in a tweet that would show your tweet to people who are interested in a specific topic, and keywords may also help people shorten the number of characters that it takes to connect their tweet to a specific topic. For example, you could tweet "Twitter hashtags are awesome for helping people connect over shared experiences. #SMM" by appending the #SMM hashtag at the end of the tweet, anyone who searches that specific hashtag will see my tweet. Since #SMM is used to refer to "Social Media Marketing" (which takes up a lot of characters), using #SMM in the tweet allows me to connect my tweet to the topic without having to use up all the characters involved in typing it out fully. Of course, this only works as long as others *know* that the #SMM hashtag is being used and what it refers to. Because if this, it's not always useful to try to artificially stimulate use of a hashtag that you create since getting widespread adoption when there are already hashtags in use might not be efficient.

For example, instead of trying to get people to use #eCommBook as a hashtag, we'll probably try to engage with people using #eComm, #SMM, #Mktg, #Marketing, and other such tags that are relevant to the topic of this book to get additional exposure. If we monitor for #SMM and respond to someone who's tweeted "I wonder how I can use Twitter to drive business to my eCommerce website? #SMM" (if we're so lucky) there's an obvious context for the engagement. Again, similar to Twitter prospecting methods previously discussed, it wouldn't make sense to just send a link to buy this book on the Barnes & Noble website if they don't have any connection. Tweeting them a reply such as "You can use Twitter to drive traffic, nurture customer communities, gather social proof, etc." will add value to them and give them exposure to our account in a way that's nonconfrontational and value adding. Similarly, tweeting them a link to a blog article on how to use Twitter for eCommerce marketing would provide them value without asking for something in return (such as buying our book). When tweeted by someone you don't know, it's natural to be curious and look at their profile to see what their background is for responding to you—and it gives them the opportunity to follow you. Also, by simply participating in hashtag conversations you can get your account seen by others who are monitoring the same topic and give them a chance to follow you even if they're not actively tweeting with the hashtag and being engaged by you.

When someone sees you engaging them or sees a tweet retweeted by you and clicks through to your profile, you should make sure that there's enough information to establish a context for your Twitter presence and encourage them to tweet. If your Twitter biography is blank, potential followers have no context for knowing what tweets from you are likely to be about. Make sure that you've filled out your Twitter biography with descriptive copy that appeals to the buyer personas that you want to follow you. Also, you can leverage your Twitter background and header image to help people visually consume more information about what your interests are and what the topics of your tweets will be. As your efforts to expose users from multiple channels to your account drive traffic to your profile page, you should be conversion oriented in design with the call to action being the impetus to follow your account.

In addition to exposing your account to others through engagement with hashtags and promotion on other channels, which are the "right" and acceptable ways of increasing exposure to your Twitter account, following others whom you'd like to follow you is a way of introducing yourself. We must point out here that aggressive following is explicitly against Twitter's terms of service and *can get you suspended or banned from Twitter*. We are not encouraging you to use this tactic, but educating you about it so that you can recognize when others are doing it as well as to protect yourself from those doing it to you and to dispel the absurd notion that you have to follow back everyone that follows you.

"Follow churning" is a practice that is explicitly against Twitter's terms of service and certainly against the spirit and intention Twitter has with the follow function. Since Twitter sends users an e-mail when someone follows them as well as gives them a notification in the "interactions" feed on their Twitter account, when someone follows you it exposes you to their account and gives them the chance to follow you back. Follow churning is the practice of following users and then unfollowing them, exposing them to your account with no intention of actually continuing to follow them and consume their tweets. Against the spirit—or even the letter—of Twitter's terms of service though this may be, it's nevertheless an effective way of artificially increasing the number of followers that you have on Twitter because it exposes your account to more people and stimulates a reflexive response for the user you've followed to consider following you back. You don't have to unfollow a user after following them; you can simply follow targeted profiles and continue following them to increase the depth of relationship and connection. However, those who seek to rapidly artificially inflate their number of followers churn the accounts that they follow at a high rate because Twitter has caps on the ratio of the number of accounts that you can follow to the number of followers that you have. You cannot, for example, simply *follow* a million Twitter profiles if you have only 100 Twitter *followers*. Twitter does this to prevent (or at least limit) the type of abuse that users who follow churn are engaging in. Their servers would become instantly overloaded, and Twitter users wouldn't be able to intelligently analyze and decide whom to follow back if there were no limits and people on Twitter were being followed and unfollowed by thousands of people every day.

In addition to user experience and technical limitations, Twitter's new monetization model—which includes "promoted accounts"—is incentivized to limit the abuse of following as a method of growing a follower base. Instead of allowing people to gain followers through free means such as follow churning, Twitter wants marketers to invest in Twitter Ads that show promoted accounts and pay Twitter to artificially grow their follower base. Be sure that if you invest in Twitter Ads to grow followers that you target well. Because Twitter followers from ads aren't "earned" (i.e., they weren't influenced by social amplification by existing followers of an account or earned through content exposure), they'll have inherently lower brand retention. Although data on this is limited so far, it's possible that—like leads and contacts generated from paid traffic sources on websites—followers generated from paid Promoted Accounts on Twitter may have a lower retention or engagement rate and therefore a lower value as a connection. Also, because of the fairly low dollar value of individual followers on Twitter, it's difficult to justify significant expenditure on Promoted Accounts to gain new followers from an ROI perspective. However, it is an effective (and legitimate) way to artificially grow your net follower base faster.

Finally, Twitter's API allows you to use certain technologies that allow you to identify contacts within your existing database that use the same e-mail address to login to Twitter so that when contacts convert organically from your website you can nurture them to connect with you on Twitter as well.

# Chapter 8:

## Managing Other Social Media Networks and Online Reviews

## Pinterest

There's been a lot made in the marketing world lately about the "visual content" revolution. Although it's not an entirely new concept, there's been a huge increase in marketers' focus on visual content after spending a few years remastering the written word. Visual content has always been important, with some studies suggesting that people process information from visual sources orders of magnitude faster as well as having more pronounced psychological responses. For example, research by 3M famously concluded that humans process information from images up to 60,000 times faster than through text. However, it was the fantastic growth and success of the image/link curation site Pinterest that reawakened the attention of marketers who had allowed their visual content to stagnate into a trite rehashing of stock photography and generic "Web 2.0" visual design schemas. Less than a year after its debut, Pinterest has already become the third most popular social network worldwide and holds the record for the fastest growing social network in history. In addition, early data indicate that traffic from Pinterest may convert at a higher rate for eCommerce companies than traffic from other social networks as well as spending more per transaction. According to a study by eCommerce shopping cart provider Shopify, the average transaction value for users referred by Pinterest is $80 – double that seen in referral traffic from Facebook in the same study. In fact, the CMO at a major eCommerce company told the authors of this book during his interview that he now uses his Facebook, Twitter, and even some of his e-mail automation for the express purpose of driving more traffic to his company's Pinterest presence. There are a number of terrific ways to use this heavily visual medium in your social media marketing plans, although the format makes the ideal approach a bit different from either Facebook or Twitter.

Pinterest is a social network that allows users to "pin," or post photos of anything they find online to specific "boards" of theirs on this network, which can be broken up by subject, color, or any other criteria chosen by the user (for example, you can have a board where you post only pictures primarily red in color). This makes Pinterest basically an online bulletin board that allows its users to show off the things that they admire, things they might like to have in the future, or things that they already have and might like to show off a bit. For an enterprise that wishes to use Pinterest to its advantage, there are a few basic ways to set up a solid, attractive account. First, it helps to create different boards that feature different products of yours. Since, unlike other social networks that are topically oriented around communication, Pinterest is primarily a network of user-curated content, it makes more sense to provide a direct, self-promotional content option for users to peruse and curate. In fact, it's not uncommon for Pinterest users to have boards dedicated to "Things I Want to Buy." By leveraging rich photography and visual content, you can help people curate your products that they want to buy. For instance, if you run a jewelry company, you might want to have different Pinterest boards for rings, necklaces, earrings, et cetera. However, if you run a company that offers similar types of products across a wide spectrum of price points, you might want to break up your Pinterest boards by price range for best results. You can also opt to use both of these approaches on the same Pinterest account, if you think it would benefit your customers. Pinterest provides for a diverse categorization schema of content, which makes it particularly useful for laser-targeting buyer personas by being able to group content into relevant groups without having to share it with the entire following like on Facebook or Twitter.

You can organize your product-oriented boards in many ways, such as category or use-case application, or even price range. For example, a jewelry company could have a Pinterest board featuring rings under $25, another one featuring rings from $25 to $100, and yet another featuring rings from $100 and up, as well as a similar series of boards for earrings, necklaces, bracelets, et cetera. The idea behind these various approaches is to make your inventory as attractive, shareable, and social media–friendly in general as you can to your target audience at large. This also makes it easier for customers who are interested in only one aspect of your business to follow certain boards of yours, whereas most traditional social networks require you to subscribe to an entire social media feed from a given account, which can annoy many users who have only a hyper-specialized interest in a company.

Make sure that the "pin" you create for each of your products redirects immediately back to your website, and be sure that the product description that you use on both your website and Pinterest is accurate, keyword rich, and conversion oriented toward your buyer personas. You can simply copy and paste your website descriptions to your corresponding Pinterest descriptions or, depending on the persona variations between your Pinterest followers and your website traffic in general, rewrite descriptions accordingly. For example, if your followers on Pinterest tend to skew younger, female, and respond well to humor and lightheartedness, it might make sense to rewrite your descriptions to be more humorous and light hearted. Additionally, as previously discussed regarding product detail page design, effective persona-oriented photography is very important—and even more so when it comes to a Pinterest presence. The previously referenced study by Shopify showed that people who are directed to a product page via Pinterest are more than 10 percent more likely to buy the item in question than if they had been referred to via other social networks.

In addition to pinning your own content, you should operate your Pinterest account with the same general purpose of regular consumers on Pinterest: curating topically organized visual content. If, for example, you're a website that sells Florida-related knickknacks and Florida-specific products like orange juice or theme-park memorabilia, it would make sense to have boards oriented around things like "Fun at the Beach" and "Florida Hat Styles" or even "People Screaming on Roller Coasters." Although you certainly *can* use Pinterest to post your product links and organize them in ways your buyer personas will find interesting, Pinterest is more than just an extension of your shopping cart's categorization. Pinterest gives you the chance to create a world of visual content related to your industry, your products, and topics that your consumers will find interesting. For example, the Florida memorabilia store could have a board of "Alligators in Weird Places" that could have amusing pictures captioned for the consumption of those who have lived in Florida. By creating "inside-joke" or topically oriented boards that reference shared experiences common among your consumers and oriented toward their personas, you can create a sense of connection and community that's difficult to replicate in any other medium. For example, a women's apparel eCommerce website could have a board of "Wardrobe Malfunctions" or pictures of apparel that's broken, snagged, or has otherwise frustrated their wearers. By creating a board that's relevant to a commonly shared experience among their consumers, they can more strongly influence people to follow their boards and be exposed to the conversion-oriented content such as product pages that you can mix into the postings and pins.

You may have heard others in the past talk about "going viral" or trying to artificially influence viral distribution of their marketing content, but it's almost universally impossible to "make" a piece of content go viral—except on Pinterest. Pinterest users, by the nature of the site as a method of curation, have a much higher velocity of amplification than on any other social network. ReTweets, for example, aren't nearly as easy to get as repins are on Pinterest. In fact, up to 80 percent of *all* pins on Pinterest *are* repins, meaning that someone else originally posted them. This means that the potential for true "viral" amplification is significantly greater on Pinterest than anywhere else. This is one of the reasons that it's important that the images you pin link to a conversion point of some kind—either a nontransactional landing page or a product detail page—and not to, for example, your homepage. You want to be able to take advantage of the amplification of your content on Pinterest and the accompanying increase in reach and exposure of your conversion opportunities.

Although there's little data yet on how consumers are using Pinterest's native search feature, marketers can use it to identify prospects on Pinterest as well. If you're a women's apparel eCommerce site and someone on Pinterest has a personal board called "Pretty Dresses," it would make sense for you to follow their board and possible engage with their content with comments, likes, and repins. Follow relevant pinners and engage with their content.

Pinterest has developed a reputation for having a fairly specific demographic of users, however. Since Pinterest is still fairly new, studies conducted by firms such as Pew Research and comScore show varying statistics that paint a similar picture: Between 60 percent and 80 percent of Pinterest users are currently female, 50 percent have children, and the average household income for Pinterest users is over $100,000. It provides an interesting new venue for social media marketers who hadn't previously had a site that had penetration into this particular—and incredibly valuable—consumer demographic that doesn't tend to be as heavily populated with early adopters of new technologies as users of other social media and social bookmarking sites. Although the demographic makeup of Pinterest is already starting to level out and will most likely continue to do so, Pinterest has particular value to eCommerce sites that have had a hard time reaching this consumer base in the past. This doesn't, however, mean that marketers who *aren't* focused on this particular consumer group shouldn't invest in Pinterest. On the contrary, given the data of increased engagement, increased transactional value, higher conversion rates, and higher amplification, it makes sense for marketers to *try* to drive more of their user base to engage with their brand on Pinterest as a strong method of increasing the LTV of individual customer contact connections. Given the topically broad, high velocity and low engagement on Twitter, for example, individual connections have a significantly lower value than on Pinterest.

# YouTube

Something that people often forget is that YouTube is one of the most widely used search engines in the world. Although commonly thought of as a social network primarily, due to its propensity for creating shareable content and the inherently sociable nature of commenting and discussing the content at hand, YouTube shares many of the common characteristics associated with a search engine. Its functions and results for specific queries are primarily based on the keywords included in the tags, title, and description of a given video.

YouTube has become a fundamental part of the social media paradigm of the modern age. The easy distribution and searchability of consumer-generated video content has fundamentally changed the way that people interact with everyday life. YouTube has taken a part of the human media experience that often eluded small-scale marketing technology and has made it accessible and mainstream to anyone with an Internet connection. The advent of extremely cheap and effective digital video equipment has helped to rapidly accelerate the adoption of online video for many causes, businesses, and individuals around the world, and has had quite a far-reaching impact. You no longer have to have an advanced suite of media production equipment or pricey professional assistance to produce crisp-looking video content. In fact, anyone with a basic webcam, a smart phone, or a $40 flip camera, combined with some free video-editing software available online, can create rich video media presentations that may include captioning, transitions, music, special effects, and much more.

## Keyword-Driven Optimization Similar to Regular Search Engine Optimization

You need to think with a similar mindset to traditional search engine optimization when optimizing your YouTube videos for maximum exposure. You should optimize the textual elements of your video to emphasize the keywords associated most strongly with the content of the video itself. Create and optimize specific product video advertisements as well as problem-oriented optimization videos that offer an in-depth illustration of the uses of these products. For example, in addition to using the key phrase "How to use a humidor digital hygrometer," you might also want to title a video "How do I measure and monitor humidity in my humidor?"

Focusing on problem-oriented optimization, product-oriented optimization, and testimonial- or review-oriented optimization will allow you to craft an effective keyword campaign using multiple phrasing variations on the same basic topic of choice.

# Types of Content for YouTube

## Product Videos

One of the most useful applications of YouTube is the ability to replicate online the real-world experience of seeing and handling merchandise for consumers. A common complaint that deters some people from purchasing online is the inability to see and handle the merchandise in person. Consumers want to see the relative size of consumer items as well as how these items work in action. Creating a video with someone handling and using the merchandise as directed, such as opening the packaging and handling any peripherals or accessories, can help online shoppers see the merchandise used in the way it was intended and provide them with the confidence needed to take a leap of faith on a digital vendor.

## Problem-Oriented Videos

Another equally important application of YouTube and other video search optimization is the use of problem-oriented optimization tactics. Instead of optimizing your title descriptions and tags around the names of specific products, optimize these phrases around the application that your target customer base might have in mind. For example, instead of titling your video "Awesome [product name]," you should create a series of videos with titles like "How do I [insert application or use of product]?"

A great deal of the search volume for YouTube is commonly focused on something called long-tail phrases, which frequently present themselves as problem-oriented sentences. By optimizing your keywords and search terms around these problem-oriented sentences, and by creating a rich catalog and high variety of content around specific problem statements in small, easy-to-search pieces, you will make it far easier for your target audience to find your content.

## Testimonials and Reviews

A third type of valuable online video content lies in leveraging user testimonials and reviews. According to Forrester Research, people are more than 90 percent likely to trust on opinion generated through a social network, testimonial, or review than they are to trust a statement made by an individual company. By encouraging, or even incentivizing, your happy consumers to help you create video content that discusses your company's products and brand further helps to overcome a classic stumbling block for many online consumers; that is, Do I trust this website enough to make a purchase? Because text content is so easily created, there can be a concern among those reading positive reviews that they're inauthentic. Video reviews personalize the testimonial to a much larger degree and increase the effectiveness of the review.

## Using YouTube to Drive Website Traffic

YouTube allows you to include notations and links within the body of the main video description itself, as well as the ability to include links in the comments, description, and other textual elements of the video. Use these options—accompanied by specific calls to action linked to your website—to drive people toward conversion opportunities relevant to the stage of the buying cycle indicated by the type of video.

For example, in a product-specific video, it might make sense for you to link directly to a product detail page that could be coupled with some type of incentive or offer of simulated scarcity. In a product support–oriented video, it might make more sense to link the viewer to related products, peripherals, and accessories, as it's probable that they have already purchased the product if they're watching a video demonstrating things such as troubleshooting techniques.

In a problem-oriented video, include a call to action directing viewers to a downloadable buyer's guide, comparison sheet, or other document that can help them move down their purchasing process. You can also generate a list of usable e-mail addresses by requiring a consumer to give this information in exchange for the valuable content you have created.

## Embedding Videos on Product Pages

Use places such as the title screen, captions, and exit screens on YouTube to display links, phone numbers, e-mail addresses, or other relevant contact information or calls to action that you would like the user to use based on what they have seen in the video. If you have planned to embed the video on, for example, a product detail page, you might include certain visual representations that direct the user toward these specific calls to action or clickable options that are also on the same page. For instance, if you're embedding a video on your product detail page, you may want to include an arrow at the end of the video that directs the viewer toward either the "add to cart" button or perhaps a secondary call to action that leads into a buyer's guide or a downloadable piece of educational information.

# LinkedIn

Although one of the most underused and less popular social networks for eCommerce, LinkedIn is perceived as the network where individual connections are worth the most, as well as the network that is most effective in penetrating and adding value to the world of B2B commerce.

## Targeting and Professional Orientation

One of the reasons that connections on LinkedIn are commonly considered to be of greater individual value than other social networks is the fact that LinkedIn users are primarily targeted by profession, employer, and skill set.

By the nature of aligning itself with a primarily professional community, LinkedIn, to a great extent, avoids the large number of legitimate yet irrelevant social accounts in the professional and B2B commerce space. Whereas Twitter, Facebook, YouTube, and other social networks have a large volume of highly engaged and active users who are not part of the conventional B2B engagement and target demographic, the connections forged on LinkedIn are primarily made between true professionals.

This is not to say that your professional connections are not actively engaged in Twitter and Facebook activities. In fact, although the percentage of professional users on LinkedIn may be higher than that of other social networks, the total number of professionals overall on the social media behemoth known as Facebook far exceeds that of LinkedIn. One of the most common misconceptions about LinkedIn— and one of the reasons that LinkedIn pay-per-click ads are capable of commanding such a high amount per click—is the assumption that LinkedIn is the best way to target corporate professionals. While LinkedIn can certainly be an effective way to network professionally, it is far from the only popular social media option available.

## Rich Targeting Data

A great advantage of marketing on LinkedIn, especially its pay-per-click marketing, is the rich and precise user data that LinkedIn allows you to mine to properly target your audience. Especially for the B2B marketing space, it can be very useful to be able to target people in specific occupations, industries, job titles, or who are currently employed at a specific company. For example, if you would like to target all of the purchasing officers at a specific company, LinkedIn allows you to do that easily with their intuitive self-serve ad platform.

This ability to pinpoint and target the specific types of professionals, companies, et cetera to whom you wish to market your site can make the high pay-per-click ad fees commanded by LinkedIn well worth the investment. If you can channel your budgeted funds toward wooing the exact individuals you have in mind, this can prove to be a very wise use of resources.

## Greater Resistance to Spam/Aggressive Deterrence

LinkedIn is the most aggressive social network when it comes to identifying and shutting down spammers and system abusers. LinkedIn uses a combination of systems that are closer in many ways to the aggressive and proactive spam-blocking features employed by Internet service providers than the more conventional social network approach of reporting and shutting down fake accounts. However, this makes it very difficult to do social-connection churning on the same scale as Twitter, for example. Social-connection churning is represented on Twitter by following and unfollowing users with a fair level of rapidity without being flagged as abusing the system. LinkedIn, by contrast, is extremely aggressive when it comes to disabling your ability to solicit new connections if a significant number of your connection requests have been rejected or ignored, which makes social-connection churning on LinkedIn nearly impossible. This makes LinkedIn a better choice to build strong and meaningful professional connections that can be relied on for advice and referrals, whereas Twitter would be the better platform for gathering individual customers and disseminating frequent updates.

More specifically, a strong reason individual connections on LinkedIn are considered to be disproportionately valuable when compared to other social media accounts is the greater inclination to action of LinkedIn users overall. The click-through rate of LinkedIn ads, for example, as well as the likelihood of one's social connections to be influenced by posts on LinkedIn, can often be much higher than the influence of a similar volume of Twitter or Facebook posts. These results can be attributed to LinkedIn's higher relative quality engagement of individual social interaction; one can be reasonably certain that they are not interacting with a spammer or scammer, and LinkedIn connections are more likely to have put effort into offering something of value on this network. Make sure that connecting to your LinkedIn account provides some real potential value to the people you contact there, and make sure that any entreaties/calls to action that you make on this network are specifically targeted to the type of people you wish to reach. Again, LinkedIn users tend to take a very dim view of Facebook- or Twitter-style generalities.

## LinkedIn Groups

Of all the social networks on which to attempt to establish yourself as a thought leader, groups on LinkedIn are perhaps the most powerful and easily targeted—especially for eCommerce B2B companies. Again, the power of these LinkedIn groups is rooted in the tendency of individual connections on LinkedIn to be particularly authentic and relevant. These groups make it easy to target or pitch an idea because, unlike building a tribe on Twitter that may involve a complex methodology of searching based on certain profile and data entry keywords, you can simply find groups on LinkedIn that are relevant to your aims and your profession and then request to join them.

The key with LinkedIn groups, as with most social media, is to add informative or opinionated value to the social network without seeming excessively self-promotional. The groups are places for people to postulate questions and get feedback, make statements about a relevant topic and/or participate in debates with professional peers, or share observations and insights that are beneficial to the social ecosystem of the group.

Although it's OK to share relevant blog articles, studies, statistics, data, and facts that you may have aggregated, analyzed, or developed that are pertinent to a specific topic and LinkedIn social group, be sure that you make genuine attempts to participate in existing conversations first. If sharing this data and engaging in blatant self-promotion is your first engagement in a group, your presence is less likely to be well-received by the group's preexisting members.

Instead of immediately posting self-promotional content, begin by answering questions in the groups and adding your insight wherever possible. That way, other members will notice you and your opinions or unique perspective. Follow up by posting your own questions that the members of the group might be able to provide unique insight or solutions for.

## LinkedIn PPC

One of the most interesting aspects of marketing on LinkedIn, as discussed earlier, is this site's powerful ability to target pay-per-click ads based on uniquely valuable and specific identifiers such as profession, job title, or employer. One of the significant drawbacks of being able to easily target decision-makers at specific corporations—which is obviously a very valuable capability—is the fact that LinkedIn paid traffic is disproportionately expensive compared to PPC ad campaigns on other social networks.

To target employees of HubSpot, for example, may cost from five dollars upward per click on LinkedIn, while targeting restaurant employees on Facebook may cost around a dollar or less. Part of this disparity in pay-per-click costs is driven by the fact that Facebook's ad creation platform was extremely weak in its ability to target based on profession and employer until recently. Since profession and employer are two of the most valuable targeting parameters, and LinkedIn was the only site that offered them, LinkedIn has been traditionally able to charge much higher prices per click. It's likely that as Facebook improves its ad-targeting criteria and platform that their ads will become more expensive and LinkedIn ads will become less expensive to compete in a changing marketplace.

If you ultimately seek high-quality professional connections that can provide you with excellent B2B marketing resources in particular, consider pouring more of your available resources into LinkedIn overall.

# Consumer Enthusiast Forums

**Niche-industry forums can help you reach enthusiastic customers on a particular subject.**

Although "birds of a feather flock together" is a tired and overused cliché, nowhere is this phenomenon more apparent than on enthusiast-oriented, vertically segmented social networking websites. One of the most valuable of these types of sites is a classic Internet consumer forum. Although consumer forums are a frequently neglected type of social networking due to their relatively archaic format that dates back to the very origins of the web, Internet forums can be extremely beneficial as part of your social media marketing mix for many reasons. For example, they can be used to facilitate customer support, consumer research, search engine optimization management, online reputation management, and even direct sales. Especially when it comes to products and industries with extremely passionate consumer populations, the typical users often find themselves compelled to discuss specific products, features, problems, uses, and issues surrounding that product and its industry.

One of the most satisfying applications of directly engaging users in consumer forums is the potential to leverage the wealth of information and insight available to build a reputation for stellar customer support. The first step to success in this matter lies with identifying issues or threats of potential relevance quickly and easily. Almost all Internet forums have an RSS feed that can be added to your favorite aggregator or reader and can then be analyzed by keyword to find threads that are relevant to your brand or company. If you can be notified every time somebody is talking about your company on these forums, it allows you to engage the community in a rapid and meaningful way. If the thread is positively oriented, you can thank the original poster and include links to special offers, educational downloadable content, newsletters, and more. (Just remember that some forums take a dim view of posting blatantly self-promotional materials right off the bat, much as the LinkedIn groups mentioned above.) If the thread is negatively oriented, which is sadly more frequent than not, the ability to respond quickly to the issue at hand and bring the engagement off-line into a classic customer support role is extremely critical. The longer a thread goes without a response from a representative of the brand or company about whom it is posted, the more mass it can gather, thus potentially eroding the core consumer base considerably. By responding quickly and directly to any problems, you can help prevent a single angry person from damaging your entire reputation within that social network.

The key is to remember the fundamentals of crisis mitigation in the realm of public relations. Keep your cool, and be polite, respectful, and helpful, and most of all, be empathetic. It is the fundamental nature of social consumer groups to take the side of consumers versus the side of a company or provider. The highest form of social crisis mitigation and customer support is offering to a particular social network a humanized image of your company as an entity that they can relate to as individuals. This can be very convincing when it comes to persuading an initially hostile audience that your company cares about their happiness and success with your product or service.

The worst-case scenario can come about if you respond slowly, poorly, or aggressively. This kind of ill-advised response to a dissatisfied consumer can lead to the thread in question generating many pages of extremely keyword-relevant content that paints your company in a negative light.

## Using Forums for Consumer Research

Another valuable application of customer forums is the ability to quickly gather feedback from your most passionate group of customers while reinforcing the perception of your brand as one that is listening and engaged at the same time. If you are considering a new product or feature of a product, posting a thread in consumer-oriented forums soliciting feedback on the subject can help to make the members of that forum feel valued as individuals and can spur an excellent degree of psychological investment in the specific product or feature when it launches. Chatting on consumer forums can also provide you with legitimate feedback and possible reactions to that new product or feature in real time. While not a perfect substitute for effective conventional market research, when used appropriately this method can give you small and extremely focused consumer-level feedback when gauging the potential reactions of your target customer base to any planned changes.

## Reputation Management

One of the most important and compelling reasons to actively and aggressively engage with and monitor relevant consumer-oriented forums lies in the potential for positive reputation management—and the potentially disastrous consequences of allowing negative attention to go unchecked.

Although all social media networks contain an inherent potential for damaging a brand's reputation, forums can be particularly dangerous for several reasons. First and foremost, consumer-oriented forums have high levels of search engine optimization potential and can frequently place many of the keywords for which you were trying to rank in search engines very highly, including branded keywords. If your company is negatively painted, it can ruin your chances of closing a sale with potential new customers who are conducting a credibility check. Although Google and other search engines have done a great job in recent years of preventing forums and other user-generated text copy websites from dominating search engine results, many of the most popular venues still rank very highly for desirable keywords.

Forums, by their very nature, are often well optimized for search. First, they're often extremely keyword-rich because of the vertical segmentation of their user base. That is, for the most part, those participating in a product-enthusiast website will be talking about the short-tail and long-tail keywords relating to that product. When a search engine indexes a given website, it analyzes keyword usage and density to determine the relevant topics and keyword query combinations for which to display that website and/or interior page. A website like a forum, with keywords that are often so narrowly focused around a very specific product, its uses, and the related keywords and terminology, can fairly be considered by the various search engines to be extremely relevant for related user queries on the subject. Therefore, a forum post featuring a user complaining about your poor customer service practices or the poor performance of your product or service in general can potentially rank very highly in search engine results not only for your branded keywords, which damage your ability to control your rhetorical ethos, but will also show up when people are doing research about product-related keywords before making a purchase from your website.

You can, however, leverage consumer product forums to help you manage your reputation and avoid many of these common pitfalls. Your first step is to create a personified company-branded profile. You'll want to use a real person's profile picture, a real person's date of birth and interests, and a real person's actual name so that forum participants have a chance to know and relate to the individual with whom they are engaging. Many enthusiast forums can be extremely resistant to retailers, manufacturers, and brands engaging in their social-networking efforts because they feel that it is an unwarranted infiltration of marketing—or spam. Remember, most people are engaged in consumer enthusiast forums to get, give, and discuss information about a product or service that they are passionate about. Therefore, it is critical to ensure that you are adding value to the forum itself and not simply spamming it by broadcasting self-promotional messages. When you make your original post, be sure to introduce yourself and include personal information about the individual who will be managing the account on behalf of your company or brand. Focus less on the history and details of the company being represented, and put your efforts toward painting the person managing the profile as a fellow enthusiast. If you can position yourself as a like-minded enthusiast who wants to be able to contribute value to the social ecosystem and establish early on that you're here to help anyone who has any concerns about a past, present, or future interaction with your brand or website, you'll gain easier and wider acceptance.

Once you've established yourself as a real person to whom other people can relate on an individual level, you will be able to start engaging in active threads relating to a particular product or industry. Instead of starting off by posting specials, discounts, coupons, or other offers, start off by filtering through the threads and see if there are any general industry or product questions being posted that you could possibly answer that are not brand- or website-specific. Again, the point is to reinforce—not only to the other members of the forum but also to the moderators who have the power and authority to ban you at will—that you're here to add value to the social ecosystem and that you will not be an annoyance or hindrance to the regular functioning of the forum. Most forum moderators understand and acknowledge that the presence of retailers adds inherent value to their website by making it a source of information, support, discounts, promotions, and more. However, it is their job to ensure the smooth and uninterrupted functioning of the forum—and they will often ban you from the forum with little or no reason if they feel your presence is an undue intrusion.

It is often a good idea to proactively message moderators that you see are actively engaged on forum pages by asking them if they have any guidelines for retailer participation in their forum. Again, these people have a relatively unlimited amount of power to ban people with no justification and at will, and on some forums moderators may abuse their power.

The key to effectively leveraging social forums for reputation management is to ensure that you respond very quickly to any threads that develop expressing an issue with your specific website or brand. Ideally, once you have had time, it'll be established within the forum community that you are available on the website as a support resource for anyone with a complaint or issue. If you develop a reputation as someone who is able to quickly and efficiently resolve issues, the other members of the forum community will often handle much of the reputation management for you and direct the original poster of any critical threads to private-message you before continuing their rant. This is the apex of reputation management within consumer enthusiast forums.

## Handling Direct Sales from Forums

There is also great potential in consumer enthusiast forums to share links that drive traffic and even to execute direct sales when users express an interest in either a specific product or problem that your products address. This is the most delicate part of working within eCommerce marketing and consumer enthusiast forums because you have to avoid the appearance at all costs of being overly self-promotional (i.e., a spammer).

There are two primary ways of doing direct sales on social media forums. The first and more commonly used method involves participating as directed on the dedicated retailer sections that many forums have, where you can post your specials, product offers, discounts, and more. For the most part, many social forum moderators will not allow you to start individual unique threads about your product or service outside of these areas. However, you can create offers either individually for each specific forum, or you can use these areas as a way to amplify your traditional offers, such as those included in your e-mail newsletters, social media postings, et cetera. Many forums permit images and basic HTML in pages and posts, so you can often simply share or repost the e-mails, specials, and other offers that you have been promoting elsewhere on the web on the designated retailer sections of these forums.

You should also make sure that users of the forum are aware of the fact that you are able and willing to give out certain discounts and coupons for people who are interested. You can make this fact known when you're doing your introductory post. I happen to have a unique coupon code available for retailer participants in forums that you can use to track the ROI of your actions therein. Additionally, offering these discounts off the bat can serve as a further method of developing trust and rapport between yourself and the forum community. This way, when people are looking for a product or service that you offer, these friendly introductions help to establish yourself as somebody that the consumer can communicate with easily and readily if they have any issues—and can also get a great deal by using the coupon that you can offer specially for that forum. By making people request a coupon, you also further simulate scarcity that increases the perceived value of the coupon.

You should also use the scanning and monitoring methods that were discussed earlier in this chapter to find forum threads posted by users who are asking for information about products or services that you offer, or who are posing questions with problems that can be solved by one of the products or services that you offer on your website. As mentioned earlier, be cautious when going about this type of thing to avoid being perceived as overly promotional and labeled a spammer. It may be best to use a proxy on the website to recommend your products and services.

When managing forum campaigns in the past, I've developed relationships with one or two well-established and well-regarded people on the forum when starting out. These people often go onto threads where my product or service could be a potential solution of their own volition and mention my site on their own. If you are unable to use a proxy in this fashion, you should be sure that you establish yourself in the community as someone who's adding value to the social ecosystem with valuable information, opinions, and commentary before you start posting any links in the forum threads.

## Running Contests on Forums

Contests are another effective marketing effort when it comes to leveraging the potential of consumer forums. Image-oriented contests featuring people using your product or service can be successful, as can soliciting product testimony or story-oriented contests. "Easter egg" contests on your website that entail asking users to find hidden images in clickable elements is another popular contest option, as is any other fun and creative type of contest relating to your product or service that can help stimulate a positive brand perception of your company. You can mention any contests that you are holding on a specific consumer enthusiast forum while simultaneously developing a greater rapport with the forum members and driving additional traffic to your website. You can reward contest winners with product prizes from your website—appropriate for the consumer enthusiast forum of choice—

such as discounts or other interesting prizes. Contests keep you engaged in the community and further enhance the perception that you are adding value to the social ecosystem outside of raw self-promotional efforts.

You can also crowdsource some of your marketing efforts using contests and consumer enthusiast forums in some cases. For example, if you are looking for a logo design, copywriting assistance, or graphic designers for your site, you might want to ask a relevant community if any product enthusiasts on the forum would like to offer their skills in exchange for money, barter, or exposure. Indeed, it can often help to have someone who knows about the product and industry you offer to handle some of the creative aspects of your business!

# Google+

When we had planned the outline for this book, Google+ was not one of the sections that had been included. Google+ was a relatively new feature from Google at the time and seemed to be just another attempt by the search giant to create a social network that could compete with Facebook, Twitter, LinkedIn, and other major social networking players. However, Google+ has several interesting and unique features that have made it a useful and interesting social network on its own merits, such as the option of grouping one's friends and acquaintances into customized "circles," as well as the inclusion of easy-to-use social engagement tools like Google+ "hangouts."

Google+ also piggybacks on the success of the Facebook "Like" button with the Google +1 concept. You can +1 pages and search results that you wish to share with your followers, which are then published into your Google+ social network just as Facebook's "Like" button does for its own users' social media feeds. Also, there's a common idea floating around in cyberspace that Google will eventually use +1 tags as a strong component of search engine rankings in the future.

Google has previously failed rather spectacularly at creating an effective social network that would achieve the necessary critical mass of users that have a valuable social ecosystem. Google Buzz, for example, was a relatively direct rip-off of the social status posting methodologies already in use on Facebook and Twitter. There was some debate about whether Google could ever effectively compete in the social media space, and whether they honestly should. However, despite the debates and their series of failures, Google pressed forward and eventually rolled out the Google+ social network. The Google+ social network can be split into two unique parts that should be considered independent of each other, even though these two aspects are designed to interact with one another.

The first and more widely known part of the Google+ network is the Google+ social interface itself. The Google+ social network's basic web interface may seem very similar to users who are familiar with Facebook. After all, with an eight-year head start on Google+, Facebook already had the opportunity to streamline their interface and concepts in an interesting way and had been able to learn how to avoid many of the pitfalls (such as buggy software and often obnoxious interfaces) that were frequently found on the platforms of their earliest competition, such as the once-formidable MySpace.

It should be noted here that as Facebook opened its doors to users around the world, its uncluttered interface, lack of malware, and general user-friendliness of Zuckerberg's brainchild effectively spelled the end of the line for the vast influence that the comparatively clunky and error-prone MySpace once commanded. As with any other aspect of eCommerce, the more user-friendly and reputable platform won out in the end. Keep this principle in mind when designing your own website and user interfaces, lest a slick competitor beat you at your own game later on!

One of the most interesting developments on the Facebook social interface occurred several years before the advent of Google+ and served as the catalyst for an idea that Google+ still considers one of its main competitive advantages over Facebook: the option of specific user lists. A common problem and challenge encountered by users of social media is the desire to filter the types of posts that can be seen by certain people in their network. Quite simply, people want to be able to vent about work without their coworkers seeing these posts, vent about relationships without their missives being readable to certain friends, post information and links without starting an argument between people with differing opinions, and generally be able to engage in social media networking with the same level of discretion as they would engage in normal social conversations.

Facebook addressed this issue by creating the concept of private lists that one can create to filter the visibility of certain posts within a given individual's social network. However, many users had problems creating these lists, and the filtered lists did not always work exactly as planned, causing quite a bit of consternation as a result. Google+ then took this concept of social media micro-segmentation to a new level by introducing circles. Although seemingly qualitatively identical to the concept and application of Facebook lists, Google+ allows you to organize your contacts into these lists (circles) in a more graphically intuitive way. Additionally, this interface and the strong support of the excellent Google team has led to few issues regarding members outside a user's intended circle accidentally seeing posts and commentary that was not meant for them. If your product or service is considered controversial in some circles, you might want to consider a stronger marketing focus on Google+ than on Facebook or Twitter. Someone who wishes to share their high opinion of your products or services with some of their contacts while hiding it from others can use their own discretion via Google+ circles from there.

Google+ also represents a powerful foray by Google into the realm of live streaming video. Although Google had previously integrated elements of video chat into systems such as Google Talk, they had never before launched a major product platform specifically designed to innovate in the video chat space. The Google hangout, as it's called, allows multiple people to be involved in a video chat display reminiscent of the talking heads of a news media broadcast. Much more engaging than the traditional conventional conference call or chat room, the live multiple streaming video element is probably one of the most innovative aspects of the Google+ social network. Google+ hangouts also allow you to collaboratively edit documents, share screens, and execute other tasks that are particularly valuable for productivity and collaboration. Google+ hangouts' aggressive new integration with the Android mobile operating system has taken the promise of mobile video chat (a promise that had been somewhat neglected throughout the recent evolution of smartphones) and made it into a new and exciting reality.

As an eCommerce professional, you can use Google+ hangouts to gather several different and loyal customers together to get feedback and suggestions, and you can use these hangouts as a wonderful and inexpensive way to have a face-to-face conference with all sorts of people and service providers around the world. Indeed, the hangout feature in Google+ can save you time, travel, and other costs associated with gathering people together for feedback and research, as well as help you save on some of the costs of running a fully functional twenty-first-century business.

However, it should be noted that outside of the moderate innovations of the Google+ hangout and the more intuitive graphical user interface improvements, the tactical marketing applications of Google+ as a social network are largely similar to those of Facebook when promoting most eCommerce ventures.

With that said, there are two key reasons why Google's current foray into social networking is something that marketers cannot ignore. First, Google has apparently decided to throw its full weight behind Google+ as a social network. Whereas Buzz, Wave, Orkut, and other failed expeditions into the social networking sphere were only moderately supported by Google's vast influence, the Google+ network reached over ninety million users in its first seven months and is projected to exceed four hundred million users—roughly half the current user base of Facebook—before its second birthday. This is partly due to Google's broad-based integration of Google+ widgets into all the Google systems. Google's goal is to create a unified user experience across all of the Google tools and platforms. This started with their introduction of the universal Google navigation bar and has continued with the addition of all the Google service products into all of the Google user interfaces. This project continues with Google compelling users who sign up for its popular Gmail service to also create a Google+ social media account. Whereas Facebook created a social network (and spawned rumors that the company would eventually use the network as a way to simply turn the site into a popular e-mail tool), Google created the e-mail tool in the beginning and is currently using it as leverage to get into the more valuable social media networking battleground.

While the ethical debates concerning Google's requirement to join their social network to take advantage of their tools from unrelated platforms continue to rage, the implications of this practice pale in comparison to the implications of Google using the frequency, velocity, and relative authority of content shared in the Google+ social network as a disproportionately strong determining factor when calculating search engine rankings. It's long been known that Google and the other major search engines have been using the number of social media shares as a factor when determining the quality and relevance of a specific piece of content on the Internet, but there are many who worry that Google might rank the shared content on its own networks more highly than similar posts on other popular social media sites. Only time will tell whether or not these fears are warranted.

Indeed, part of the reason that many online marketers today are so enthusiastically pushing their social networks and brand connections into active participation on Google+ is simply the widely held belief that content shared in Google+ will eventually become a very strong search engine ranking signal that can best the influences of Facebook, Twitter, or LinkedIn.

By the very nature of the fact that Google controls the vast majority of the world's search engine traffic, Google is able to compel marketers to actively attempt to leverage their user bases into Google+ to improve their chances of benefiting from user shares via this network as a strong search signal. By hijacking the relative network effects of the vast community of Internet marketers and professionals that use their services, Google is able to ensure that Google+ will not suffer the same fate as their other social network ventures by tying this new social media platform to the all-important online marketing factor of organic search engine optimization.

The second element of Google+ that marketers should educate themselves about is the Google +1 button. Although theoretically an integral part of the Google+ social network platform itself, the Google +1 button's application across many facets of the web are what make it unique. On the surface, it seems very similar to the Facebook "Like" button or the "share on Twitter" button. When applied as part of the social media sharing options on a web page, this is basically the case. However, Google +1 buttons are also appearing in search results next to individual website listings. This indicates that Google is considering +1 shares in search results as well as other web page shares to be strong signals of search engine relevance and authority. Because of this, and because of the potential for the Google +1 button to become an increasingly important signal in search engine relevance, marketers are engaging in concerted efforts to influence users to engage with the Google +1 button as well as with the Google+ network itself. In fact, Google recently released an update that indicated that shares made on the Google+ network with the +1 button would be considered more important in determining search engine relevance, authority, and eventual ranking than equivalent shares made on the mighty Twitter social network.

Although the fundamental concepts and tactics of engaging with consumers in Google+ are the same as on other social networks, influencing consumers and users to share your content and +1 your results and pages is likely to become increasingly important to marketers as Google continues to factor activity in the Google+ social network as a particularly strong indicator of search engine authority. There was much buzz when Google first developed the Google+ system surrounding whether or not Google+ would be the network to sink Facebook, just as Facebook once sank MySpace. Based on the lack of substantive differences between the fundamental natures of Facebook and Google+, as well as the massive number of users that each venue enjoys, this scenario is extremely unlikely at present. Although you may see no greater ROI from your engagement on the Google+ network in terms of actual sales that you might see on Facebook, forums, Twitter, LinkedIn, and the myriad other social networks throughout the world, Google's ability to leverage their massive search volume to cajole marketers into actively using their social media platform—unlike the failed experiments of Google's other social networks—Google+ will become increasingly relevant regardless of any substantive differences between this social network and Facebook.

# Online Reviews

There are many good reasons to be concerned with the online reviews that your company or brand receives. First, online reviews are often used by consumers as part of their regular buying cycle research phase. Consumer reviews are significantly more trusted—nearly 12 times more—than descriptions that have been written by manufacturers (eMarketer, February 2010). Seventy percent of people online tend to trust the opinions of unknown users, (Econsultancy, July 2009), while 61 percent of people rely on ordinary user reviews for product information or research before a buying decision is made (Razorfish, 2008).

Regardless of the statistics you use, it's clear that consumer reviews can very strongly influence someone's decision whether or not to buy from your website. Keep in mind that there are many venues and many reasons for somebody to write an online review of your product, service, or company.

## Managing Bad Reviews

No matter how great your product or services are, or how wonderfully polite and helpful your staff is, you will always get some negative reviews. You must focus on keeping the ratio of positive to negative reviews drastically weighted in favor of positive reviews. Although users heavily weight the opinions of online consumer reviewers, they understand that primarily people who go through the effort of reviewing a product or service are those motivated by negative emotions as opposed to positive emotions. Therefore, you can and should strive to offset any negative reviews by having enough positive reviews out there to convince potential customers to consider your negative reviews to be statistical outliers.

It's also important that you engage with negative reviews quickly and efficiently. Earlier in the chapter, we discussed how to interact with negative reviewers in consumer enthusiast forums. A similar methodology can be applied to consumer review forums where you are able to reach out and comment on positive and negative reviews.

# How to Get More Reviews

### E-mail Marketing

When it comes to garnering online reviews via e-mail, there are several techniques that you can employ to increase the number of testimonials on your product or service across the web. For best results when it comes to turning new customers into loyal, repeated users who will be happy to give you their business in the future, the trick to eliciting a positive review lies in striking a balance between excellence in providing what was expected of you on time and in full, as well as remembering that abusing the e-mail addresses given to you by your customers can and will be seen as annoying, spammy behavior. With that said, if you can successfully build an effective campaign using these resources from the bottom of the sales funnel, you should have no problem when it comes to passionate customers recommending your products or services to others on their own.

As mentioned above, using behavioral triggers to nurture a greater number of click-throughs should be of primary importance when it comes to compiling a follow-up e-mail marketing missive. Make it easy for customers to leave a review of your product or service by adding an easy-to-find link to a popular review site in the body of your e-mail. Yelp reviews can prove to be a great option, and PayPal reviews, should you use this company as a payment processor, can prove to be a boon to your business as well. Make sure that the links you provide as behavioral triggers designed to induce a customer to leave their opinions on your enterprise are directed specifically to your company's page listing rather than to a generic site homepage for added customer convenience and a greater probability of positive results. Again, the more steps it takes for a user to complete any task online tends to directly result in the decline of these tasks being completed at all, so make things as easy and direct as possible!

When it comes to avoiding the appearance of spam in your e-mail marketing missives, it is important to limit your post-purchase contact with an existing customer to no more than two e-mails on the subject. More than two follow-up e-mails are likely to annoy your users, getting your e-mails increasingly sent to spam folders worldwide and encouraging less-than-satisfied customers to leave a scathing review. Remember, a key part of online etiquette is valuing the time and bandwidth of other users, so do your best to ensure that the people who are receiving your missives only include those who genuinely care about what you have to say.

With that said, a good way to encourage new customers to leave you a review might be phrased via the "Alarm Clock" technique. This type of phrasing is geared toward framing your request for a review in a positive manner, restating your commitment to excellent customer service, and encouraging direct feedback to make right any deficiencies in the product or service provided. For example, one might send a post-purchase e-mail that says something to the effect of, "Since you haven't left an online review, we were wondering if you had any suggestions for us on how to improve our service to the level where you feel compelled to shout it from the rooftop—which is the only level of customer satisfaction that we'll accept!" This type of phrasing offers a concrete call to action, a specific desire to ameliorate any less-than-satisfactory aspects of a transaction, and emphasizes that your primary goal is to please the customer whenever possible.

# Chapter 9:

## eCommerce E-mail Marketing

E-mails are generally used to remind contacts about your store while enticing them back to your site to take an action, likely to purchase from you again—thus increasing the contact's lifetime value. Influencing the lifetime-value economics is commonly considered a function of sales and pricing but actually plays an important role through e-mail marketing. eCommerce marketing departments can influence the lifetime value of a customer at many stages, although two are the most obvious and critical.

E-mail marketing can be used to assist in setting the pricing of individual products to help optimize the process of cross-selling related supplementary items and up-selling items with additional features or functionality. eCommerce e-mail marketing can also be used to influence the lifetime value of customers is through the ongoing process of remarketing—or bottom-of-the-funnel nurturing. Simply put, this is the process of selling more products to customers who've already purchased from you in the past. Leveraging marketing automation to engage with prospects who have not returned to the website, who purchased an item with valuable related supplementary products that provide an opportunity for cross-selling, or customers who purchased an item with consumable components that have to be repurchased are all effective ways of leveraging remarketing in the bottom of the funnel. eCommerce marketers can also leverage automation to engage with prospects who expressed a behavioral interest in specific categories in which there is some price volatility or in which there are occasional discounts to incentivize purchase.

# Preparing for E-mail Marketing

Knowing how to properly prepare your database for e-mail marketing is the first step to success. Preparing for e-mail marketing begins with database segmentation. Database segmentation is the process of organizing your e-mail contacts into lists that will be engaged with through e-mail marketing. Segmentation of e-mail contacts into targeted lists begins with monitoring and measuring customer and lead behavior, preferences, and buyer personas. Segmentation is then accomplished by organizing e-mail contacts into lists defined with criteria of measurement and site behavior. Segmenting your database allows you to ensure that each group of recipients receives the most relevant, targeted, and timely e-mail messages ultimately leading you to higher engagement and better e-mail marketing.

It should be noted that the best way to accomplish segmentation is with software that can make dynamic lists based off of criteria you provide. Dynamically creating and segmenting lists defined by contact behavior will help ensure accuracy and can greatly aid in e-mail marketing performance. An alternative to using software to create dynamic lists would be manually keeping track of the criteria in a program like Microsoft Excel.

Dynamic e-mail marketing lists are created through organizing contacts based on criteria that you define. Common criteria to define in list building generally consist of a contact type, engagement levels, site browsing behavior, and shopping behavior. For example, a basic form of list creation based on criteria would be segmenting your database into two lists of customers and noncustomers. You would message your customers with the goal of increasing brand awareness and repeat-purchasing behavior. You would message your noncustomers with the goal of getting them to make a first-time purchase. A slightly more advanced list would be created by organizing your contacts into lists based off of categories purchased. For example a pet-supply company would segment their customers into groups of contacts that have purchased from each of their top-level categories of different pet types, thus being able to send dog-related coupons to those contacts that have purchased dog products while sending cat related coupons to those contacts that have purchased cat products. A more advanced list would be created by organizing your contacts into groups of engagement level. Contacts that have opened five or more e-mails while visiting your site twenty or more times without making a purchase show a high engagement level. Creating this type of list would allow you to e-mail an inciting offer to only a subset of your contacts that meet this highly engaged criterion but have not purchased from your store before.

# Noncustomer Segmentation Best Practices

Segmenting and targeting e-mail contacts that have given you their e-mail address by filling out a form on your site but have not completed a purchase is known as lead segmentation. The goal of lead segmentation is to provide recipients with relevant e-mails with the dual purposes of fueling brand evangelists (basically your happiest and most loyal customers) and converting leads into customers.

Three common lead-segmentation criteria to setup are:

- Blog subscribers—users that have subscribed to blog updates
- Top-of-the-funnel leads—users that have given you their contact information but have not completed a purchase
- Abandon-cart leads—users that have started a checkout but have not completed a purchase

A contact that has downloaded an offer like a coupon or a buyer's guide but has not completed a purchase is classified as a lead. A contact that has subscribed to your blog can also be classified as a lead. Even someone that has started a purchase but has not completed that purchase can be classified as a lead. However, these contacts should be segmented and messaged differently than your customers.

Users that have subscribed to your blog and have not completed another offer on your website should only receive e-mails alerting them of new blog posts. Blog subscribers have expressed interest in your content and could become brand evangelists that share your website pages across their various networks. You should be optimizing your blog posts with calls to action advertising new offers to entice blog subscribers to move to a more qualified lead or customer.

Users that have downloaded one of your offers such as a coupon or buyer's guide but have not completed a purchase can be e-mailed relevant information and specials to help them convert into a customer. Send these leads a mix of your best content and special offers to help bring them closer to a purchase or at the very least keep your company in mind when they are ready to purchase.

The third, and perhaps most valuable, type of lead segmentation is an abandoned-cart lead. Users that start a checkout process but do not complete their checkout have identified themselves as the highest quality of lead an eCommerce marketer can generate. Capturing abandon-cart leads is most commonly accomplished by requiring a two-step checkout process—a user must submit her name and e-mail address before proceeding on to payment and shipping information. Abandon-cart leads should be treated with care and should not go onto a regular mailing distribution list like specials, coupons. or newsletters.

## Customer Segmentation Best Practices

Segmenting customers into different lists based on interest or purchase behavior is known as customer segmentation. The goal of customer segmentation is to send more targeted and relevant e-mails to customers to increase the average LTV of a customer by generating more repeat purchases. Two common customer segmentation criteria to set up include:

- Category or product purchased—segment customers into different lists based on the category or products they have purchased.

- Most valuable customers—identify the customers that have spent the most money in your store to find the most valuable.

Segmenting customers into different lists based on the criteria of category, brand, or product purchased can be one of the most effective ways of identifying top-performing categories and targeting customers based on their interests. For example, an online golf store may create a dynamic list based on the criteria of a customer purchasing a golf club. This would be accomplished by setting criteria "any item purchased contains the words 'golf club.'" This would create a list of all customers that have purchased a golf club and would be updated dynamically as new customers purchased golf clubs. This list of customers could be sent monthly specials on golf balls, golf bags, or any accessory for a golf club. Recipients of these updates would find highly targeted e-mails more useful than an advertisement for a new golf club, something they recently purchased.

An example of brand or product segmentation could be seen from an online clothing retailer identifying customers that have purchased a particular brand or product. This list could be alerted when new arrivals of that brand come in stock or special discounts have been applied. Customers that have purchased a particular brand are likely to be interested in new updates on that brand, special coupons, promotions, and even blog articles written on that brand.

A second way to segment customers is by identifying the most valuable customers based on average amount of purchase and total revenue generated. Incentivize these valuable customers to continue to purchase from you and to become evangelists of your brand. Let them know that you value their business and would like to reward them with exclusive offers, updates, and coupons.

## Demographic Segmentation

Another common form of segmentation is the demographics of your contacts. Segment your contacts based on the information you know about them from checkout and offers you have on your site, such as joining a VIP program. Gender, date of birth, and geographical location are common demographics to segment. Where recipients of your e-mail live can greatly affect their buying habits and is a great place to start your segmentation. You should have the geographic location of your contacts from the shipping and billing address provided to you in their checkout process. Use this data to send relevant specials and promotions. For example, a clothing retailer may want to message contacts living in northern states about a new winter jacket collection, whereas they would message contacts living in southern states about a new light fleece collection. A smart online clothing retailer may even look at weather patterns to send timely e-mail specials to historically rainy climates like Seattle, Washington. They may advertise a special on rain gear to Seattle contacts on a day that it is actually raining there. This highly relevant and timely e-mail could convert at a higher rate than a general one-off e-mail blast to all contacts.

# Basic Behavior-Driven Segmentation

A basic form of behavior segmentation is accomplished by segmenting engaged users versus unengaged users. This is done by tracking opens and clicks of your e-mail sends as well as

the behavior that was done by the user after clicking a link. Segmenting based on opens and clicks can help you reduce the frequency of e-mails to unengaged users as well as experiment with different subject lines and e-mail content for those that have not opened or responded to an e-mail. Segmenting based on activity on-site after clicks is an advanced form of segmentation that can help you understand and target your lists in more efficient ways. Below are a few behavior-segmentation lists to implement:

- Has never opened e-mail
- Has opened e-mail but never clicked a link
- Has visited site from e-mail more than once
- Has purchased from e-mail

Behavior-driven segmentation can help you qualify the content of your e-mails by measuring the engagement of the end-user at both the macro and micro levels. Measuring the total number of contacts lost from an e-mail send will help you identify if the content of your message needs to change or not. Perhaps your e-mails are not relevant enough and your contacts start to treat them as spam and unsubscribe, thus losing your contacts and diminishing the value of your database. Measuring metrics like open and click-through rates can be leading indicators to losing contacts. Seeing a trend in dropping open and click-through rates from your e-mail sends should alert you to either change the message of your e-mail content or engage in further contact segmentation.

# Advanced Behavior-Driven Segmentation

An advanced behavior-driven e-mail marketing list would be created by dynamically segmenting your contacts into macro and micro buyer persona groups developed through abandon-cart activity and site-browsing behavior. If a user comes to your site and starts a checkout for, say, a television, but does not complete the purchase, we can assume that this user is interested in purchasing a television from you and could be categorized into a macro-level persona group based on the type of television that was in the cart. For instance, a higher-end television would indicate a different persona type than a lower-end television and could be the basic criterion used for a macro buyer persona group. Developing a micro persona from the macro would require tracking the abandon-cart user's behavior on your website. What pages did they visit? Did they read any blog articles or buyer guide's focused on your micro persona? Did they look at televisions better suited for sports or cinematic experiences? Capturing the browsing behavior would allow you to categorize the abandon-cart user into a targeted micro-persona group that would allow you to send a targeted and relevant series of e-mails aligned with their specific interests.

Define the behavior a contact can take on your website that would categorize him into your macro and micro buyer persona groups. Then setup dynamic lists from that criterion. Here are a few examples that we recommend:

- Buyer persona lists from products or categories added to cart or purchased
- Buyer persona lists from pages viewed
- Buyer persona lists from links clicked within e-mails

Your open rates, click-through rates, and revenue generated from e-mail marketing will never be higher than when you engage in behavior-driven, buyer-persona marketing.

# Executing E-mail Marketing

The first and most important thing you want to ensure in your e-mail marketing efforts is that you are complying with the Controlling the Assault of Non-Solicited Pornography And Marketing Act (CAN-SPAM). Much like privacy laws regarding direct mail through the postal service, sending e-mail also has binding privacy legislation that must be followed. The easiest way to stay compliant is by following these three simple rules:

1. Always include your company information and physical location address in all e-mail communications.

2. Make it easy for users to unsubscribe from your e-mails by including an unsubscribe link in all e-mail marketing communications.

3. Honor opt-out requests promptly.

Most e-mail marketing software will automatically require you to conform to CAN-SPAM before allowing your e-mail message to be sent. However, it is important to be aware of, as

you are ultimately responsible for any e-mails that you send.

After ensuring that your e-mails are compliant, you can start to enhance the effectiveness of your e-mail marketing efforts. Effective e-mail marketing should always begin first by segmenting your database into targeted lists. Effective execution of e-mail marketing will consist of maintaining high deliverability rates while sending targeted and relevant messages in both timely and automated fashions to buyer persona types. There are many tactics to employ and test within the execution of e-mail marketing that we will be covering. E-mail template design, subject-line testing, using dynamic tokens, using the psychology of anticipation, and behavior-based automation are important tasks to engage in to improve your e-mail marketing efforts. However, all engagement and testing will be for naught if your deliverability rate is suffering because of poor practices.

# Maintaining High Deliverability

E-mail deliverability rates are important and can easily plummet without proper monitoring and marketing execution. Your e-mail deliverable rate is calculated by dividing the total number of delivered messages by the total number of sent messages. An undeliverable rate is calculated by dividing the total number of messages never received by the intended recipient (i.e., undeliverables) by the total number of messages sent.

For example, if you send 100 e-mails and 25 were returned due to bad addresses, the undeliverable rate would be 25 percent. To calculate the deliverable rate, you need to take the total number of e-mails that were delivered (75) and divide this by the total number of e-mails sent (100). In this case, the deliverability rate would be 75 percent. An undeliverable rate of 25 percent is not good at all and would be a concern for you if your e-mail sends average this amount. In fact, if your e-mail deliverability bounces exceed 3 percent, then you have entered a red-flag zone. You are within normal parameters if the undeliverable count is between 1 and 2 percent.

The following best practices should be implemented to ensure high deliverability rates.

Never send an e-mail to someone who has not consented to receive e-mails from you. This includes not buying lists from third parties. Bought lists put you in danger of sending e-mails to invalid e-mail addresses, spam traps, and unsuspecting recipients—putting your odds of being reported as spam very high.

Avoid spammy subject lines. Create enticing and informative subject lines that get to the core of your e-mail message. Write a subject line that you would feel comfortable opening in your own inbox. Never write in all capital letters and avoid excessive punctuation like multiple exclamation marks. Don't use numbers or characters in place of letters either.

- Example of a spammy subject line: WIN F*r*e*e iPad2 OPEN THIS N0W!!!

- Example of a good subject line: Collection of Fall Winter Jackets on Sale

Send e-mails with consistent frequency. You might consider sending weekly, biweekly, or monthly communications, but for every company the timing varies. Run experiments, from two a week to one a month, and measure your complaint, unsubscribe, and bounce rates. Should you see a spike in those numbers, slow the frequency of your message down.

Make it easy for recipients to unsubscribe from your e-mails. Always include an unsubscribe link in every e-mail that you send. It should be easy for users to unsubscribe from your e-mail communications. Even better, organize your e-mails into subscription types, so that when a contact clicks your unsubscribe link, they see all the different types of e-mails that you send. A user may not be interested in receiving your newsletters but could stay interested in your deals and promotions. Allowing users to unsubscribe via subscription types will lower your overall unsubscribe rate while still executing your e-mail marketing within best practice guidelines.

Keep e-mail marketing sends to a low volume if you do not invest in e-mail marketing software and instead use your own corporate server. Sending more than 1,000 identical messages at a time from a specific server is a red flag from ISPs and could result in your e-mails being marked as spam at alarming rates.

Invest in an e-mail service provider (ESP) that is dedicated to ensuring high deliverability rates. There are a variety of ESPs to choose from that will enable to you to execute e-mail marketing at high standards. We recommend that you ensure that whichever ESP you choose that it integrates with your shopping-cart database of contacts. Automated, behavior-driven e-mail marketing will be much more difficult if your ESP does not connect with your shopping cart. HubSpot for example offers a high end ESP that is connected to a contacts database which enables seamless segmentation and targeted email marketing.

# E-mail Template Design

All e-mails that you send out, whether one-off's or automated should be designed for both deliverability and user experience. You want your e-mails to be attractive, engaging, and informative, and provide value in a way that is designed for readability in all e-mail clients We are not going to go into great detail on how to actually code e-mail templates. Instead we want to focus on ensuring that you are aware of e-mail template code best practices so that you can check to make sure your templates are conforming to host standards.

Two main elements to be aware of are that your e-mail templates should be designed with tables while using inline CSS. HTML tables should control the design layout of the e-mail while the CSS controls the presentation. Inline CSS should control elements such as font size, text alignment, table shape, color border, and height. E-mail services that are browser based, like Gmail or Yahoo, will strip out certain CSS tags such as DOCTYPE, BODY, and HEAD tags, making your e-mail preview fine to you, but terrible by the e-mail recipient. For these reasons you should avoid referencing any external CSS.

You should also refrain from using Javascript and rich-media files in your e-mails. Most e-mail clients will have the ability to view rich-media files turned off by default. Instead you will want to include an image of your video player with a play button as the screenshot that links to the video hosted on a website page. Using rich media in this fashion has the side advantage of bringing users to your website through your e-mails, increasing your click-through rates and the quality score of your e-mails.

An e-mail template that has strong visual images will almost always perform better than e-mail templates stuffed with lines and lines of text. Consumers are most likely to be attracted to clicking on visual elements; this is especially true when targeting consumers. Just about all one-off e-mail sends should include visual elements. Some behavior-based automation e-mails may be best sent with plain-text only e-mails, but these will be far and few between for eCommerce e-mail marketers.

All of the images used in e-mail templates should be sized appropriately and include ALT text. (ALT text is a text description that can be added to the HTML tag that displays an image. Most images will not load by default in most e-mail clients and will instead require a user to "display images" before any images are loaded. However, these clients will load the ALT text associated with images.) Including images of large file size will slow the loading time of the e-mail by the recipient, likely leading to them deleting the e-mail message before your image is even displayed. Make your image-file sizes as small as possible without losing their visual integrity. This will prevent long e-mail load times.

## Segmented One-Off E-mail Sends

Time-sensitive promotions or newsletters are the most common application of sending one-off e-mails. One-off e-mail sends will always be more effective when sent to segmented lists of your contacts. Holiday-themed promotions, special events and promotions, new-product announcements, and limited-time offers are great reasons to send one-off e-mails. Overstocked item blowouts, newly released products, and special offers that aren't significant enough to warrant a "build-up" campaign are effective uses of one-off e-mail sends. These are more effective applications because they're disruptive of customer expectations and less likely to be archived, skipped, or ignored without being read.

It is important to plan a monthly or quarterly schedule of one-off e-mail sends before executing. Look at a calendar and outline all of the upcoming holiday events that you could have promotions for, and examine your current inventory and identify items for limited-time offers. Make a list of any upcoming inventory that you can have promotions around. Make a list then apply the list to a calendar.

We recommend that you send at least one scheduled one-off e-mail a week to your segmented database of contacts. Product-inventory and holiday-themed specials should always be tailored to segmented lists.

You should be conscious of not being overly promotional when sending one-off e-mails, even when advertising holiday sales, new product inventory, or special offers. You can do this by combining relevant content with products and sales in the e-mail. Identify blog articles, how-to videos, buyer's guides, and frequently-asked-questions pages to use in combination with your e-mail marketing. For example, a great structure of a one-off e-mail send may look something like this:

Header with coupon code

Featured blog article on topic of e-mail

Featured item on topic of e-mail

Featured item on topic of e-mail

Behavior-driven e-mail Communication


## Abandoned-Cart E-mail Marketing

Abandon shopping-cart nurturing is one of the most effective e-mail marketing tactics that you can use as an eCommerce marketer. eCommerce sites lose out on many potential sales simply because customers abandon their carts in the middle of shopping, and it's not always because they're no longer interested in purchasing the product (although that might be true in some cases). A great way to recover these customers without investing a lot of cost and effort is through the deployment of abandoned-cart e-mails.

An abandoned-cart e-mail is an e-mail sent to a customer who initiates a shopping event by adding items to his or her online shopping cart but leaves the site before completing the order. These e-mail messages can serve a number of functions depending on the customer because there are a whole host of reasons why shopping-cart abandonment may happen, both from the customer's and retailer's end.

Causes of Shopping Cart Abandonment from the Customer's End:

- Internet connection times out
- Tab/browser accidentally crashes/closes
- Shopper must unexpectedly leave computer
- Unexpected final price after taxes and shipping are added (a.k.a. "sticker shock")
- Concerns about website data security
- Intent to purchase at a later time or date
- Simply not ready to purchase yet
- Loses interest in product

Causes of Shopping Cart Abandonment from the Retailer's End:

- Registration required (no guest check-out)
- Technical issue with the web page
- Complex, confusing, or complicated web forms
- Selection of payment options is lacking
- Limited shipping types and destinations

## How Abandoned-Cart E-mails Can Help

Since there is little you can do as a retailer to fix problems that originate from the customer's end, an abandoned-cart e-mail is the single-most effective countermeasure you can take to combat these issues. As for the errors originating from the retailer's side, of course you should be working toward solving these problems. But you should still be sending out abandoned cart e-mails. Why? They will still be effective in encouraging the customer to try again, and by tracking certain metrics regarding conversion, they can even help you pinpoint trouble spots and road bumps on your website over time.

Make sure your eCommerce page captures the customer's e-mail address as early as possible in the ordering flow so you can reach out to all your customers no matter how far down the ordering "funnel" they get. Some websites will also ask for a contact number to reach the customer by phone, but most customers consider this to be intrusive when coming from online retailers. Unless your product or website is so complicated that it merits voice support, stick with the e-mail address. You can always add a hotline number to your abandoned-cart e-mail to make it convenient for your customers should they wish to call you. Include a link that takes the customer directly back to their shopping cart.

The further along in the ordering process a customer is, the sooner you should send an abandoned-cart e-mail. If they abandoned their cart relatively early in the ordering "funnel," wait a few days to remind them about their purchase. If sending more than one e-mail is feasible, you can also consider a tiered approach, where a series of automated e-mails are sent at different time intervals following an abandonment episode. It is recommended to send the first within an hour of cart abandonment, a second within twenty-four hours, and a third and final reminder at the seventy-two-hour mark. Any more than this and your customer might start to cry "spam," so be aware of the impact that too many reminder e-mails can have.

It's also important to include a statement addressing why your customer is receiving the e-mail. Make sure it doesn't sound too Big Brother-ish and that you're watching his or her every move on your site. Simply notify the customer that his or her transaction was not completed, and offer some guidance back to the cart. Be sure to include contact information at the end of the e-mail in case the customer had an unanswered question that will help complete the transaction.

## Sample Template for First E-mail

Hello [Insert Recipient Name],

Thank you for visiting [Insert Company Name]!

We noticed that you didn't complete your order, and we wanted to do everything we can to help. To complete your order in two minutes or less, simply revisit your shopping cart by clicking this link [Link to Shopping Cart].

If you have any questions about our products or services, please contact us using one of the following methods:

[Insert Phone Number] or [Insert E-mail Address]

Please let us know if there is any other way we can help.

Thanks,

[Personal Signature]

# Chapter 10:

## Experimental eCommerce Marketing and Analytics

Most webmaster analytics hold little value for actionable intelligence in marketing decisions. Metrics in this category would include page load time and length of time per site. While a functioning website is important to user satisfaction and repeated sales, tracking webmaster analytics is an inefficient use of time for most marketing specialists. Avoid compiling useless data sets on optimizing website performance and work toward actionable intelligence on the behavior patterns of your customer base and the efficacy of current marketing strategies.

Track the types of content that drive traffic and lead to engagement among your customer base. If fans go wild over photographs of the CEO's dog or humorously written profiles of your hard-working employees, consider adding more of this type of content to various platforms. When examining the correlation of marketing campaigns to a new surge of customers, fan engagement, or page views, be sure to include all measurable factors. If your company Facebook page has driven new visitors in the last several days, examine the correlation of traffic and individual posts until you identify the one associated with the surge.

Web analytics that can be enormously useful to an eCommerce marketer can include the geographic origin of unique page views and search terms associated with first-time visitors. Another essential marketing analytic is the origin of the page view, particularly when the visit is converted into a new customer. Your business can benefit immensely from determining which social media platforms, strategies, and campaigns are driving traffic and which aren't, because it can easily lead to actionable intelligence.

Combining marketing analytics with your current customer relationships management program can provide what is known as closed-loop analytics, which are among the most effective ways to determine your actual ROI for each active marketing campaign or social media platform. The term "closed loop" is inspired by the fact that you are essentially filtering data to only include qualified leads or closed sales, essentially closing off data points which did not actually contribute to your company's bottom line.

Implementing closed-loop reporting is relatively simple for organizations that are already actively tracking leads or customers using software such as Salesforce when combined with closed-loop analytics technology from HubSpot. Closed-loop data can also be manually tracked using Excel. Regardless of how you choose to build your closed-loop reports, be sure that this data includes several critical fields: the initial source of the visit, percentage of visits converted into a lead, and percentage of leads converted into customers. Once a closed-loop analytics system is implemented, you can begin determining the true value of your marketing campaigns and social media efforts. Closed-loop data also holds fascinating potential for analysis beyond ROI and efficacy of marketing campaigns. Studying channels of arrival, page views, and purchase tendencies of your customers could reveal patterns that even help you determine how and where to most effectively market individual products or services offered by your organization.

Dollar for dollar, tracking closed-loop data could be the most valuable source of actionable intelligence you mine from web analytics. The basic analysis of the percentage of new page views converted to a sale are the closest you can come to hard numbers on how you should be spending your time. The results of your closed-loop analytics can be surprising. You may find that lengthy blog entries yield far fewer results than pithy tweets. It is important to consider that while closed-loop marketing analytics are invaluable, they aren't infallible. Human behavior can change drastically due to myriad external factors, and even closed-loop marketing data is a snapshot with relatively limited forecasting potential.

Be sure to understand that certain social media efforts may appear to have a limited ROI when examined through the perspective of closed-loop data, particularly for a young organization. The intrinsic value of engaging with fans on a social media platform cannot always be measured immediately or financially. You may find that Twitter leads to page views, or that certain social media platforms are just not an effective use of your time from an ROI standpoint. However, it is essential to keep in mind that social media can assist with customer satisfaction. Relationship maintenance is increasingly important among savvy consumers, who can ruin a dozen potential customer relationships by sharing a link and negative personal experience with their Facebook friends. Social media may not appear to pay when viewed through the context of closed-loop data, but it shouldn't be abandoned. Consider the value of maintaining relationships and open-dialogue with customers in addition to the hard, actionable numbers derived from closed-loop analysis.

While the enigma of human behavior will likely never be fully understood, web analytics can help a modern marketer discover patterns in the actions of their customers. As one of the unique challenges of eCommerce marketing is maintaining customer relationships electronically, marketers can derive actionable intelligence through easy data reporting. Be smart with your time and make sure you are tracking the best data for intelligent-decision making. Ignore silly vanity metrics and useless webmaster analytics, focusing on using web analytics to develop relevant marketing information. Invest in a reliable closed-loop marketing system for contemporary reporting on your ROI across social media platforms and marketing campaigns.

# Analytics

Marketing can feel like a continual process of trying to see patterns amid the swirling chaos of human decision making. Accurate, comprehensive data sets have historically served as the backbone of effective marketing campaigns. To most efficiently study your current customers and increase your potential for clients, you should have a thorough understanding of each type of analytics and data set that can drive eCommerce marketing. Immerse yourself in the terminology related to modern marketing and data tracking to effectively analyze your company to the next level.

Blogs are surrounded by their own type of language, and companies that rely on their written words for inbound marketing traffic should make a concerted effort to learn the important terms. Blog traffic is among the most basic measures of your company's visibility on this particular platform. Track the number of visitors per day and their source of origin. Track the search terms customers and visitors used to find your blog by search engine. These terms and phrases can offer particular value for search engine optimization and fine-tuning your current product descriptions. The number of blog subscribers should also be tracked because this metric can offer quick insight into the overall health and appeal of your content. If you are able to discern a statistically significant decrease in subscribers following a change in posting schedule, authors, or types of content, you can extrapolate that your new blogging style offers less mass appeal. Excessive frequency of content can also lead to a drop in number of subscribers.

While the number of comments on each blog post can be the easiest way to track post popularity, you should expand the ways an individual post's efficacy is examined. Check out the number of shares each post received on Facebook or Twitter. The number of individual views per post or clicks to your company website are also a highly effective means of viewing exactly what types of content are viewing sales. For organizations with multiple blog authors, you can examine what styles or writing and tones resonate best with potential customers. Finally, a particular benefit of blogging for small to mid-sized businesses is the opportunity to improve search engine rankings and establish credibility in their field by generating up inbound links. Check out which types of posts have generated the highest amount of inbound links from being quoted by other bloggers, electronic news sources, or websites. Highly technical or specialized content will likely be quoted most often, which add a particular value to the types of blog posts that will likely bore the majority of your fan base.

Analyzing reactions, inbound links, comments, and shares on social media will likely reveal the value of varied types of blog posting. Witty writing or socially controversial posts may generate a great deal of comments or social media shares, offering visibility and branding potential to your organization. Highly technical posts probably won't make a splash on Facebook, but you could enjoy a new surge of traffic or sales when the data points or carefully written, technical descriptions in the post are quoted by a reporter at a community news website. Tracking various types of blog analytics, including traffic, search terms, comments, shares, and inbound links can offer actionable intelligence to help you develop a blogging strategy with a high potential for maximum ROI.

Search engine optimization is among the more challenging measure of performance metrics. Search engine ranking is determined by highly complex and dynamic algorithms, particularly for the largest and most popular search engines. Algorithms can change several hundred times per year, making it nearly impossible to entirely optimize your site for each new version of the algorithm. Keep in mind the quality, quantity, and recent content remain among the biggest content-driving search engine ranking, all of which can be optimized through well-written blog entries on a consistent basis. The frequency at which your content receives inbound links can positively affect search engine ranking, increasing your incentive for occasionally including highly technical material. Tracking your inbound links is among the best ways to measure your blog's SEO potential.

Recent changes in major search engine algorithms have reduced the incentive for organizations to churn out low-quality content packed with salient keywords as fast as possible. While keyword use in tags and the content body are still highly relevant to your search engine ranking, inbound links and other measures of quality have been given an increased rank. Avoid the temptation of writing or purchasing bad content to maximize keyword presence on your website or blog. You'll likely find this approach hurts instead of helps, as you lose subscribers, reputations, and potential for engagement with customers. Pure maximization of keywords without accompanying quality is never a good approach for an intelligent marketer.

Marketers can be tempted to ignore analyzing unwieldy sets of SEO data in favor of simpler social media metrics. If your organization drives any business through pure search engine traffic, maximizing your SEO potential is essential. Compile a dynamic list of keywords and search terms that are highly relevant to your mission or products. Examine and track your ranking among similar eCommerce organizations for these important keywords. Achieve and maintain a high ranking on these particular keywords through quality content, inbound links, and frequent updates to the website.

One of the most effective ways to determine the particular weight associated with each keyword or search term is through visits. This metric reveals how much search engine traffic is driven to your web page through each individual keyword.

Rank the keywords in the order in which they are driving traffic to your web page. Viewing the keywords in order of traffic can help you identify which keywords offer the best ROI for inclusion in social media marketing and content. Use these keywords as much as possible.

Don't forget to derive actionable intelligence from developing a list of low-ranking keywords that are highly relevant to your product or mission as actionable intelligence. Avoid losing traffic and sales to your competitors unnecessarily due to a lower inclusion rate of these salient terms. Keyword ranking is among the most dynamic metrics of eCommerce marketing. Due to the ever-changing content of eCommerce websites, which is driven in part by the increasing prevalence of business blogs and frequent updates to search engine algorithms, it is essential to frequently examine your keyword ranking to identify the terms with the highest potential. Keep yourself educated on relevant industry buzzwords and the hottest terms related to your products and services. Create as much relevant content and social media promotion as practical for your marketing team to respond to changes in important keywords.

Social media metrics should be examined carefully, with marketers making every effort to wade through vanity metrics (metrics that have no actionable application) to access truly actionable intelligence. While your number of Twitter and Facebook followers truly offer limited value as a metric, you should make an effort to ensure your number of followers is increasing over time. While net followers is a vanity metric, it can offer some perspective on the quality and appeal of your social media outreach. Pay more attention to tracking social media engagement, which is among the best measures of your true impact on Twitter, Facebook, and other platforms. Likes and comments indicate that your content is being viewed and read by your followers. Make every effort to maintain an active, engaged presence by issuing quality, thoughtful responses to engagement from your fan base. Ignoring comments and likes, particularly when they include questions, can discourage engaged followers from future engagement. Responding to social media engagement should be performed on an ongoing, daily basis to create the strongest impression of availability to current and potential customers.

Facebook and blog content shares and ReTweets are better than comments and likes because these indicate that your social media content is genuinely resonating with fans of your business. Identify which types of content are being shared with fans, treating this intelligence as low-cost marketing with a high return of unique website traffic and new business. Including social media content that isn't directly relevant to your company mission, such as intelligent discussion of current or local events, often inspires shares among fans while driving attention to your company name.

While maintaining an increase in followers on various social media platforms is a limited indicator of your social media marketing health, calculating the percentage of followers who are engaged is a better metric. Look at percentage engagement on a frequent basis and determine which types of content are inspiring fans to break the barrier of silently follower social media to voluntarily engaging with your company. Identifying the types of content that are converting followers into engaged fans and emulating the topics and tone whenever possible is among the best means of improving your organization's social media marketing impact.

The bounce rate of your landing page can offer valuable insight into the appeal and effectiveness of page layout and content. Bounce rate is calculated by determining the number of potential customers who click through from social media or other referral methods and then immediately leave your company website. Unaffiliated referral sites and web directories are an ineffective means of judging bounce rate, due to the fact that marketers have little control over the associated content. Landing page bounces occur because the content on the target page does not live up to the expectations created by the source of the link. Focus on click-throughs from your biggest traffic drivers, which will likely include search engine traffic, e-mail marketing campaigns, and social media. Ignore bounces that occur when your company name or URL is searched by a potential customer, focusing on keyword searches relevant to your product or content.

Avoid creating a sketchy first impression by making sure that the keywords or linking social media content associated with the landing page match. Nothing drives away potential business faster than content that does not appear connected to the text describing the initial link. Avoid creating a dishonest or disorganized first impression by accurately describing the contents of the landing page when promoting the link. Ensure that the text on the landing page is clear, concise, and includes inspiring calls to action. Avoid unnecessary information, extraneous explanation, and promoting unrelated products or services on landing pages whenever possible. Testing the efficacy of your landing page content and layout is among the best means to reducing bounce rate. Ensuring potential customers who have made the effort to click through are impressed by your content is essential to the success of driving business through search engine and social media marketing efforts.

Tracking e-mail marketing metrics can be among the more difficult analytics to track, due to the dynamic nature of e-mail databases. Focusing on driving new subscriptions is critical because the size of your e-mail database should grow at a high rate compared to followers on social media platforms. Compared to social media, e-mail accounts have an extremely high rate of abandonment or closure by users. Expect an approximate turnover rate of 25 percent a year, which can seem shockingly high. Increasing your list size by 25 percent annually is necessary to simply maintain the extent of your e-mail outreach, without any attention paid to other factors such as the rate at which recipients are unsubscribed from your e-mail campaigns.

Use the rate at which members of e-mail database opt out receiving communications as an indication of the quality and relevance of your content. If your opt-out rate exceeds 5 percent following each new mass mailing, use this intelligence as a strong indicator that the quality and quantity of your e-mail marketing should be examined in depth. Subscribers are most often tempted to opt out of e-mail campaigns due to an excessive frequency of e-mails, poor content quality, or irrelevant information. One of the best ways to effectively communicate with members of your e-mail database on a regular basis without overwhelming readers is creating segments in your e-mail database using as many demographic and purchase history methods as practical.

Divide your e-mail list into loyal customers, one-time customers, and future customers. Separating subscribers by every available demographic metric, including age, gender, and geographic location can help marketers tailor content optimally. While sending one hundred e-mails per week to ensure that each age group in a given state are receiving relevant content that reduces the risk of unsubscribing would offer an optimal ROI, this method is impractical for most eCommerce companies. Evaluate the number of individualized e-mail campaigns you can reasonably draft each week or month to segmenting your e-mail list into too many categories for intelligent, personalized outreach efforts.

Sender score is a complex metric that can dramatically affect the efficacy of your e-mail campaigns. A low sender score can prevent your subscribers from even having the option of reading your carefully crafted content, taking advantage of special offers or making purchases from your company. Sender bounce rates, defined as the percentage of e-mails which are sent to invalid e-mail accounts, can decrease your sender score. Maintaining your e-mail database on a consistent basis is critical to maintaining effective e-mail marketing campaigns and ensuring your content isn't destined for the spam folder of recipients.

The best way to warm a subscriber score is by sending e-mails to a dedicated segment of your e-mail database. Choose a list of loyal customers who have previously expressed warm satisfaction with your products and services to ensure a positive response. Your sender score can be damaged by recipients marking the e-mails as spam, and an initial poor rating can be difficult to raise. Craft marketing e-mails with particularly appealing special offers, such as a free e-book or repeat customer discount to ensure a high open rate. Warming an initial sender score through marketing directly to the portion of your e-mail database that will not mark the content as spam can set a strong precedent for future e-mails to less loyal customers and prospects.

Sender score can also be negatively affected with a low open rate, which is a simple metric to track the efficacy and relevance of e-mail marketing campaigns. Strive to maximize your open rate by crafting eye-catching subject lines. Personal appeals, amusing anecdotes, or promises of free content or a good deal in a subject line might increase the open rate among members of your e-mail list. Avoid passive or boring language or excessively wordy phrases. Treat subject lines like Twitter content. Focus on achieving the perfect blend of clever, eye-catching and informative text in as few words as possible.

Offering redemption on e-mail marketing and social media can be an indication of both the extent to which your content is being viewed and the appeal of your special offers. Examine the types of products that are redeemed most often by your followers in addition to the presentation styles. If your customers and fan base go wild over informational e-books, expand the rate at which you are releasing these free products to entice page views. If you have a low redemption rate on special offers, examine the methods in which you are presenting the products. A clever tweet or Facebook update could enhance appeal, as could a well-worded blog entry that summarizes the value of the content contained in the e-book. Carefully examine the redemption rate of special offers to avoid wasting time crafting products irrelevant to your customers and base of followers that will not have a positive impact on your bottom line.

Your organization's Net Promoter score can help you determine the extent of customer loyalty and salvage relationships. This metric is derived from data from customer surveying following a purchase. Determining customer satisfaction is critical in eCommerce marketing efforts, because modern consumers often fail to directly communicate mild dissatisfaction with customer service representatives. Instead of seeking resolution in-house, consumers will often use personal social media accounts to bash your organization. Though complaints to friends and followers through social media are often inevitable, they can have a devastating affect for eCommerce companies. Organizations marketing a niche product to well-connected consumers run a particularly high risk of losing business if they don't make an effort to salvage relationships with dissatisfied customers. Improving the visibility of your customer service contact information or creating content about your organization's commitment to customer service can help efforts to maintain a strong reputation among competitors and customers, but using net promoter score metrics to maintain relationships is a significantly more effective method of avoiding widespread customer complaints.

Ensure you are e-mailing surveys to customers following each purchase, even for dedicated, loyal buyers with a long purchase history. You can include multiple questions on these surveys to derive data critical for strengthening other marketing campaigns, but ensure the surveys are sufficiently simple and easy to maximize the response received. Each mailed survey should ask the question critical to net promoter score, which is how likely recent customers are to recommend the product or company to a friend. Provide a range of response options that range from 0 to 10. Customers who express total satisfaction, defined as the top two points of the response options are defined as promoters. Customers expressing dissatisfaction, which are the bottom six points of the survey options, are detractors who present a liability for maintaining a strong online reputation. Subtract the percentage of total response by detractors from the percentage of promoters.

Avoid taking information from surveying personally, because respondents are unlikely to be in the middle ranges of the points, which are defined as passives. These consumers are satisfied by their experience purchasing from your organization but were not sufficiently satisfied to have been converted into repeat customers. Keep in mind that the Net Promoter score is often driven by customers who experienced a satisfaction rate at the more extreme ends of the satisfaction spectrum, whether that is entirely negative or positive. Use the Net Promoter score as a tool for outreach and reputation maintenance, not an entirely accurate gauge of overall customer satisfaction. Maximize the number of customers responding to your satisfaction surveying by ensuring the e-mails are appealing, personalized, and trustworthy. Include your company logo and the full name and contact information of a customer service representative with your organization to add weight and legitimacy to the survey outreach efforts.

Make a concerted effort to reach out to detractors in the most personalized and solution-driven manner practical for your customer service team. Offer resolution while gleaning information about the source of their dissatisfaction to minimize the number of detractors in the future. Make every effort to quickly apply information from detractors for best business practices. Use all information gleaned from postsale e-mail surveying to segment your e-mail database for effective marketing. Treat promoters as loyal customers, and offer special deals whenever possible to the passive members of the middle of the scale to avoid losing their business. Distinguishing your company and providing the best deals possible to passives is critical to maintaining their business and converting these customers to promoters of your company's mission and products.

Defining and tracking conversion assists, simply defined as the most convincing pages on your company website, could be among the most effective marketing practices your company can adopt. Pages that are frequently viewed before a visitor is converted into a customer are defined as conversion assists. Tracking this metric to define your most potent content could offer the highest ROI of any actionable intelligence you undertake. Promote these web pages as often as possible in social media and e-mail campaigns. Identifying conversion assists can help you transform leads into customers and prior customers into frequent buyers.

Figure out which web pages are viewed frequently before an initial sale, and split these pages into elements that could be contributing to their relative success. Examine the type of content, topics, and even page format. The tone or visual layout of the page could be contributing to these pages' success at converting website visitors into customers. You could be surprised by which pages are your highest converters. If your company's mission statement, biographies of executives, or content detailing green practices have a proven record of closing sales, treat these metrics as actionable intelligence and expand on their success in every way possible. In addition to frequent promotion of these pages, create more marketing materials that expand on these proven performers for social media and blog content.

Patterns among successful pages could be obvious or difficult to identify. Use the information gleaned from tracking conversion assists to boost the performance of web pages and blog content not listed among top conversion assists. In addition to producing more content that emulates proven high performers, editing the format, tone, or content of existing information can boost overall success.

Adopting a thorough practice of tracking marketing analytics can seem truly daunting. Avoid overcomplicating the process by remembering the goal of identifying the methods that can offer the highest ROI. Identify the social media content, blog content, and landing pages that resonate among your customers and fan base. Use engagement, which includes comments, shares, ReTweets, e-mail opens, and offer redemption, as the best measure of the quality of your efforts. Make the effort to maintain a high net promoter score by personally reaching out to your detractors, and analyze your top conversion assists to improve your bottom line.

## Experimental eCommerce Marketing

When most people hear about "experimental marketing," they think of marketers running experiments to improve a specific key performance indicator. While marketing experimentation is very important, and in fact is covered in depth in the next section, "experimental marketing" actually refers to how marketers can—and should—design, test, and refine new-buyer personas. We talked in great detail earlier in the book about defining buyer personas, but simply defining a small number of your buyer personas once doesn't sustain an ongoing strategy. Because attraction-based inbound marketing is not, nor will it ever be, a laser-targeted and perfect science, you'll always be attracting traffic to your site and converting nontransactional leads that aren't your intended buyer persona. Instead of ignoring these leads entirely or—worse—overinvesting in creating content that attracts and messaging that influences these personas, you should silo them into individual experiments where you analyze the unit economics that are unique to them. For example, there may be traffic that you're getting right now that, if you invested more in creating content to attract them, would have *better* unit economics and make for better customers. It's also entirely possible that they'd be a worse business, either by having a higher cost-of-customer acquisition or by having a lower LTV.

Buyer personas are also not a static issue. You can decide that a certain persona doesn't make sense to focus on now, but that doesn't mean that economic factors in the future or changes in your products or business models won't make them a good persona in the future. The only way to know for sure so that you don't distract your marketing team from the core business which you, hopefully, have already defined and know is profitable, you should create small-level experiments to test different buyer personas on an ongoing basis. One of the wonderful aspects of inbound marketing is that it's fairly agile. If you decide to target a new persona, you simply have to start creating new content and messaging to attract and influence them.

An experiment should always have a hypothesis, and buyer persona experimental marketing is no exception. Let's discuss some primary hypotheses you can test.

## First Hypothesis: We can effectively sell to these leads.

If you're able to identify and define that you're getting traffic from another personas that you'd like to test, it's because they're already converting as nontransactional leads where you're gathering information that indicates that they're different. The first challenge is whether or not you can create messaging in e-mail and social media that's going to convert the existing leads that you're getting into paying customers. Often, different buyer personas will require different language, different positioning, and even different products or accessories to get the most out of their purchases. You should first experiment with e-mail segmentation and automation with existing contacts that you're converting that are a unique buyer persona to see if you can get the lead-to-customer conversion rate to make sense.

While testing this hypothesis, you may find many instances where your initial expectations for the psychographic dimensions of the persona are flawed or incomplete. Before investing in testing any other hypotheses, you can use this phase to properly refine the buyer persona.

## Second Hypothesis: This buyer persona makes a good customer.

As we discussed in the beginning of this book, it no longer makes sense to focus on trying to attract and convert buyer personas that are only going to convert once. You're not going to make the COCA:LTV balance make any sense, since you're going to get "Amazoned" and run into retailers who are willing to make less money than you. When deciding whether a specific buyer persona makes sense to invest in, you should make sure that their average transaction value, their purchase frequency, and even any additional strain they may add to your support infrastructure (some personas really like to call and complain, and that's a business expense) is in line with them being a significantly valuable customer.

## Third Hypothesis: We can attract more of these types of visitors.

Once you've decided that you can convert the traffic you're getting into leads, convert the leads into customers, and that you're customers make sense from a unit-economics perspective, you're next task is attracting more of these visitors to your site. The same fundamentals of traffic generation apply (organic, paid, social media, and offline sources), but each source will have to be treated in a different way. You may need to create content around a different facet or application of your product. You may need to optimize around different keywords. You may have to focus more heavily on a different social network. You'll need to see whether or not you have an actual ability to gain penetration into the online audience for this persona, which is going to come down to whether or not you can create and promote effective content to attract the persona.

Essentially, experimental marketing begins with the middle of the funnel, progresses to the bottom of the funnel, and then—if it makes sense—addressing growth at the top of the funnel. Given how good the unit economics and market outlook are for the persona after you're done testing it, you may want to shift your strategy to address more of a specific persona.

# Tactical Experimentation and Testing

The only intelligent way for marketers to improve the performance of their funnel metrics is to conduct tests and experiments. Since the dawn of professional marketing, we've relied primarily on the opinions and gut feelings to make decisions about how to improve the performance of our campaigns. Simply, the technologies and methodologies to effectively conduct marketing experiments didn't exist in the pre-Internet world. It wasn't feasible to, for example, conduct tests to increase the performance of billboard or television ads. The media providers didn't have the infrastructure built to serve different samples of a TV commercial, for example, to randomized segments of an audience, and the response to these ads was typically so low and so difficult to attribute that there wasn't a significant, measurable metric by which we could have measured the impact anyway.

Unfortunately, much of this same psychology has trickled into the modern era where marketers are too inclined to go with their gut rather than conduct proper, methodical experiments with significant metrics to improve their performance. This is one of the greatest dangers in modern marketing organizations, when marketers ignore data entirely or simply accept the performance of their efforts as the best they're going to get without trying to improve. Simply put, it's a lazy and a behavioral relic of the *Mad Men* era that marketers ignore the fact that eCommerce websites have the ability to track almost every possible behavior and marketing activity that influences and drives them.

Although there are a number of highly skilled and qualified researchers conducting ongoing experiments and analysis to develop best practices for inbound marketing, there are significant differences in the sample populations of each website that make the blind application of best practices ineffective. Since all of these experiments rely on behavioral analytics, and every website's buyer personas respond—by their nature—in different ways to messaging and stimuli, it's impossible to say that what works for one website (or what works when massive sets of data from many websites are analyzed as a whole) will work specifically for your website. Therefore, it's more important that you use the data and methodology from these researchers to design and conduct experiments on your own site rather than simply designing your interfaces and marketing efforts based on the results of experiments conducted on unrelated consumer sample populations.

The most fundamental experiment is the single-variate A/B test where one version of the element or tactic (called the "control" or "version A"—which is often the existing version) is served to a randomized subset of the overall population while a second version (called the "treatment" or "version B"—which has a single element modified from the control) is served to another subset of the same population. There are two very important factors when conducting variate testing to keep the experiment "clean" and have the results be significant and accurate. First, you should ensure that each version or treatment you're testing has only one element that has been modified from the control. If you change multiple elements—for example the headline of a landing page *and* the number of forms *and* the image on the page *and* the structural layout of the page—you won't know *which* of the elements that you modified was the modification that drove the change in behavior. You can test multiple variables but only if you do so methodically by creating iterations of the multiple combinations of variables to see if there's a specific mix of variable changes that are driving the greatest impact on the outcome of the experiment.

To drive the highest velocity of change and be able to reach levels of statistical significance as rapidly as possible, you should focus on testing the most disruptive elements first and making decisions as soon as you reach an acceptable level of statistical significance. For example, it makes sense to test a red versus blue color for a call to action, which is likely to drive a significant change in behavior, before testing whether an exclamation mark drives more clicks than having no punctuation (which, if it drives any change in behavior at all, will be so small that the experiment will have to have a massive sample size before drawing a conclusion). At the other end of the spectrum, it's not always necessary to let an experiment run for an excessive period of time and refine the experiment data to an extremely precise confidence interval before ending the experiment, drawing conclusions, and testing another variable.

It's important that conclusions that you draw have an adequate level of statistical significance, but for the purposes of this book we're not going to dive deeply into *how* to determine statistical significance and assert that all of the following experiments should continue until they have a statistically significant result based on the change in behavior and an adequate sample size. Every test that you conduct should have a hypothesis and a key metric. For example, "Changing the Landing Page's Image Will Improve the Conversion Rate by at Least 5 percent."

# Landing-Page Conversion Rates

The key performance indicator for nontransactional landing pages (such as download pages for e-books or buyer's guides) is the conversion-rate percentage. The conversion-rate percentage is the number of times the form on the landing page is filled out and submitted divided by the total number of visitors to the landing page. For example, if a landing page gets 10,000 visits and 1,000 visitors fill out and submit the lead generation form, the conversion rate of the landing page is 1,000/10,000 or 0.1 or 10 percent. The assumption is that if all variables remain the same, one out of every ten people who visit that landing page will fill out the form and become a prospect lead that you can nurture. Improving this metric is a function of the design and messaging of the page, which has some specific variables that you can test:

## Layout

One of the most disruptive elements (or element that will create the greatest change in behavior through optimization) of a page is the layout of the various elements. The position on the page of the headline, the form, the image, testimonials, the copy, et cetera, can all influence in what order and how quickly a visitor processes the information and makes a decision about conversion. The configuration of elements horizontally and vertically can make a difference. Should the page copy be on the left, below the image, so it gets read after the image is seen but before the form is seen? Should the form be above the "fold" (the point where a visitor has to scroll to see it) so that the conversion purpose is obvious? By testing the layout and configuration of the various elements of your landing page, you can change the order in which a visitor processes the information and influence their decision-making process in converting.

## Hero Image

We've previously talked about the impact of imagery and visual content on rapidly communicating messaging and value propositions to website visitors. Visitors to landing pages undergo a very brief period of evaluation before deciding to convert, and the "hero image" (the main, disruptive image on the page) is a key element of rapidly communicating a persuasive-value proposition. Should the image be a graph of product performance? Should it be of a person that's reflective of the visitor's buyer persona? Should it be bright and loud or dark and subdued? Should it have multiple elements, such as star-outlined copy emphasizing the value of the offer? Many variables unique to your specific landing page can be tested with the hero image, and because of its ability to communicate a persuasive-value proposition so rapidly it should be among the first of the disruptive elements that you test.

## Form Fields

The number of fields and the type of information that you ask for in the form is going to have a significant impact on the amount of people that successfully convert on your landing page. For example, if you're just asking for a first name and an e-mail address, you're likely to get more submissions than if you ask for first name, last name, e-mail address, mother's maiden name, and the brand of the visitor's first pet's favorite squeak toy. However, this isn't to say that you should always try to have the shortest possible form. If the information you're collecting is valuable for your persona identification and segmentation efforts that will help you more accurately nurture this person, then you should ask the question even if it has an acceptable impact on conversion rate. For example, if your statistically significant test concludes that asking for "primary television use" causes the landing-page conversion rate to drop from 20 percent to 18 percent, but knowing that information helps you create e-mail and social nurturing messaging that significantly improves the conversion rates further down the funnel, the lower conversion rate on the landing page may be an acceptable consequence.

The types of fields can also impact the conversion rate on landing pages. For example, radio buttons, check boxes, and dropdown menus may have a higher conversion rate than open-ended text boxes that require more intellectual investment from the visitor. It's worth testing what types of fields generate the highest conversion rate and most accurate and valuable reporting and segmentation for you.

Another metric of the number and type of questions asked on a landing-page form is the quality of data you receive. Some recent research data has suggested that long forms with complex questions are more likely to be answered with inaccurate data as the visitor tries to complete the form rapidly without regard to your database's need for accurate information. Data accuracy is a difficult metric to measure and corroborate, but it's something that makes sense to keep in mind and possibly analyze as a secondary KPI when testing the number and types of form fields.

## Headline

The headline, along with the hero image, is one of the most important visual elements of the landing page as it's an obvious influence on a visitor deciding what the landing page is about and what its value proposition is. Should the headline be a question? Should it be a statement? Should it be the title of the offer or a statement about the consumer pain point that the offer provides information on? By testing the headline of the landing page to be as persuasive and descriptive as possible, you can significantly influence how quickly a visitor comprehends the value proposition and improve the percentage of visitors that convert.

## Submission-Button Design

The form's submission button can also influence the conversion rate of the landing page. It can be used to more clearly define the result of the action ("Download Your Free Guide Now!"). It can appeal to the problem the offer is addressing ("Learn How to Plan the Perfect Party"). It can be used to ask a question ("Are You Ready?"). The standard copy and design is of a simple, often gray button that just says "Submit." However, most websites that test this find that landing-page visitors don't like to "Submit." In addition, a small button with a subdued color such as gray might not be attractive enough to draw the visitor's eye and incentivize conversion. Although, as with all of these landing-page elements, it's possible that your optimized conversion structure will have the normal button configuration, and many websites find that the messaging and design of the submission button can positively impact conversion rates.

## Copy Organization

Since visitors to a landing page have a limited amount of time to consume the persuasive information about what the offer is, you should test the structure and organization of the descriptive copy on the page. Should the copy be short and sweet or long and detailed? Should it be bulleted, enumerated, or in paragraph form? Should the paragraphs be broken up in different ways?

The copy on the landing page is one of the deeper, more influential elements to those visitors who aren't going to be influenced by optimization of the headline, image, and form. It's the opportunity to make the persuasive case to the visitor. By testing the length, type, and configuration of the copy, you can influence how quickly and how much information the visitor can process before making a decision about converting.

## Value Proposition

The value proposition of the landing page has to do with how you position the reason that the visitor should provide their information in exchange for the content as a whole. Most of the individual elements themselves have the option of testing the value proposition on the micro level, but on the macro level the entire landing page has an overarching value proposition that you can spin and emphasize. eCommerce companies are good at crafting value propositions for product detail pages with the understanding that they're *selling* something to the visitor to the page. Marketers should think of landing pages as product detail pages for the content offer. You're selling an item of value (the content offer) in exchange for something of value to the consumer (their contact information). The more and more valuable the information you're asking for, the higher the "price" that you're asking someone to invest is. Alternatively, the greater and more convincing the value proposition for the content offer, the more value you're offering in exchange for the price. You can A/B test what value proposition you're emphasizing to see which method of framing the value you're "selling" has the greater impact.

## Rhetorical Appeal

There are three primary modes or appeals of rhetoric: Logos (the logical appeal), Pathos (the emotional appeal), and Ethos (the credibility or authority appeal). Which rhetorical appeal is most persuasive for your site visitors is very much a function of the psychographic dimensions of your buyer personas. Should you emphasize on the landing page the detailed, logical argument for converting on the page? Should you make an emotional proposition for how the offer will help? Should you emphasize the credibility of the data the offer is based on or its author? A/B testing which appeal has the greatest impact on conversion rate and then correlating that to the form data that you're using to identify the buyer persona can actually help you define the psychographic dimension of responsiveness to rhetorical appeal for each of your individual buyer personas, and you can even apply that lesson elsewhere in your marketing.

## Social Proof

Social proof and testimonials or reviews of the content *can* have a significant, positive impact on the conversion rates of landing pages depending on your buyer persona. If your product primarily appeals to early adopters, however, this may not be true. You should test the effectiveness of different types of social proof on the overall conversion rate of the page. Should you group social proofs together? Should you have just one? Should you have none? Should you use reviewers who reflect a particular demographic profile? Testing all of these questions and correlating the results to the identified personas based on form-field submissions is another method of refining psychographic persona characteristics similar to rhetorical appeal.

# Calls-to-Action Click-Through Rates

Basic "button" calls to action (CTAs) on your site have five primary elements: the color, copy, shape, size, and value proposition. CTAs are typically thought of as button and clickable elements on your site that take visitors to product detail pages or to nontransaction-offer landing pages, and these are certainly valuable pathways to test. However, eCommerce marketers often fail to test the most important CTA on their website: the "Add to Cart" button. Data generated by HubSpot customers using the CTA testing tool showed up to a 1,500-percent increase in the conversion rate of their product detail pages simply through A/B testing their "Add to Cart" button's five primary variables. However, most marketers simply accept the "Add to Cart" button that came stock with their eCommerce website's design without acknowledging that it's a conversion web element for which they should take responsibility.

For both primary CTAs like "Add to Cart" and secondary CTAs to landing pages, you should again focus on the most disruptive elements first. The primary color palette is a good starting place for testing. In general, you want your CTAs to violate the color scheme that's surrounding them. They should be visually distracting and obvious as the desired point of engagement for visitors. However, exactly *which* color is most effective is going to be unique to each website and is something that can be determined only by experimentation.

After working your way through variations on the primary color palette, you can work on the copy of the CTA itself. The copy isn't necessarily what you're saying, it's *how* you say it. Punctuation, sentence structure, diction—all of these elements can influence how effectively you're communicating the value proposition of why someone should click. When testing this feature, it's important to also track the click-to-submission rate to ensure that you're not abusing the copy to increase the click-through rate (which is a good and valuable metric) at the expense of the landing page's conversion rate (which is the more important metric) by confusing the visitor or improperly setting or aligning expectations with what they're seeing when they have to actually convert.

The shape of the CTA should—like the color—be disruptive from the overall design. In general, most websites use square or rectangular CTAs with either edged or rounded corners, but that doesn't mean that that's the most effective shape for your website. You can test any number of shape configurations to see what draws the attention of the visitor's eye while still communicating the fact that it's a call to action. Users of the Internet understand that standard button shapes are clickable, and while designing your CTA in the form of a

Tyrannosaurus Rex may *sound* like a cool idea, it may actually lower the click-through rate by preventing people from recognizing it as a CTA. However, we're not going to say this is absolutely true, and if you *want* to test a T-Rex iteration as part of your due diligence as a marketer, then that is your prerogative.

The size, similar to the shape, is a relatively standard function of most website's designs. In general, clickable web elements that are larger are more disruptive of the graphical layout of the page and will get more clicks. However, in some cases smaller CTAs that add more white space around them might get a higher CTR. This is another variable whose impact will change based on your unique site design and the layout of your web elements, and is worthy of testing.

Value proposition, as opposed to copy, isn't just *how* you're saying something but *what* you're actually saying the value of the offer on the landing page is. Again, this is a variable that you should monitor to ensure that the click-to-submission rate isn't affected. For example, you can alter the CTA to say "Click Here for Your FREE Pet T-Rex!" and probably get a higher click-through rate based on the high perceived value of that offer, but when it takes them to a landing page with copy specifying that they're downloading an e-book about your product's industry, the conversion rate of the landing page will suffer. However, you can here test the rhetorical appeal of the value proposition as well as what you emphasize as the valuable part of the offer.

Of course, in addition to standard-design button-type CTAs there is an infinite universe of combinations for CTAs with buttons inside buttons and varying designs. The five basic variables we've discussed here are universally applicable, but your particular design may have many other disruptive variables that you can—and should—test.

## Social Media Experiments

In previous chapters we've defined some of the key performance indicators (KPIs) of social media, and they vary from site to site. However, there are some KPIs that are fairly universal that you should test.

The click-through rate of the links that you share on sites like LinkedIn, Facebook, Twitter, and Google+ can be affected by the copy, tone, and descriptive value proposition of the post in much the same way that a CTA communicates and persuades someone to click. In addition, the timing of these posts can significantly affect their click-through rate. If the majority of your audience is on Twitter during the late evening hours, it might not make sense to focus your tweeting efforts on times during the business day, even if that's when *your* team is online. You should test different configurations and copy for social postings as well as experimenting with posting at different times of the day. Although your buyer personas should attempt to guess at what times and days of the week each persona type is engaged with social media, you should test those theses by modifying the types and frequency of your posts as well as exploring different days of the week. You might be surprised, for example, by the number of your social connections who are more highly engaged with social media on the weekends when they're not distracted. You may find that your audience is, in fact, composed primarily of night owls, and you should schedule posts overnight. Text and timing are the two most important variables to test when trying to get more clicks.

The frequency of posts is also a variable for you to test. In addition to possibly impacting the click-through rate and the net number of clicks, frequency may negatively or positively impact social-follower attrition. People may unfollow you if you're not posting enough of the types of content that they find valuable, and they may unfollow you if you're posting too frequently. Particularly on high-engagement sites like Facebook, high-posting frequency may lead to lower engagement rates and follower attrition.

You should also experiment with different types of media. Especially on sites like Facebook and Google+ that are getting better at emphasizing visual content, it might be *more* beneficial in terms of driving clicks if you post (for example) a visually engaging image and then accompany it with a shortened link in the comment or caption instead of posting links in the traditional manner. You should experiment with all of the different types of media posting that's available to you to see which ones most strongly benefit your key performance indicators.

# E-mail Marketing Experiments

E-mail is one of the most heavily studied marketing activities in the eCommerce arsenal. However, that means that we all too often accept as true "best practices" that may not necessarily be applicable to our audience. Each aspect of the e-mail influences a different metric and should be analyzed accordingly.

The open rate is primarily a function of the subject line. The open rate is a peculiar metric because it's one of the most inaccurate metrics in all of Internet marketing. Because open rates are primarily measured by e-mail service providers (ESPs) using the number of times that a single-pixel image they automatically include in the e-mail is loaded, the huge number of inboxes that have images disabled by default underreport the number of opens that an e-mail receives. However, when conducting an A/B test with adequate sample size, you can adjust for this with the assumption that (given adequate sample size) a similar percentage of recipients in each test population will have images disabled. If this becomes weighted on one list, the test could become significantly influenced and the results could be invalid. This is why randomizing the contact lists that you test with—instead of sorting by form submission, or chronologically, or by any other variable that might be weighted in favor of users of a particular type of inbox or types of personas who more frequently disable their images—will likely lead to skewed and invalid experiment results.

In the subject line there are a huge number of possible variables that you can test, including (but not limited to):

- Subject-line length
- Usage of punctuation such as exclamation marks
- Usage of special characters such as brackets
- Formulating the subject line as an interrogative versus a statement
- Tone of voice and level of humor
- Value proposition and what's emphasized
- Personalization such as first name or company name
- Inclusion of specific words such as "Free"

- Use of traditionally technology-added e-mail elements such as "Fwd:" or "Re:"
- Sending as a person instead of a brand

Testing your subject lines should be an ongoing process that's very highly aligned with your buyer personas. For example, if the persona you're e-mailing has a high level of responsiveness to humor, then a humorous subject line is worth testing. If, however, the persona you're segmenting on is highly analytical and data-driven, you should test inclusion of data in the subject line. You can also test their responsiveness to familiarity versus professionalism and many other variables.

The click-through rate, which is the end metric most valuable in terms of measuring e-mail engagement, is a much more accurate metric to track. It's easier for most ESPs to track who clicked which links than it is to measure open rate, since click tracking isn't a function of the end-recipient's ISP or inbox, but of the destination site and/or the ESPs use of redirects. To influence the click-through rate of the e-mail, there are again a large number of variables similar to the variables available for testing on a landing page. You can test:

- Length of copy
- Plain text versus use of HTML design
- Usage and placement of images (such as the percentage of your e-mail that is composed of images that may, as referenced earlier, not actually show up for the recipient if their inbox has them disabled by default)
- Type and design of images and other graphics
- Personalization, such as first name or company name
- Behavioral information, such as product images based on their history
- Inclusion or exclusion of specific pricing
- CTAs within the body of the e-mails themselves
- Links within the copy of the e-mails
- Composition and organization of the copy (e.g., use of bullet points versus paragraphs)
- Social proof or testimonials

- Organization of offers within the e-mail

- Inclusion and prominence of nontransactional offers and content, such as blog articles

- Tone and familiarity, such as usage of humor

- Disruptive, nontraditional personal elements, such as inclusions of postscripts

In addition to testing the e-mails themselves, testing *your* behaviors and the impacts that they have on the performance of the e-mails is very important. The frequency with which you send e-mails may positively or negatively impact your list's attrition. The time of day and day of the week that you send e-mails may also strongly impact the performance of both the open rates and the click-through rates of your e-mails. Again, just because *your* marketing team is engaged during regular business hours doesn't mean that you won't be more successful if you e-mail early in the morning or on the weekends. You should control for the variables of time of day and day of the week when A/B testing as well. You can't conduct a test of the subject line using version A at 8:00 a.m. on Monday and send version B at 6:00 p.m. on Thursday and effectively compare those two results, since the change in the timing may have impacted the result more significantly than the variable test itself. In fact, what variables perform best at what times may even be different. For example, an interrogative subject line may work best Monday mornings, but an exclamatory subject line may perform better on Monday afternoons. It's all dependent on how the individual buyer personas consume and respond to your messaging and marketing, and it should be tested to the fullness of the permutations that you have available to you to ensure that you're getting the maximum benefit from your e-mail marketing efforts.

# Chapter 11:

## Inbound Campaign Marketing for eCommerce

A lot of marketers we talk to think that the more marketing activities they do, the more results they will yield. These marketers may place regular ads in newspapers and magazines or perhaps even post new sales information to social media accounts like Twitter, Pinterest, and Facebook. However, there is no goal or consistent theme of promotion through the major vehicles of online promotion activities: search, social media, and e-mail marketing. These marketers are in danger of creating ineffective marketing environments that are not operating with the highest efficiency for increased website traffic, prospects, and sales.

For example, some marketers will rely on social media promotion for the majority of their marketing activities. These marketers will post an interesting product to Pinterest on a regular basis. They will schedule tweets to twitter advertising products and promotions. They may even promote new blog articles and products on Facebook as well. These are all great activities to driving traffic and potentially even sales from social media but have two glaring problems. First, there is no goal associated with the social activities other than being engaged in social media. Second, the marketer is only using one channel for marketing and does not seem to have a concrete reason to be engaged in those channels.

Solely focusing marketing efforts on single marketing activities, such as social media, without goals for the activities is inefficient, ineffective, and can be a waste of time and resources. Just doing marketing activities for the sake of doing them is not effective either. Posting to Twitter or Facebook can help gain more exposure for an online store, but is it effective alone? What is the posting to Twitter or Facebook accomplishing? What are the traffic and sales goals accompanied with the social activities? Are you making progress toward the goals or staying stagnant? E-mailing your contacts once a month can generate a few more sales, but is the e-mail generating the maximum amount of sales? Are you actually diluting the value of your list by e-mailing your contacts information that unappealing? Tracking open rate, click-through rate, and overall contact engagement for e-mail campaigns will help you measure the successfulness of e-mail marketing, but how does that fit into the overall picture of your marketing efforts? Creating a new category page in your store may help with visibility within organic search, but is it enough? Will that help maximize your marketing efforts? We say no.

Marketing activities like e-mail marketing, social media, and search optimization are essential to overall success, but they must be used together for maximum return on your marketing efforts. Orchestrated and defined inbound marketing campaigns conducted through search, social, and e-mail channels focused on achieving specific, measurable, attainable, relevant, and timely goals will maximize your marketing efforts and produce the most ROI of you and your team's time. These are the basics of campaign marketing and the guiding principle that will take your marketing efforts to the next level of success.

The concept of using multiple channels to achieve a goal is not a new one or one that we are inventing. Campaign marketing has been used quite successfully by thousands of companies across B2B, B2C, and eCommerce industries. However, the concept of campaign marketing for eCommerce is a relatively new one that we want to explore in detail. The goal of this chapter is to maximize your return on marketing time and effort by establishing highly effective marketing eCommerce campaigns.

ECommerce campaign marketing focuses on achieving goals, usually of increased online traffic, prospects, and sales through the orchestrated promotion of products or offers through multiple marketing channels. For example, an organized campaign with the goal of increasing a specific product's sales should have an orchestrated marketing campaign. The campaign should include a blog article promoting the sale, a landing page advertising the sale (ideally with functionality on the page for the consumer to contact you for more information via chat or form), social media promotion of the sale, and a segmented e-mail send to your existing contacts telling them of the new sale. This is a much better approach than simply putting the item on sale in your store and hoping that people find it—even better than just promoting the sale on Facebook and Twitter.

An important distinction to note in campaign marketing is that campaigns will come in all shapes and sizes and generally will have distinct focuses and goals. Some inbound marketing campaigns will focus on driving more traffic to the online store. While other inbound marketing campaigns may focus on driving more prospects and sales, it is OK to have different focuses for your inbound marketing campaigns. In fact, it is very important to know the focus of a marketing campaign before executing it. Focus often comes when goals and deadlines have been set. Therefore, before beginning any marketing campaign, you should set a specific, measurable, attainable, relevant goal within a specified timeframe. These types of goals are called SMART (specific, measurable, attainable, relevant, timely) goals and should be the catalyst behind your marketing efforts. Your inbound marketing campaigns will be the plan executed to achieve your SMART goals.

## SMART Goals

SMART goals were first introduced in 1981 by George T. Doran in the November 1981 issue of *Management Review*. SMART goals have been widely used to achieve key performance indicators for project-management performance and even personal development ever since. SMART goals are important because they keep you focused, accountable, and motivated in an organized fashion. Use SMART goals as the backbone of your marketing efforts to stay efficient and focused on driving your eCommerce sales through the roof. To understand how to develop SMART goals, examine the criteria describing the characteristics of each letter in the acronym.

The first-term, *specific*, stresses the need for a nongeneralized goal, one that is significant, simple, and specific. A goal of "doing better on Facebook" is not specific. A goal of "increase Facebook traffic by 20 percent" is significant, simple, and specific. Yet it is not perfect. Specific goals can be made even better by defining what should be accomplished, for example, why is it important to be accomplished and who is going to accomplish it? "I will increase Facebook traffic by 20 percent because Facebook traffic converts at a higher rate than paid search" is an excellent example of a specific goal.

The second term, *measurable*, stresses the need for criteria measuring progress toward the achievement of the goal. If a goal is not measurable, it is not possible to know whether you are making progress toward successful completion of the goal. Measuring progress toward your goal will keep you on track and help you reach target dates and experience the achievement that spurs on continual effort required to reach the goal of eCommerce sales growth. Increasing website sales is not as good of a measurable goal as increasing website sales by 20 percent each quarter. Be sure to strive for meaningful yet manageable measurements for your goals.

The third term, *attainable*, stresses the importance of goals that are realistic. It is OK to have a goal that encourages yourself and your team to achieve higher performance but important for that goal to be realistically attainable for motivation. Attainable goals should neither be out of reach nor below standard performance. Identify goals that are important to you but are realistically attainable over specified periods of time. Growing your website traffic by 10,000 percent in one month is not realistic or manageable for achieving meaningful and manageable progress. "Growing organic search traffic by 75 percent in three months through a regular blogging schedule" is an attainable goal.

The fourth term, *relevant*, stresses the importance of choosing goals that matter and are result based. For example, a goal of "Growing the number of Facebook fans by 1,000 in three months' time" is specific, measurable, and attainable but lacks relevance. A relevant goal is one that's important to your boss, your team, and your organization. A goal that supports or is in alignment with other goals of your company would be considered a relevant goal. A goal of "increase the number of Facebook fans by 1,000 in three months' time to double social media traffic and sales" is a relevant goal to the entire company.

The final term, *timely*, stresses the importance of setting goals within a specific timeframe. A commitment to a deadline helps you and your team focus your efforts on completing the goal on or before the due date. Timely goals prevent goal-related tasks from being overtaken by day-to-day responsibilities that invariably arise and distract you and your team from achieving primary goals. A timely goal will always set the criteria of when the goal should be accomplished by. "Decreasing paid search spend by blogging three times a week" defines a timeframe but not one relevant to the goal. "Decreasing paid search spend by 75 percent in two months through traffic-generation campaigns" is a timely goal that can motivate and align you and your team.

# Developing SMART Goals

A common goal is "increase online sales." I'm sure that all eCommerce marketers reading this book would like to increase online sales, so let's use this as an example goal and develop it into a SMART one.

First we need to make our goal more specific. "Increase online sales of category X" is specific because it focuses on a specific category instead of just "online sales." Next we need to make it measurable. "Triple online sales of category X" is specific and measurable. But this goal is likely not attainable, at least not in a timely fashion. "Increase online sales of category X by 75 percent" is likely a more attainable goal. But why are we focusing on category X? How is that category relevant? We now need to make our goal more relevant. "Increase online sales of our most profitable category, category X, by 75 percent" is much more relevant. But when will the goal be achieved? We need to place an obtainable timeframe around the goal to make it realistic and attainable. "Within three months' time we will increase online sales of our most profitable category, category X, by 75 percent." This goal is specific, measurable, attainable, relevant, and timely. A SMART goal if we have ever heard one.

Congratulations! You just learned how to take the vague goal of "increase online sales" and transformed it into a real goal that can align and motivate you and your team toward success. You will want to replicate the model of SMART goals for every marketing campaign you employ.

All of your marketing goals from this point forward should always be specific, measurable, attainable, relevant, and timely. No longer will you tell yourself or your boss that you will focus on doubling website sales. No longer will you tell yourself or your boss that you are going to be more effective in social media. No longer will you tell yourself or your boss that you're going to increase conversions through e-mail marketing. You instead will start telling yourself and your boss SMART goals—specifically SMART goals that focus on generating results for your business.

We have found that the best SMART goals focus on generating increased traffic, prospects, and/or sales.

For example:

- Traffic goal—"Achieve a first-page organic search ranking on Google of highly converting keyword phrase 'XXX' within six weeks"
- Prospect goal—"Within four months, generate thirty-five prospects a month for underperforming division 'XXX'"
- Sales goal—"Extend the LTV or our current customer base we will increase click-through rates of our e-mail sends to 20 percent within three months"

SMART traffic goals are generally accomplished with campaigns focused on driving more traffic to specific pages or sections of your website. Traffic campaigns can use many different types of marketing activities, but all should generally be focused on achieving the SMART goal. A common assumption of traffic campaigns is that they are solely focused on content creation and social media promotion. Although these tasks are core to traffic campaigns, they should not be the only tasks used. E-mail marketing, for example, is a great resource for driving traffic to the site that some marketers overlook in traffic focused campaigns.

SMART prospect goals are generally accomplished with campaigns focused on generating more sales-ready prospects for a business. This concept may seem foreign to strict eCommerce sites, but are common knowledge and essential to B2B eCommerce sites. Medical-product eCommerce sites largely sell to hospitals and universities. Although these medical websites have a shopping cart and allow single purchases, they rely on a steady flow of bulk purchases from businesses. Education-product eCommerce sites often sell to individual teachers but target school administrations and universities for larger and more consistent sales. Both sites are eCommerce but have a real need of generating sales-ready prospects from their target businesses. Setting SMART prospect goals are necessary for success.

SMART sales goals are generally most successful when accomplished with campaigns focused on generating revenue from specific categories or products lines. Segment the goal of generating more online revenue into targeted categories or product lines for more focus on success. Most retailers will have the most success of achieving a SMART goal of increasing online sales if they focus on generating campaigns for a specific product line. However, there is no reason that multiple campaigns cannot be run at the same time, so pick three or five different product lines and run three or five targeted campaigns at the same time. Set goals for each campaign and watch the overall sales number rise.

SMART goals focused on generating an increase of traffic, prospects and sales will keep you and your team focused on moving the needle of eCommerce success. SMART goals will make you more focused, efficient and yeah, smarter. We all want an increase in sales, but what are the goals that you are going to set before yourself to get there? Start writing down your goals and expand them into SMART ones.

## Achieving SMART Goals with eCommerce Campaign Marketing

SMART goals, by nature, will rarely be exactly the same from company to company, campaign to campaign. The specificity of a goal makes this so. However, most SMART eCommerce goals generally focus on generating either more traffic, prospects, or sales—sometimes a combination of all three. Campaigns can be of different aggressiveness as well. Some campaigns will use only a couple of targeted marketing activities whereas more aggressive campaigns will engage in more activities to drive more engagement. The aggressiveness of a campaign is generally derived from the scope and scale of the goal. The larger the goal, the more aggressive the campaign.

Your specific goal should generally fall into a broad category of increased traffic, increased prospects, and/or increased sales. Campaign marketing will be the vehicle used to achieve these SMART goals and can be customized to the specificity of your goal.

## Accomplishing SMART Traffic Goals

We are going to use an example traffic goal to demonstrate how to outline both a basic and advanced marketing campaign to accomplish the example SMART traffic goal. The campaigns outlined below use suggested activities, not required ones. Feel free to model your campaigns after our examples or, preferably, use our models to mold a campaign right for your business.

Goal: "Increase overall monthly traffic to top sales performing category X by 50 percent within three months' time."

Before we begin to outline the campaign tasks to accomplish this goal, we need first to gather some data and answer a couple of questions. A central number to the success of the campaign is the amount of traffic that category currently receives a month. If the traffic to that category is 1,000 visits, then you need to achieve at least 1,500 visits by month 3. So now you should update your goal to state, "Increase overall monthly traffic to top sales performing category X to 1,500 visits a month by X date." The next question to answer is, What are you currently doing to drive traffic to that category? This will help you to determine if you need to either create new marketing activities to promote the category or simply increase the activity of your existing activities. For instance, if you are already blogging once a month on the category, you should probably increase that velocity of those blog posts to at least once a week to hit your goal.

Basic Campaign:

1. Write and schedule blog articles on the topic of the category to post once a week onto your blog. Start with first developing blog article titles aligning with the category topic, ideally targeting a buyer persona. Achieving the goal within ninety days means that you have twelve weeks to work with. This means that you will need to develop twelve blog articles.

2. Promote the blog articles on social media. At the most basic level of promotion, you should be promoting the articles on Twitter, Facebook, and any other relevant communities to your industry at least one time. (See the social media chapter for best practices.)

3. Identify most popular products within your category and promote them on social media. At a basic level of promotion, you should be promoting the products on Twitter, Facebook, and any other relevant communities to your industry at least once per week. (See the social media chapter for best practices.)

4. Use e-mail marketing to promote the blog articles and specific category. You should have a new blog article every week on the specific category. And you should develop e-mails that advertise both the new blog article and a hot item within the category. Send a weekly

e-mail to your contacts with both the blog article advertised and the promotion of a specific item within the desired category.

5. Analyze the organic, social, and e-mail traffic to the category pages on a weekly basis. If you are not on track to meet the goal after three or four weeks, consider engaging in an "Advanced Campaign."

Advanced Campaign:

1. Write and schedule blog articles on the topic of the category to post five to ten times a week onto your blog. Start with first developing blog article titles aligning with the category topic, ideally targeting a buyer persona. Achieving the goal within ninety days means that you have twelve weeks to work with. This means that you will need to develop sixty to 120 blog articles.

2. Promote the blog articles on social media. At an aggressive level of promotion you should be promoting the articles on Twitter, Facebook, and any other relevant communities to your industry at least once per day. (See the social media chapter for best practices.)

3. Identify most popular products within your category and promote them on social media. At an aggressive level of promotion, you should be promoting the products on Twitter, Facebook, and any other relevant communities to your industry at least once per day. (See the social media chapter for best practices.)

4. Use e-mail marketing to promote the blog articles and products within the category. You should have at least one blog article a day on the topic of the specific category. And you should develop e-mails that advertise both the new blog article and a hot item within the category. Depending on the desired level of aggressiveness, send either a daily or biweekly e-mail to your contacts with both the blog article and the promotion of a specific item within the desired category advertised.

5. Analyze the organic, social, and e-mail traffic to the category pages on a weekly basis. If you are not on track to meet the goal after three or four weeks, consider increasing the velocity of blog posts, social media publishing, and e-mail sends. In some cases there may be a necessity to investigate purchasing PPC ads targeting the category if you start to fall short of your goal.

Both the basic and advanced campaigns use the three primary drivers of inbound marketing to accomplish the SMART goal in an orchestrated manner targeting a specific purpose. These are the types of marketing activities to engage in to move the needle for traffic growth.

Regardless of the specificity of your traffic goals, you should be engaging in inbound marketing campaigns with a similar structure to the campaign detailed above. Most traffic campaigns will consist of:

1. Organic traffic promotion tasks

2. Social media promotion tasks

3. E-mail marketing promotion tasks

4. Analyzing performance on a regular basis to determine aggressiveness levels of campaigns

Aligning your marketing efforts in this way will help you achieve your goals while making you a more effective marketer.

## Accomplishing SMART Prospect Goals

The following is an example of prospect goals to demonstrate how to outline both a basic and advanced marketing campaign to accomplish a SMART goal. The campaigns outlined below use suggested activities, not required ones. Feel free to model your campaigns after our examples or, more preferably, use our models to mold a campaign right for your business.

Goal: "Generate 250 sales-qualified prospects in six months' time."

Before we begin to outline the campaign tasks to accomplish this goal, we need first to gather some data, answer a couple of questions, and make an important distinction between a lead and a sales-qualified prospect.

A lead, or someone filling out a form on your website, may not be qualified for a sales representative to talk to. For instance, someone downloading a top-of-the-funnel offer like an e-book from your site may not be ready or interested in talking to a sales representative to buy your product. However, someone filling out a bottom-of-the-funnel offer like a "Contact Us" or "Free Assessment" form is generally more sales qualified. Identify which forms and offers on your site that mark a lead as a sales-qualified prospect. Your first task of the marketing campaign will be making BOFU sales qualified forms and offers if you currently have none.

Next you may need to distinguish how many leads you are currently generating a month and how many of those leads convert into sales-qualified leads. This will take a bit of gut-feel generalization if you have never set out to achieve SMART prospect goals before. Until you gather enough data to determine the percentage of leads to sales-qualified prospects, you will need to make an informed approximation goal of leads to sales-qualified prospects. For example, using an advanced prospects campaign focused on generating both leads and sales-qualified prospects may have the approximation of 50 percent conversion rate of leads to sales qualified. This would mean that you would need to generate approximately 500+ leads through TOFU offers to come close to your goal of 250 sales-qualified prospects generated through TOFU conversions.

It is possible and feasible to skip the TOFU approach of converting lead to sales qualified prospects and focus entirely on promoting sales-qualified offers. Although it is important to note that the majority of first-time visitors will not convert on your BOFU offers so it may take more promotion and effort to reach your goal of 250 sales qualified prospects by solely focusing on a BOFU offer.

If you have engaged in prospect generation before, you should identify how many sales-qualified prospects you are currently generating a month. On average, how many leads does it take to generate a sales-qualified prospect? Use these numbers to make your goal of "Generate 250 sales qualified leads within six months" more specific. You may need to update your goal to something like "Generate 750 leads from offers 'X, X, and X' with the goal of generating 250 sales-qualified leads from offers "X, X, and X' within six months' time."

If you decide that you are focused solely on the promotion of sales-qualified offers to hit your goal, you should follow the structure of the basic prospect generation campaign outlined below. If you instead decide to apply both TOFU offers and BOFU offers to achieve your goal, you should follow the advanced prospect-generation campaign outlined below.

Basic Prospect Generation Campaign:

1. Develop or decide on BOFU offer(s) to generate sales-qualified prospects. A common tactic is to take a "Contact Us" form and spin it to be a "Free [Insert Topic] Assessment." An education site selling self-help books may make "Free Education Collateral Assessment" or "Free Lesson Plan Assessment" to attract teachers and administrators interested in investing in new adding new education books to their school. They may even make a "Buyer's Guide for K–12 Science Books" that would generate prospects more ready to purchase than someone downloading a "Free Science Experiment Lesson Plan" guide. Whatever your industry, develop either one or a few BOFU offers that would identify a lead as a sales qualified prospect.

2. Make a website page(s) advertising the offer(s). This page should include a form that must be filled out to get the offer—a landing page.

3. Make call-to-action buttons advertising the offer. Call-to-action buttons are images used to advertise an offer, generally to be placed on your website. The call-to-action image should link to the landing page. Call-to-action buttons should be placed on highly trafficked and relevant website pages to the offer. For instance, the education website should place call-to-action buttons advertising the "Free Lesson Plan Assessment" offer on pages like:

- Homepage
- Lesson Plan category pages
- Lesson Plan product detail pages
- Blog Homepage
- Blog articles discussing lesson plans

4. Develop a blogging plan to promote the offer(s). Write and schedule blog articles on the topic of the offer(s) to post once a week onto your blog. Start with first developing blog article titles aligning with the offer topic, ideally targeting a buyer persona. Achieving the goal within six months means that you have approximately twenty-four weeks to work with. This means that you will need to develop twenty-four blog articles on the topic of the offer(s).

5. Promote the offer(s) on social media. At a basic level of promotion, you should be promoting the offer(s) on Twitter, Facebook, and any

other relevant communities to your industry at least once per week. (See the social media chapter for best practices.)

6. Use e-mail marketing to promote both the offers and blog posts aligning with the topic of the offers to your existing contacts. Develop at least one e-mail purely advertising the new offer. Next, you should develop e-mails that promote both the new blog articles and the bottom of the funnel offer(s). These e-mails should be sent on a weekly basis. These e-mails should have a core focus on the blog articles with call-to-action buttons advertising the offer within the e-mail ad copy.

7. Analyze the organic, social, and e-mail traffic to the offer landing page(s) on a weekly basis. If you are not on track to meet the goal after two or three months, consider engaging in an "Advanced Campaign."

Advanced Prospect Generation Campaign:

1. Generate TOFU offer(s) on the topic of the BOFU offer(s).

2. Build landing pages for all offers. Consider creating variations of each landing page and engage in A/B testing for increased conversion rates. (Reference the Experiments chapter for more information.)

3. Write lead-nurturing e-mails for TOFU offers. These e-mails should be focused on promoting both BOFU offers and the best blog articles on the topic of the BOFU offers. For best results, use automation tools to send these e-mails automatically to leads.

4. Create call-to-action buttons for all offers. Consider creating variations of each call to action and engage in A/B testing for increased conversion rates. (Reference the Experiments chapter for more information.)

5. Develop a blogging plan to promote the offer(s). Write and schedule blog articles on the topic of the offer(s) to post three to five times a week onto your blog. Start with first developing blog article titles aligning with the offer topics, ideally targeting a buyer persona. Achieving the goal within six months means that you have approximately twenty-four weeks to work with. This means that you will need to develop 72 to 112 blog articles on the topic of the offer(s).

6. Promote the offer(s) on social media. At an aggressive level of promotion, you should be promoting the offer(s) on Twitter, Facebook,

and any other relevant communities to your industry at least once per day. (See the Social Media chapter for best practices.)

7. Use e-mail marketing to promote the both the offers and blog posts aligning with the topic of the offers to your existing contacts. Develop at least one e-mail purely advertising the new offer(s). Schedule these offer focused e-mails to be sent three to four weeks apart. Next, you should develop e-mails that promote both the new blog articles and the top and bottom of the funnel offer(s). These e-mails should be sent on a biweekly basis. These e-mails should have a core focus on the blog articles with call-to-action buttons advertising the offer within the e-mail ad copy.

8. Analyze the organic, social, and e-mail traffic to the category pages on a weekly basis. If you are not on track to meet the goal after two to three months, consider increasing the velocity of blog posts, social media publishing, and e-mail sends. In some cases there may be a necessity to investigate purchasing PPC ads targeting the offers if you start to fall short of your goal.

Both the basic and advanced campaigns use the three primary drivers of inbound marketing to accomplish the SMART goal in an orchestrated manner targeting a specific purpose of generating sales-qualified prospects.

Regardless of the specificity of your prospect generation goals, you should be engaging in inbound marketing campaigns with a similar structure to the campaign detailed above. Most prospect generation campaigns will consist of:

1. Offer development tasks

2. Organic traffic promotion tasks

3. Social media promotion tasks

4. E-mail marketing promotion tasks

5. Analyzing performance on a regular basis to determine aggressiveness levels of campaigns

Aligning your marketing efforts in this way will help you achieve your goals while making you a more effective marketer.

# Accomplishing SMART Sales Goals

Outline both a basic and advanced marketing campaign to accomplish the example SMART sales goal. The campaigns outlined below use suggested activities, not required ones. Feel free to model your campaigns after our examples or, most preferably, use our models to mold a campaign right for your business.

Goal: "Increase online sales of high margin 'product X' 20 percent in two months' time."

Before we begin to outline the campaign tasks to accomplish this goal, we need first to gather some data and answer a couple of questions.

To identify the amount of acceptable variation in your pricing, first you will need to identify how much revenue the product is generating per month. This will be your base number that will help shape the campaign to achieve your goal. Let's say that 'product X' generated $5,000 in revenue last month. Increasing this by 20 percent would mean that by the end of the second month, you will need that product to generate $6,000 in revenue—basically increasing its sales by $1,000. Next you will need to know the average sales price versus costs for the product. How much revenue is generated per product sold at the average sales price? Let's keep the math easy and say that you generate $100 profit when the product is sold at $300. This is important to know if you plan on discounting the product-to-increase-sales velocity. If you were to discount the product with a 20 percent off sale, your revenue per unit sold will change, and you will need to sell more units. Figure out the total number of units you need to sell to reach your goal, taking into account sale discounts if this a tactic you are going to engage in. You may need to update your goal to be more specific: "Sell 'X' number of units of 'Product X' to generate '$X of revenue' within two months time."

Now that you know the number of units you need to sell to reach your revenue goal, you can start to develop a marketing campaign to reach that goal.

Basic Sales Generation Campaign:

1. Determine which of your existing macro and micro buyer personas would be most interested in the product. This will be a very important

step to ensure that all content created to promote the product will be targeted at the right consumers.

2. Create incentive for targeted consumers to purchase the product. Discounting the specific product is a common tactic to take to create incentive. However, this tactic is completely optional and not the only tactic available. Creating a package promotion where you offer the target product in a bundled deal with another complementary product could create incentive. For example, you may make a bundled deal where if you purchase the target product, you get a low-cost item for free or at a discounted price. A popular and effective low-cost item to be used in the bundled deal are company-branded low-cost items like hats or T-shirts.

3. Create call-to-action buttons linking to the target product to be featured on relevant and highly trafficked pages. A clothing retailer focusing on a particular jacket should place these call-to-action buttons on pages like:

- Homepage
- Jacket category pages
- Blog homepage
- Blog articles

4. Develop a blogging plan to promote the product. Write and schedule blog articles on what would be of interest to your macro and micro buyer personas to post once a week on your blog. Start by developing blog article titles of interest to your buyer personas. Achieving the goal within two months means that you have approximately eight weeks to work with. This means that you will need to develop eight blog articles of interest to your buyer personas.

5. Promote the target product or bundled deal on social media. At a basic level of promotion, you should be promoting the offer(s) on Twitter, Facebook, and any other relevant communities to your industry at least once per week. (See the Social Media chapter for best practices.)

6. Use e-mail marketing to promote both the product or bundled deal and blog posts aligning with the topic of the offers to your existing contacts. Develop at least one e-mail advertising the product. Next, you should develop e-mails that promote both the new blog articles and the

BOFU offer(s). These e-mails should be sent on a weekly basis. These e-mails should have a core focus on the blog articles with call-to-action buttons advertising the offer within the e-mail ad copy.

7. Analyze the organic, social, and e-mail traffic to the offer landing page(s) on a weekly basis. If you are not on track to meet the goal after three or four weeks, consider engaging in an "Advanced Campaign."

Advanced Sales–Generation Campaign:

1. Determine which of your existing macro and micro buyer personas would be most interested in the product. This is a very important step to ensure that all content created to promote the product will be targeted at the right consumers.

2. Create incentives for targeted consumers to purchase the product. Discounting the specific product is a common tactic to take to create incentive. However, this tactic is completely optional and not the only one available. Creating a package promotion where you offer the target product in a bundled deal with another complementary product could create incentive. For example, you may make a bundled deal where if you purchase the target product, you get a low-cost item for free or at a discounted price. A popular and effective low-cost item to be used in the bundled deal are company-branded low-cost items like hats or T-shirts.

3. Develop a specific landing page promoting the product with a discount or the bundled deal. Consider creating variations of these landing pages and engage in A/B testing for increased conversion rates. (Reference the Experiments chapter for more information.)

4. Create call-to-action buttons for promoting the target product. Consider creating variations of each call to action and engage in A/B testing for increased conversion rates. (Reference the Experiments chapter for more information.) Place these call-to-action buttons on highly trafficked and relevant pages.

5. Develop a blogging plan to promote the product. Write and schedule blog articles on that would be of interest to your macro and micro buyer personas to post three to five times a week onto your blog. Start with first developing blog article titles of interest to your buyer personas. Achieving the goal within two months means that you have

approximately eight weeks to work with. This means that you will need to develop sixteen to forty blog articles of interest to your buyer personas.

6. Promote the target product or bundled deal on social media. At an aggressive level of promotion you should be promoting the product and associated blog articles on Twitter, Facebook, and any other relevant communities to your industry at least once per day. (See the Social Media chapter for best practices.)

7. Use e-mail marketing to promote both the product or bundled deal and blog posts aligning with the topic of the offers to your existing contacts. Develop at one to three e-mails purely advertising the product. Next, you should develop e-mails that promote both the new blog articles and the targeted product or bundled deal. These e-mails should be sent on a weekly basis. These e-mails should have a core focus on the blog articles with call-to-action buttons advertising the offer within the e-mail ad copy.

8. Analyze the organic, social, and e-mail traffic to the offer landing page(s) on a weekly basis. If you are not on track to meet the goal after three or four weeks, consider increasing the velocity of blog posts, social media publishing, and e-mail sends. In some cases there may be a necessity to investigate purchasing PPC ads targeting the offers if you start to fall short of your goal.

Regardless of the specificity of your sales-generation goals, you should really be engaging in inbound marketing campaigns with a similar structure to the campaign detailed above. Most sales generation campaigns will consist of:

1. Buyer persona development

2. Incentive to purchase target product or categories tasks

3. Organic traffic-promotion tasks

4. Social media–promotion tasks

5. E-mail marketing–promotion tasks

6. Analyzing performance on a regular basis to determine aggressiveness levels of campaigns

Aligning your marketing efforts in this way will help you achieve your goals while making you a more effective marketer.

## Accomplishing SMART Traffic, Prospects, and Sales Goals Simultaneously

It is best to be focused on specific tasks and goals while having a clear determination and focus on achieving those goals. However, the world does not always conform to simplicity, and you will be tasked to achieve several goals within a specified time period. Fortunately, inbound-marketing campaigns can run parallel to each other and can often be used to spur the success of one another.

Did you catch the theme in the campaigns that we built for traffic, prospects, and sales goals? Each campaign had a focus on engaging in organic, social, and e-mail-related tasks. These tasks should be present for inbound marketing campaigns to ensure optimal success and can all work together to achieve traffic, prospects, and sales goals.

Let's say that you are tasked with a goal from your boss of "Double online sales by the end of the year." As you know, this is not a SMART goal. You, as an educated marketer, know to break up this goal from your boss into actionable SMART goals to be accomplished with inbound marketing campaigns. We urge you to develop traffic, sales and, if applicable, prospectus goals to accomplish the original goal from your boss. You may develop goals such as:

- Grow social media traffic to product pages from our highest converting social media site, Pinterest, by 200 percent within three months' time.

- Increase the effectiveness of our e-mail marketing campaigns—we will grow the total number of contacts within our database to X within four months.

- Increase sales of our most popular categories, 'X, X, and X' by 75 percent within four months.

These SMART goals are all aligned at achieving the goal from your boss, "double online sales by the end of the year." These SMART goals will also set you up to develop actionable, measurable plans to show your boss—making you look like the marketing genius that you are.

Setting specific, measurable, attainable, relevant, and timely goals to be obtained with inbound marketing campaigns consisting of organic traffic generation, social traffic generation, and e-mail generation tasks will set you up for success.

CPSIA information can be obtained at www.ICGtesting.com
Printed in the USA
BVOW08s1130080714

358479BV00035B/1282/P